£32.50
(not costed to F)

EDMONTON GREEN
LIBRARY
36-44 SOUTH MALL
N9 0NX
TEL: 081-807 3618

THE POLITICS AND ECONOMICS OF THE POLL TAX: MRS THATCHER'S DOWNFALL

John Gibson consistently predicted that the introduction of the poll tax would cause the Government far more severe problems than either Ministers or their advisers anticipated. This book includes a detailed explanation of the changes in local taxation resulting from the replacement of domestic rates by the poll tax. The Government's reforms are analysed within a framework of economic and public choice theory. Whilst some elements of the reforms are supported by this analysis, the overwhelming drawbacks of the poll tax are exposed. The deficiencies in the presentation of Mrs Thatcher's 'Flagship' policy are documented. The closing chapters provide a powerful critique of the Government's handling of the introduction of the poll tax in England and describe the important role of the poll tax in Mrs Thatcher's downfall.

JOHN GIBSON

John Gibson is a Senior Lecturer at the Institute of Local Government Studies, University of Birmingham, and has published widely in academic journals and the local government press on the issues of local government finance and central-local government relations.

The Politics and Economics of the
POLL TAX
Mrs Thatcher's Downfall

JOHN GIBSON

EMAS LTD
339 Halesowen Road, Cradley Heath, Warley,
West Midlands B64 6PH, UK

© EMAS LTD, 1990

ISBN 0 947817 40 9

All rights reserved. No part of this publication may be reproduced, stored in a retrieval system, or transmitted in any form or by any means, electronic, mechanical, photo-copying, recording or otherwise, without the prior written permission of EMAS Ltd, United Kingdom.

TYPESET BY THE SCRIBES, STUDLEY, WARWICKSHIRE
PRINTED BY THE CHAMELEON PRESS LTD,
LONDON, UNITED KINGDOM

PREFACE

This book is concerned with both the politics and the economics of the poll tax. I have been predicting, since 1985, that the introduction of the poll tax would lead to political unpopularity for the Conservative Government, and that the tax would not achieve its objective of improving local accountability. My argument was that when the tax was ultimately introduced, the fine rhetoric of courage and high principle exhibited by Conservative ministers would be replaced by panic and regret when actually confronted by voter hostility. However, there were doubts. In September 1987, I had witnessed a large audience of senior Conservative councillors giving, what was I thought, excessive respect to the Minister of State, Michael Howard, when he was explaining the new tax, and asking little more than whether the Government would provide funding for the cost of posting an increased number of bills. Perhaps I was out-of-touch. Perhaps the poll tax wasn't a massive error which would incur massive political costs. Perhaps the tax would be possible to administer.

The downfall of Mrs Thatcher, in which the poll tax had an important role, has answered these questions. It was Mrs Thatcher and her favoured policy advisors who were out-of-touch. One can now see that there has been a major deficiency in the advice filtering through to the inner circles of this Government. The use of economic and public choice theory has been extremely partial - with awkward bits, which question either the desirability or possible success of the poll tax, simply being ignored. Certainly, the then Chancellor of the Exchequer, Nigel Lawson was ignored when (as he has recently recalled) he said in the cabinet committee on local government finance that the poll tax would be "completely unworkable and politically catastrophic".

This is a great pity because my own view is that there have been some positive achievements under Mrs Thatcher's premiership, especially (i) the important victories over militancy and aggression in industrial disputes, (ii) the rejection of corporatism and of the presumption that interest groups must be bought off to achieve some desirable consensus, (iii) the increasing reliance upon market forces, and (iv) a resistance to the extension of bureaucratic allocation of resources and rationing. There have, of course, been some major drawbacks, including the unnecessary depth of the 1979 to 1981 recession in Britain.

The book provides both a thorough background to the introduction of the poll tax, and its redistribution of local tax burdens between different areas and households, compared to the previous rates-block grant system. It also applies economic and public choice theory to evaluate the desirability of the reforms, taking into account the predicted political reactions resulting from the application of this theory. Approximately one third of the material (see Acknowledgements) was written prior to 1990 with the rest written mainly between January and September 1990. Completion of the book was then delayed to add Chapter 18 following the contest for leadership of the Conservative party in which Michael Heseltine's proposal to do something (anything?) to reduce the problem of the poll tax played an important role.

I would particularly like to acknowledge the important encouragement to my work on local government finance provided by Kingsley Smith and John Kirkby, respectively Chief Executive and County Finance Officer of Durham County Council. In addition much valuable and necessary information has been provided by finance officers of the various local authority associations, including Martin Pilgrim, Helen Quigley, David Madsen, and Keith Beaumont of the Association of Metropolitan Authorities, John Blundell and Robert Haywood of the Association of District Councils, Stephen Hughes and Steve Lord of the Association of London Authorities, and Ian Ward and Peter Williams formerly of the Association of County Councils. Also I am grateful to my colleagues - Ian Blore, Graham Dawson, John Stewart, Bruce Walker, and Peter Watt (co-author of Chapter 11) - at the Institute of Local Government Studies, for reading and discussing parts of the manuscript. I should also mention the helpful interest in my work provided by Bob Bennett, Richard Jackman, George Jones and Tony Travers, of the London School of Economics, Peter Smith of York University, and Peter Jackson of Leicester University. Responsibility for any remaining errors in the book are, of course, mine. Finally, I would like to thank Clive Richards of EMAS for patience in awaiting the final manuscript, and my wife Anna for tolerating my long absences at the type-face.

ACKNOWLEDGEMENTS AND SOURCES

The following list indicates where the original versions of material making up the whole, or part, of the relevant chapters first appeared. I am extremely grateful to the publishers of the journals concerned for permission to republish.

Chapter 9. **Policy and Politics.** June 1987.

Chapter 10. **Policy and Politics.** June 1988.

Chapter 11. **Government and Policy.** August 1989.

Chapter 12. **The Political Quarterly.** July-September 1989.

Chapter 13. **Local Government Chronicle.** 1 April 1988.

Chapter 14. **Public Service and Local Government.** June 1987.

In addition, Durham County Council kindly gave permission to republish the material which makes up most of Chapter 6. I am also grateful to Glen Bramley and his co-authors for permission to reproduce diagrams from their article published in **Policy and Politics**, January 1989.

CONTENTS

Preface
Acknowledgements

1.	Introduction	1
2.	Rates, expenditure and the problem of local accountability	7
3.	The Government's analysis	35
4.	The redistribution of the tax burden: area analysis	49
5.	The redistribution of the tax burden: household analysis	81
6.	The comparative impact of poll tax and rates revaluation	97
7.	Revaluation on capital values	111
8.	Accountability and efficiency	117
9.	The poll tax: further accountability considerations	135
10.	Rates and accountability: some better evidence	147
11.	Poll tax versus privatisation: comparing two Thatcher flagships	167
12.	The presentation of the poll tax	183
13.	Poll taxes in other countries: the Japanese poll tax	203
14.	The electoral problem	209
15.	The implementation problem: description	217
16.	The implementation problem: analysis	237
17.	Evaluation: accountability, evasion, and equity	247
18.	Mrs Thatcher's downfall: the future of the poll tax	255

Bibliography 263
Author Index 279
Subject Index 283

1.
INTRODUCTION

The Government's reasons for introducing its thorough overhaul of the system of local government finance in Britain can best be quickly conveyed by the statement of the Secretary of State for the Environment in the House of Commons at second reading of the Local Government Finance Bill:

> The objectives of the Bill are first, to abolish the inequities of the present domestic rating system; secondly, to make local councils more responsive and accountable to their electors; and thirdly, to provide badly needed protection for business ratepayers. It will achieve those objectives first by replacing domestic rates with a fairer community charge: secondly by establishing a uniform business rate and thirdly by introducing a simpler and more stable grant system. Together, these proposals will provide the essential linkage between those who use, pay and vote for local services.[1]

After this concise introduction he proceeded to go into more detail:

> ... Excessive local spending has plagued governments of both political colours. ... We have had some success. ... but it is still too high. ... We have a system in which control of local government's ... spending is vested in 35 million electors. Yet ... 20 million of the local electorate make no direct contribution to the cost of local services. Under the present system half of local revenue is raised from businesses which are defenceless against exploitation by authorities, particularly those controlled by the Labour party ... The domestic rating system is also unfair. Many who benefit from local services pay nothing towards them. Payments based on rental values bear little relationship to ability to pay and even less to their use of local services.[2]

Obviously there is a very strong linkage in the Government's view between its perception of the weaknesses in local accountability and the high and excessive level of local government spending.

Local authorities in Great Britain were responsible for net expenditure of nearly £40,000 million in 1987/88 - over £770 per head of population. This was 23% of general government expenditure (see Table 1.1, p.2). However, these public expenditure figures understate the relative importance of local authorities because they are net figures, after the subtraction of substantial income from charges for services (£5,800 million in England in 1987/88), especially housing rents, and from sales of capital assets - both of which are a much greater proportion of local government than central government gross expenditure (Heald, 1989).

Table 1.1: Total public and local authority expenditure, Great Britain, 1987/88 (£ million)

Local Authority public expenditure:

Relevant expenditure	32,005
Other current	4,383
Total current	36,388
Gross capital	7,219
Receipts	- 3,656
Net capital	3,563
Total local authority expenditure	39,951
Public Expenditure Planning Total	145,744
General Government Expenditure	171,829[a]

Note: a = UK figure

Source: *The Government's Expenditure Plans 1989-90 to 1991-92, Ch. 21, Cm 621*

Rates had long been the only tax available to local government in Britain. In England they financed approximately 55% of the relevant (ie mainly net revenue) expenditure of local authorities - in Scotland the comparable figure was 44% and in Wales 33%. Their yield in 1987/88 (see Table 1.2) was nearly £17 billion, the fourth largest source of government revenue.

The rates, like a number of property taxes in other countries, had also been a relatively unpopular tax both with domestic ratepayers and business ratepayers. There had also been periodic outbursts of increased taxpayer protest against rates. These had usually been associated with rating revaluations or significant rapid changes in local tax levels caused by either escalating inflation or changes in the grant system. One such phase occurred in 1974 when Mrs Thatcher was shadow Environment minister and the Conservative's manifesto for the October general election included the following commitment:

> ... within the normal lifetime of a Parliament we shall abolish the domestic rating system and replace it by taxes more broadly based and related to people's ability to pay ...

However, that election was lost and when the Conservatives won the 1979 election under the leadership of Mrs Thatcher, the abolition of domestic rates had slipped to an uncertain secondary priority below the reduction of direct taxation.

Table 1.2: Government Receipts, 1987/88 (£ billion)

Income Tax	41.5
National Insurance Contributions	28.7
VAT	24.1
Rates	16.9
Corporation Tax	13.7
Petrol, derv, etc	7.8
Interest and dividend receipts	6.3
All other receipts	34.7
Total receipts	173.7

Source: Financial Statement and Budget Report, 1988-89

Within two years heavy rate increases, particularly in London, had occasioned fresh protests and the pressure on the Government persuaded it to embark on a new search for a replacement to domestic rates and it published a Green Paper 'Alternatives to Domestic Rates' in December 1981. The House of Commons Select Committee on the Environment was then also stimulated into investigating the subject in 1982. The outcome of all this was the Rates White Paper of 1983 (Department of the Environment, 1983).

This White Paper had concluded that domestic rates did have some major strengths and should be retained, but subject to powers to limit rate levels in high spending local authorities. Indeed the White Paper stated that no other tax should be introduced because there was no consensus in support of any alternative local tax. Poll tax itself had been rejected by the Government because (Department of the Environment, 1983, para. 2.9 p.12):

> ... the tax would be hard to enforce ... A new register would ... be needed. But this would make the tax expensive to run and complicated, particularly if it incorporated a rebate scheme. Without a rebate scheme a poll tax would bear harshly on people with low incomes ... The government agree with the Environment Committee that this option should be rejected.

This surely looked as if it would be the end of any search for an alternative to domestic rates for the foreseeable future. Indeed the then Secretary of State for the Environment, Patrick Jenkin, made a speech to the Conservative Central Council in March 1984 which stated that the Government had abandoned the search for an alternative to the rating system "in the course of the present Parliament" (Langdon, 1984).

It would not be unfair to say that any commentator who had predicted in 1984 that, within a few years, a Conservative Government would have abolished domestic rates and replaced it with a poll tax would have been judged to have completely lost touch with reality. The weight of historical and international experience has been such that a poll tax has always seemed to be a political non-starter. In England the last major attempt to levy a poll tax in 1377 had been a major cause of the Peasants' Revolt of 1381.[3] Following its use in the southern states of the United States after the civil war as a device to limit the voting power of the newly emancipated slaves, poll taxes had been forbidden under the American Constitution. In addition, poll taxes introduced by the British in a number of their African colonies had withered away in the 20th century, surviving only in Nigeria and Papua New Guinea.

However, within less than 15 months of Patrick Jenkin's speech in Birmingham the Government had decided to abandon domestic rates and seek legislation, in the then, present Parliament, to replace them with a poll tax in Scotland, and to follow quickly after the next election with similar legislation for England and Wales. The proposals were laid out a Green Paper, titled 'Paying for Local Government', (Department of the Environment, 1986a) published in January 1986.

There was still no consensus in the country. In fact early opinion polls registered a considerable majority against the introduction of the poll tax. However, the need for consensus, stressed as so important in the 1983 Rates White Paper, was obviously no longer paramount. Indeed, despite Mrs Thatcher's immediate attention to the inner cities on the night of her third election victory, it was the poll tax which she gave the status of the "Flagship" policy of her third term of government[4] in June 1987.[5]

The obvious question is what had caused the rapid change in the Government's approach to local government finance? There are two main explanations. The first is that there were grave weaknesses in local accountability, which urgently required action but that these had become apparent only recently to the Government because of its efforts to control local government spending. The Green Paper supplied this line of argument when it stated (Department of the Environment, 1986a, para. 1.32):

> The flaws have always been inherent in successive systems over many years. But the inevitable tensions that have arisen - in a period when a Government, for the first time since the war, has been seeking to exercise significant restraint over local authority spending - have highlighted their importance.

It may still be difficult to understand why after nearly 5 years of such efforts at control by March 1984, plus the two major investigations in the early 1980s already mentioned, within another twelve months there were suddenly revealed to the Government flaws not apparent in 1984. It is so difficult in fact, that it is better to move on quickly and consider a second explanation.

The second explanation is that it was simply a response to the political outcry caused by a rating revaluation in Scotland in 1985. Such outcry, especially by Conservative voters, gave the Scottish Secretary, George Younger, with the support of Mrs Thatcher, the impetus to succeed in overcoming the widespread doubts of other members of the cabinet regarding the replacement of domestic rates by a poll tax.

Objective and plan of this book

Even without Mrs Thatcher giving the reform of local government finance its flagship status, the changes in the system would merit analysis because they represent by far the largest change in the system in the twentieth century and Britain will become the only country in the world with a poll tax raising a significant amount of revenue. The objective of this book is to apply the methods of political economy to the reform of local government finance. The book will analyse both the politics and economics of the reforms.

Given that the ostensible case for the reforms rests on weaknesses in local accountability, Chapter 2 will describe the recent historical background including two previous analyses of weaknesses in the system of local government finance, followed in Chapter 3 by a description of the Government's own analysis. There then follows a detailed consideration of the redistribution of the burden of local taxation in Chapters 4 to 7. The redistribution is given considerable weight because it is a fundamental prerequisite to the evaluation of the reforms given in Chapters 8 and 9 which includes predictions of the interacting political and economic effects of the reforms. Chapter 10 provides evidence that rate increases actually did have an effect during local elections in the 1980s. Chapters 11, 12 and 14 analyse the pure (or, rather, not-so-pure) politics of the reforms and suggests reasons why the poll tax will be much less viable politically than the Conservatives' other innovatory flagship policy of privatisation. Chapter 13 gives a brief examination of poll taxes in other countries. Chapters 15 and 16 examine the decisions made on grant aggregates, business rates, and the standard spending assessments during the winter of 1989/90, and the initial impact of the introduction of the poll tax in England in 1990. Finally, Chapter 17 gives an overall evaluation.

Notes

1. House of Commons, Parliamentary Debates, 17 December 1987

2. House of Commons, Parliamentary Debates, 17 December 1987

3. The tax was used to finance the 100 years war with France. A register of the population maintained in order to collect the tax recorded a fall of one-third in the population of England in the four years from 1377 to 1381 (Dobson, 1973). There have also been occassional municipal poll taxes.

4. There is, in fact, a strong link between the two subjects. This is because the stated purpose of the reform of local government finance is to remove what the Government has perceived as major weaknesses in local accountability - with the worst weaknesses in the inner cities.

5. This was a very strange flagship because it had hardly been mentioned during the election campaign.

2.
RATES AND SPENDING: THE PROBLEM OF LOCAL ACCOUNTABILITY

The Government's reforms were designed to repair what it perceived as serious weaknesses in local accountability - weaknesses which it saw as leading many local authorities into excessive levels of spending. This chapter will show how the issues of local government spending, local taxation and accountability, emerged as important problems and were analysed during the period between 1974 and the publication of the 1986 Green Paper.[1] Particular attention will be paid to the practical working theory of the control of local government expenditure which was operated by both Labour and Conservative governments during this period. [The appendix to this chapter explains the main features of the new grant system introduced in 1981 and contrasts it with the 1970s grant system]. There will also be a description of two significant analyses of the problem of local accountability made during these years. The first is that of the majority report from the Layfield Committee on Local Government Finance. The second is the analysis of Foster and Jackman, who later acted as advisers to the Conservative Government in 1985.

The Rates Crisis of 1974

By the early 1970s local government had experienced over 10 years of significant real growth - local authorities' final consumption expenditure had risen from over 5.2% of gross domestic expenditure in 1960 to 7.4% in 1972. However, a major part of this large growth in expenditure had been financed by increases in central government grants. The Labour Government increased the proportion of relevant expenditure[2] in Great Britain financed by grants from 51.1% in 1964/65 to 56.4% in 1970/71. This trend continued until 1974/75 by which time it had risen to 65.3% in England and Wales. In addition the share of the domestic sector in the total rate yield had been cushioned by the introduction in 1966 of a domestic element grant giving general relief to domestic ratepayers, as well as means tested reliefs for low income ratepayers.

By 1974 a combination of a number of factors generated considerably increased taxpayer anger and resistance to rates. First, in 1973 there had come into effect the first rating revaluation since 1963, and this had inevitably caused a significant redistribution of local tax bills, despite the amelioration offered by reliefs to householders of one-half of any rate increase above 10%. Second, the reorganisation of local government in April 1974 had added to the growth of local government expenditure, which was already reflecting the ambitious growth expectations of the time.[3] There was also a natural tendency for discontinued authorities to leave little in the way of reserves for the new authorities. Third, at a time when local authority treasurers expected to face both growing cost inflation during the financial year 1974/75 and growing spending commitments, the initial grant support offered had been based on overoptimistic official estimates of inflation. Finally, there had been another disturbance to rate bills caused by a late change, imposed by the newly elected Labour Government, in the distribution of rate support grant, especially the alteration of differential flat reliefs in the rate poundage (i.e. tax rate) applying to domestic householders in different areas of 7p to 40p to a uniform 13p in England and 33.5p in Wales.

The inflationary background was such that the rate of increase in prices rose from 10% at the end of 1973 to 19% at the end of 1974, before ultimately peaking at 27% in August 1975. Domestic rate payments increased by an average of over 11% in 1973/74 and 21% in 1974/75, and, as is shown in Table 2.1, increases were largest in English non-metropolitan areas.

The level of public concern was such that there was much discussion in the media about local authorities' extravagance and several ratepayer groups were formed which put forward candidates in local elections and a number of successful results were achieved (Nugent, 1979).

The Layfield Committee

The Conservative party's response to the rates crisis was its manifesto commitment to abolish domestic rates at the general election of October 1974. The Labour Government had by then already made two responses to the rates crisis. First, after the financial year had started a large amount of extra grant was given to local government, and special relief for householders was introduced at the rate of 60% of any rate increase in 1974/75 exceeding 20%. Also an increased level of grant support to local government was offered for the next financial year 1975/76. Second, the Government appointed the Layfield Committee to carry out an investigation into the problem of local government finance. Against some expectations the Committee sat for two years and produced a fundamental and wide ranging review of the issue of local government finance and central-local government relations.

Table 2.1: Percentage changes in the general rate 1974/75 compared to 1973/74

	Non-domestic %	Domestic %
Inner London Boroughs	28	10
Outer London Boroughs	37	22
Metropolitan Districts	50	39
Non-metropolitan Districts (England)	56	45
Non-metropolitan Districts (Wales)	55	-6

Source: CIPFA (1975, Table 3.9)

It was the Layfield Committee which put accountability at the centre of the debate on local government. Given the tension between the public's desire for higher levels of local government services but concern over local tax levels, it diagnosed that the system of local government finance was seriously flawed. It argued that the growing dependence of local authorities on central government grant in the 1960s and early 1970s had confused accountability for local government expenditure and the issue of where accountability for that expenditure should be placed.

The confusion in accountability was seen as a source of weakness in securing the control of local government expenditure (Layfield Committee, 1976 p. 72, para. 25):

> Effective control of expenditure cannot be ensured in a system where local accountability has been seriously weakened, unless central accountability provides that control. Centralisation of expenditure decisions is the inevitable end to which a system depending on high and increasing grants, and associated with an inflexible and politically sensitive local tax, must lead. There is an alternative - namely to

revive local accountability. Local councils would be responsible to their electorates for both the expenditure they incurred and the revenue they raised and, above all, for increases in either. It need not be incompatible with the government's proper concern over the totals of local expenditure.

Layfield emphasised the role and responsibility of central government and central departments in the increase in local government expenditure. The centre had been responsive to the demands of interest groups for improvements in the provision of particular services and, at the same time, sensitive to the demands of many ratepayers that the burden of increased real expenditure should not be placed upon the rates. The result was a situation where citizens as local taxpayers had secured extra goods and services whilst bearing little real increase in local tax costs. Layfield argued that the bonds of accountability between local councillors and the local electorate had been damaged by the presence of too much grant and increases in grant in previous years. In such a situation all the pressure from service professionals, councillors, and recipients of services, was being placed on the centre to finance expansions in services.

The route to greater local accountability suggested by the majority report of the Layfield committee was to reduce central government grant and to replace this reduced source of finance by a local income tax. The priority concern was to increase the proportion of local tax to expenditure - there was no emphasis on increasing the tax contribution of particular electors but rather with a general increase in the local tax burden on those with the ability to pay. The increase in the proportion of local taxation to local expenditure would increase financial accountability and local electoral accountability because it would make 'local councillors more accountable to the local electorate in their taxation and expenditure'.

However, by the time that the committee reported in 1976 the rates crisis was subsiding. The rate of inflation was falling and attempts to rein back the growth in local government spending were succeeding and this was partly responsible for the fact that rates increases started to reduce, and to fall below the general level of inflation (see Table 2.2). In addition, rates increases in 1976/77 and 1977/78 had been assisted by the use of funds accumulated by many local authorities' overcautious budgeting in 1974 and 1975 (Lynch and Perlman, 1978).

Thus when eventually the Government made its response to the Layfield Report in a Green Paper published in July 1977 the rates crisis had disappeared as a political priority (Department of the Environment, 1977).

The Labour Government was not willing to contemplate such a radical step as the introduction of a local income tax. The Green Paper rejected the need to make any fundamental redefinition of the relative responsibilities of central and local government. The most significant proposal was to introduce a new unitary grant chiefly on the grounds that it would make the level of spending and efficiency of each local authority more visible and understandable to local ratepayers.

Table 2.2: Rate increases compared to inflation, 1975/76 to 1978/79 (England and Wales)

	Increase in:		
	Non-domestic rate poundages %	Domestic rate poundages %	Retail prices index[a] %
1975/76	30.4	22.6	14.8
1976/77	6.9	9.1	18.9
1977/78	10.3	15.0	17.4
1978/79	6.4	9.6	7.9

[a] Annual increase as at April of the relevant financial year.

Sources: Department of the Environment (1989) and Department of Employment (monthly).

Curbing local expenditure: an important theory

The financial crisis faced by the Labour Government had necessitated borrowing from the I.M.F and it had been forced into seeking cuts in public expenditure. The largest cuts came in capital spending but reductions were also required in current expenditure. The Labour Government was the first government for a long time which actually sought to reduce the real level of local government's current expenditure. For this purpose there was a well established theory which could be implemented. This theory was well known in both Whitehall and Westminster and, the then Labour Chief Secretary, Joel Barnett, later recalled the theory explicitly (Barnett, 1982, p.75):

My main concern was with total local authority expenditure ... we were always discussing how best to exercise control ... The main source of control was the size of the Rate Support Grant. As Chief Secretary, I would be arguing for as low a grant as possible, on the grounds that it would squeeze local authorities, who, not wanting to increase rates excessively, would be compelled to cut expenditure.

The main point to stress here is that the strategy of using reductions in central grant to secure reductions in local authorities' expenditure is risky because, other things being equal, it will add to the level of rates or rate increases. This is because the reductions in grant will not - other things being equal - be matched by the level of expenditure reductions.[4]

Despite this danger the Labour Government proceeded to reduce the real level of grant provision to local government. The ratio of aggregate exchequer grant to expenditure levels at Rate Support Grant Settlement, after peaking at 66.5% in 1975/76, was cut back to 65.5% in 1976/77 and more sharply to 61.0% in 1977/78. At the same time the growth in expenditure supported was less than the rate of inflation facing local authorities. In this context the expenditure figures increasingly came to be seen much more as centrally approved levels rather than simply as forecasts or projections as in earlier years.

In fact local government achieved the cutbacks in planned expenditure requested by the Government with real cuts in volume occurring between 1975/76 and 1977/78 without generating real rate increases. The reason for this was that the 'other things being equal' proviso did not apply. The important change which had occurred was that a large body of local authorities had moved from Labour control to Conservative control. Such changes in political control were significant in expenditure reduction terms (see Gibson, 1985; Barnett, 1982).

The success of the attempt to eradicate the real growth in spending was publicly acknowledged by the Secretary of State for the Environment in his Rate Support Grant statement in December 1977 when he thanked local authorities for their efforts. By the end of 1978 the pressure on local government was eased. The fact that local government had achieved the desired standstill in real levels of expenditure, and perhaps the imminence of a possible general election led to a resumption of planned growth for local government in the Rate Support Grant Settlement for 1979/80. This change in direction was very short-lived however, because the plans were quickly reversed on Labour's loss of office to the Conservatives at the enforced general election in May 1979.

The fast developing "crisis" in central-local relations:

The years since the Conservatives took office have been marked by a fast developing crisis in central-local relations (Bramley, 1985; Jones and Stewart, 1982). The crisis centered on the issue of local government spending. The Conservatives were committed to reductions in public expenditure and in the levels of taxation. In fact the cuts now requested from local government were very much larger than the small ones requested a few years earlier (see Table 2.3).

Table 2.3: The Conservative Government's spending plans (1979 survey prices)

	1979-80 Estimated £m	1980-81 Plan £m	% Change
Central Government			
Total	52,032	51,665	- 0.7
Local government			
Total	18,113	16,996	- 6.2
Education, Science, Arts	8,140	7,736	- 5.0
Environmental services	2,271	2,237	- 1.5
Law and order	1,865	1,921	+ 3.0
Social services	1,367	1,276	- 6.7
Transport	1,762	1,667	- 5.4
Housing	2,466	1,914	- 22.4
Other	243	245	+ 0.8

Source: *The Government's Expenditure Plans 1980-81 to 1983-84* Cmnd 7841, Tables 1.3 and 1.5

However, the Conservative Government did not rely simply on cutting grants to local authorities. It also changed the grant system because it thought that it encouraged higher levels of spending. The Secretary of State for the Environment, Michael Heseltine, explained to the annual statutory meeting presenting the Rate Support Grant (RSG) Settlement in November 1979:

> ... the present rate support grant arrangements are based on the assumption that need is demonstrated by authorities' expenditure. Resources element provides the same marginal rate of grant support to a local authority's expenditure regardless of how extravagant that expenditure might be. Furthermore, high spending

authorities can actually attract to themselves a larger share of the resources grant at the expense of other more prudent authorities. Needs element is distributed on the basis of an analysis of past expenditure patterns. The consequence of this is that if authorities with high levels of expenditure all decided to maintain or increase their levels they could create a feed-back that enhanced their measured needs.

Within such a system it is very difficult to convince authorities that it is in their interest to economise, for to do so might over a period reduce their eligibility for central government support. At its simplest, this phenomenon is known as the "problem of the overspenders".

The new grant system involved the following changes designed to increase the disincentive on spending. First, the needs and resources element grants were combined into a composite block grant with a reduction (known as the 'taper') in the rate of grant support on expenditure above a 'threshold' - itself set 10% on average above the measure of each authority's expenditure needs. Second, the methods chosen for measuring expenditure needs were based much more on client group numbers and attempted to avoid, as far as possible, the use of past expenditure data, thus reducing the possibilities of 'feedback'. Finally, the measures of expenditure need were published for the first time in order to make explicit which authorities were 'overspending'.

However, despite the introduction of the block grant for the 1981/82 financial year there was a notable failure to secure cuts of more than a small proportion of the ambitious request for an unprecedented year-on-year cut of nearly 6% in real terms. A mid year request for submission of revised budgets in order to secure elimination of an £800 million excess current expenditure over the Government's provision, set the scene for an escalation of the crisis. The Department of the Environment's press notice of 3 September 1981 announced the results. It noted that the original overspend on current expenditure at November 1980 prices had actually increased by £15 million:

> most local authorities (257 out of 413) have ... reduced their expenditure ... from ... original budgets by £196m in line with the Government's request ... a small number of authorities have ignored the Government's request for economy ... The total increase by these local authorities is £211m of which £167m is attributable to just 3 authorities."

The three authorities were the Greater London Council (GLC), Merseyside County Council, and the West Midlands County Council. All three were new Labour administrations replacing Conservative administrations and in each case it was the introduction of fare reductions in passenger transport which gave a sharp boost to their budgeted expenditure.

There could be no clearer demonstration of the important effect of political control, and changes in political control, at the local level, on expenditure policies. We will return to the comparative failure of the Conservative's attempt to control spending and the new rates problem which it generated after considering the important alternative (to Layfield) analysis of the problem of controlling local expenditure and local accountability.

The expenditure and local accountability problem again: Foster and Jackman's analysis

Foster and Jackman (1982) argued that under the rating system increased pressure placed on local tax levels brought about by grant reductions, would not have much effect on local authorities' expenditure. This was because of weaknesses in local democratic accountability - weaknesses which had not been much affected by the introduction of the block grant system. One new feature of the analysis was the emphasis on problems caused by large discrepancies for groups of electors and ratepayers between local taxes paid and the value of benefits received.

They identified four linked sources of weakness in local accountability:

(1) Non-Voting Ratepayers - although more rates were raised from local businesses than local residents, local businesses had no votes and their owners often lived outside the authority. This weakness would not be alleviated by the Layfield remedy of cutting central government grant.

(2) Domestic marginal contribution - the open-ended contribution of the non-domestic sector to marginal spending combined with the rate poundage equalisation objective of the system meant that domestic ratepayers' contribution to the marginal £1 of spending varied widely between authorities and was usually well below £1. In contrast to Layfield, they argued that it was the marginal local tax cost to the domestic sector of extra spending which was far more important than the average local tax cost or proportion to total spending as an influence on spending decisions. They showed that the introduction of the block grant in 1981/82 had brought little change in the amount of marginal spending met by domestic ratepayers and therefore had had little impact on local spending (see Table 2.4, p.16). This subsidy at the margin was seen as resulting in too high a level of spending and a major drawback to the achievement of accountability in local finance.

Table 2.4: Cost to domestic ratepayers of £1 of marginal spending (in pence)

	Pre Block Grant 1980/81 (1)	Block Grant 1981/82 (2)
London:		
ILEA	25.9	42.2
Camden	24.3	24.3
Hackney	48.9	45.8
Kensington & Chelsea	51.3	126.7
Lewisham	51.4	44.4
Westminster	16.0	16.0
Barnet	67.4	67.1
Bexley	48.6	54.0
Newham	40.8	45.1
Metropolitan:		
Manchester	34.1	35.9
Liverpool	33.3	29.4
Sheffield	28.2	34.6
Newcastle	34.0	39.6
Birmingham	41.0	38.1
Solihull	52.4	54.7
Kirklees	23.6	23.2
Leeds	30.3	28.4
Shire Counties:		
Avon	37.5	35.8
Buckinghamshire	53.1	55.0
Cleveland	32.1	30.6
East Sussex	52.4	48.6
Northumberland	32.7	31.7
Nottinghamshire	34.0	31.5
Somerset	36.7	37.4
Suffolk	38.2	38.3
Surrey	57.1	53.0
Warwickshire	44.8	45.3

Source: Foster and Jackman (1982)

Rates and Spending: The Problem of Local Accountability 17

(3) Non-Ratepaying Voters - three groups of voters paid either no or very little rates: (i) non-heads of households, (ii) lodgers and other renters, and (iii) those ratepayers on supplementary benefits or receiving rate rebates.

(i) Non-heads of households. Although they expected spouses' to be sensitive to the rate bill received by the head of household they regarded this as much less true of children over 18 still living at home. However this latter group comprised only a small number of voters,

(ii) Lodgers and other renters. This group they regarded as unlikely to have much awareness of the effect of rate bills on the rents they paid.

(iii) Those ratepayers on supplementary benefits or receiving rate rebates. The numbers in this category had been growing partly because of the increase in the number of old-age pensioners but more importantly because of the spectacular increase in the level of unemployment in the early 1980s.

(4) Disproportionate Benefits - those who receive benefits in excess of their rate costs, usually those with school-age children or in council housing, can be expected to support high levels of expenditure, although as Foster and Jackman argued, this should be counterbalanced by those receiving below average benefits. However, in addition, they suggested there was another group which received disproportionate benefits from local government spending and therefore supported high levels of spending: namely local government employees.

Considering the above points, Foster and Jackman concluded that

there may be various groups of voters who, rationally and fully informed of the financial consequences, may vote for higher rates.

They had a number of proposals designed to improve the situation. First, the conversion of the grant system into a genuine lump-sum or block grant and a standard national rate poundage for all non-domestic ratepayers. The local yield from the standard non-domestic rate poundage could be deducted from the overall grant entitlement of a local authority. This would mean that all increases (or reductions) in an authority's spending would fall on the enfranchised domestic ratepayer rather than on the unenfranchised non-domestic ratepayer. However, they still saw a place for resource equalisation and stated that their proposals provided an opportunity for a more equitable system of resource equalisation based on average household incomes rather than rateable values. This package would lead to large domestic rate rises in the cause of imposing greater self-restraint on local electorates. If this were regarded as unacceptable due to the inequitable distribution of the burden of domestic rates then "rather than abandoning the search for local accountability, we would argue for substituting a local income tax in place of rates".

Second, with regard to the problem of non-ratepaying voters they restated their view that financial accountability could only be improved by bringing home the cost of expenditure increases to these voters. However, they could not suggest any reform using the rating system which would achieve this for those over 18 and for renters. For those receiving rate rebates they were aware that their argument was leading them in the direction of a suggested reform which would arouse strong political objections: "we can only state that it is impossible both to protect those on low incomes from having to pay rates, and at the same time to have a financial discipline bearing upon low-income voters".

Foster and Jackman argued that the increase in domestic taxation under their main proposal would result in more people voting and on more local issues rather than, as commonly perceived, largely along national party lines. One novel proposal here was that elections should be held for one-third of seats every year in all local authorities and that they should be held in February with the budgetary proposals of all parties on view rather than as at present in May after the budget has been decided.

The increasing rates problem: the 1981 Green Paper

As with the previous Labour administration, the Conservative Government attempted to reduce local government expenditure by reducing grant. However, their requests for cuts were much larger and the relevant circumstances were much less propitious.

As stressed earlier, grant reductions will lead to extra rate increases because each £1 of grant reduction will lead to expenditure reductions of less than £1, with the residual being made up by extra recourse to local taxation. Special factors, namely the fact that many local authorities moved to Conservative control, kept down rate increases during the grant squeeze of the late 1970s.

When the Conservatives applied the same medicine conditions were changing and the traditional operation of the national-local political cycle was against them. Newly elected Labour authorities had higher spending plans than their predecessor Conservative authorities. By mid 1981 there had already been three years showing a strong rising trend of rate increases, with the worst effects being felt in Inner London where rate demands rose by nearly 40% after 1981/82 budgets were set (see Table 2.5), although in nearly all areas the increase was above the general trend of inflation (see Table 2.6).

However, later in 1981 there was an additional problem caused by supplementary rate demands from a number of authorities. An important source of these demands was the additional precept required by the GLC. The ambitious spending plans of the GLC resulted in extra grant losses. The source of these were the addition, by mid 1981, of expenditure targets for individual local authorities with special grant penalties for overspending these targets, to the basic block grant system. [For a more detailed explanation of the high rate increases of this period see Gibson and Travers, 1986.]

Table 2.5: Average rate payments, Inner London

	£	Annual increase %
1978/79	176.76	
1979/80	206.87	17.03
1980/81	284.02	37.29
1981/82	397.02	39.78

Source: CIPFA, Financial, General and Rating Statistics (annual)

Table 2.6: Rate increases 1981/82

	Domestic %	Non-Domestic %
Inner London	36.5	26.3
Outer London	30.5	25.9
Metropolitan	26.7	23.3
Non-metropolitan	12.0	10.1

Source: CIPFA, Financial, General and Rating Statistics, 1981/82

The level of rate increases was also particularly high in a number of provincial cities where unemployment was rising rapidly in the recession, with the latter also leading to a slump in business profits. Thus to the discontent of many domestic ratepayers there were added many protests from the business community and renewed calls for another investigation into the problem of the finance and role of local government (Birdseye and Webb, 1981).

The response of the Government was the publication of a Green Paper 'Alternatives to Domestic Rates'. This paper gave a clear impression that there were great difficulties in finding an alternative source of revenue, especially because a number of major objections were made to the possibility of a local income tax.

Consideration of the responses to the Green Paper, as well as the House of Commons Select Committee on Environment's Report of its own investigation in 1982, led the Government to the opinion that there was no suitable alternative to domestic rates. However, the Government did feel that it needed to do something to offer protection from high rate levels in local authorities.

This need had become urgent by the spring of 1983 when the Government decided to call a general election. There had been little sign of success for the Government in its aim of reducing local government spending during 1982 and 1983, and although the general level of rate increases abated in many areas they were still well above inflation. There was little likelihood of the rates problem improving, given that the general level of grant support was being reduced - from 59.1% of planned relevant expenditure in 1981/82 to 56.1% in 1982/83 and 52.8% for 1983/84 - and the special grant penalties for local authorities exceeding their targets were being stiffened as part of the strategy of putting downward pressure on spending.

Local government had been warned that increases in central government's powers would be sought if 'overspending' by local authorities persisted[5] and, facing an apparent impasse on alternatives to domestic rates, the Conservatives promised in their election manifesto that they would seek powers to control the level of rates in high spending local authorities.

The Conservative victory at the general election was thus quickly followed by the publication, in early August 1983, of the White Paper 'Rates' (Department of the Environment, 1983). The case for seeking direct controls put in the White Paper were:

(1) that excessive local spending "may lead to other important spending programmes having to be curtailed" (para. 1.6) including capital investment programmes;

(2) that high business rates have "major consequences for competitiveness and jobs" (para. 1.7); and

(3) high local rates "feed into the Retail Price Index (RPI) and help to generate pressures for compensating pay increases throughout the economy" (para. 1.8).

The White Paper discussed the increase in rate levels (para 1.22):

> Between April 1979 and April 1983 domestic rates in England increased on average by 91% while the RPI rose by only 55%. ... This increase in rates was equivalent to an average increase in the domestic rate of 72p in the pound across the country. But this average disguises a wide range of individual increases which varies from over 160p to just over 40p ... the root cause of this large increase in rates has been local government's failure to meet the Government's spending plans. Had it done so, rate increases would on average have been below the general rate of inflation.

It then proceeded to put the responsibility for high rates and overspending on a minority of authorities by stating that, whereas the 80% of authorities spending at or near to target in 1983/84, taken as a group, showed no growth in the volume of current expenditure between 1978/79 and 1983/84, the other 20% had increased their expenditure by about 8% in volume over the same period. It also emphasised that in 1983/84 75% of the budgeted overspend of £771million on the aggregate of local authority targets in the RSG settlement was due to only 16 authorities. Of these the GLC accounted for £300million and the ILEA for £100million (para. 1.26).

In addition it stated that the targets themselves had been based on a total public expenditure provision which had been adjusted upwards to take account of local authority overspending.

> The Public Expenditure White Paper published in March 1980 (Command 7841) looked for a cut of 5.6% in volume terms between 1978/79 and 1981/82 and for continuing economies thereafter. But in England local authorities' budgets for 1983/84 show current expenditure 4% higher in volume terms than actual expenditure in 1978/79: that is no less than 12% higher than the planned total first proposed for that year in Command 7841 (para. 1.27).

Table 2.7 (p.22) shows the annual process of upward revision of government expenditure plans measured in terms of 1983/84 prices. Compared to the plans in the March 1981 Public Expenditure White Paper the upwards revisions of late 1981 and summer 1982 had resulted in a 10.8% increase in current expenditure plans for 1983/84.

22   *The Politics and Economics of the Poll Tax*

Table 2.7: Revisions to government plans for local government current expenditure, (England £ million 1983/84 Prices)

White Paper	1981/82	1982/83	1983/84
Cmnd 8175 (Mar 81)	18226	17852	17700
Cmnd 8494 (Mar 82)		18902	18720
Cmnd 8789 (Feb 83)			19620

Source: Public Expenditure White Papers listed and current expenditure price indices constructed by Lincolnshire County Council.

The Rates Act of 1984 made possible the operation of both selective and general rate limitation schemes, with the latter remaining as a reserve power. In its first year 18 local authorities were selected. Although these were unprecedented new powers in England,[6] much criticised even by a number of Conservative backbenchers, the Government must have hoped that the problem of local government finance would now recede. When announcing the rate capped authorities the Secretary of State, Patrick Jenkin, stated:

> My announcement today brings the first fruits of our manifesto commitment to protect ratepayers in the highest spending areas in the country. The 18 authorities selected for rate capping together cover about one in five of ratepayers in England. ... Ratepayers in those areas will now be protected. Their rate increases will be lower than they otherwise would have been. This will be good for them and their employment prospects, and good for the national economy. ... Ratecapping is also good news for responsible councils which until now have had to bear a heavy share of the economies we have sought from local government. They have suffered because of the severe and persistent overspending of a minority of overspenders. By curbing the overspenders I am now able to take the first step to set fairer targets for low spending councils.[7]

The statement also shows that the Government was sensitive to criticism that the separate system of targets bore unfairly on prudent lower spending (meaning mostly Conservative controlled) councils, where targets were often below GRE. As explained in the appendix, targets and penalties were scrapped after 1985/86 and replaced by stiffer basic block grant mechanisms.

Rate increases were noticeably lower in 1984 (see Table 2.8) and the Government may have temporarily hoped that its problems were over, and might have been especially encouraged by the fact that both the volume and the real level of expenditure of English local government fell in 1985/86 (Department of the Environment, 1989, Fig. 6, p.10) to below the real level of 1983/84. In addition, as Table 2.9 shows,

Rates and Spending: The Problem of Local Accountability 23

the level of spending above Government plans was also at its lowest since the introduction of the block grant. Ironically this was the year in which the Government began to frame its plans for the abrupt end of the rating-block grant based system.

Table 2.8. Domestic Rate Poundage Increases, 1981/82 to 1986/87 (England)

	Domestic rate poundage:		Retail prices index:
	p	% increase	% increase[a]
1981/82	122.3	22.2	12.0
1982/83	140.4	14.8	9.4
1983/84	150.2	7.0	4.0
1984/85	159.9	6.5	5.2
1985/86	173.3	8.4	6.9
1986/87	196.7	13.5	3.0

[a] Annual increase as at April of the relevant financial year.

Sources: as Table 2.2

Table 2.9: % Excess of Budgets over Government Plans

	Current Expenditure	Total Expenditure
1981/82	8.4	9.5
1982/83	7.0	7.7
1983/84	4.4	3.8
1984/85	5.1	4.1
1985/86	4.3	1.3

Source: ACC (annual).

In August 1984 the Audit Commission had published an extremely critical report on the block grant distribution system (Audit Commission, 1984) - a report which encouraged renewed pressure from critics of the system both outside and, more significantly, inside the Conservative party. The Government's response, given by Patrick Jenkin's announcement to the Conservative Party conference at Brighton in October 1984, was that the new local government minister Kenneth Baker and junior minister William Waldegrave were to mount a departmental inquiry into local government finance. This inquiry was to look at the distribution of rate support grant, the balance between local and exchequer financing of council spending, the strengthening of local accountability and the raising of local revenue.

At the time this was justifiably interpreted as the start of yet another inconclusive search for reform of the system (Travers, 1984). The reason why the departmental inquiry resulted in the radical proposals for reform was the accidental coincidence of the studies with the widespread protest against rate increases which erupted in Scotland following a revaluation which had its impact on Scottish households with the arrival of rate bills in April 1985. This led to much more pressure being put on what had, for six months, been a low key inquiry and quickly led to a series of public speeches by Ministers putting emphasis on the need for thorough reform on this occasion. (Department of the Environment, 1985; Waldegrave, 1985). In the summer of 1985 there followed a series of Government leaks to the press suggesting that poll tax was now seriously under consideration as a replacement for domestic rates. The publication of the Green Paper set out the radical proposals for the reform of the system of local government finance in Great Britain based on the scrapping of domestic rates and their replacement by a poll tax.

APPENDIX 2A:

THE NEEDS AND RESOURCES ELEMENTS AND BLOCK GRANT SYSTEM

Rates have been levied on the basis of the annual value of property and paid by the occupier. Assessment of rateable values has been the responsibility of the Commissioners of the Inland Revenue. The general principle of valuation of domestic properties has been that of estimating the rent a property would command in a free market if the occupier paid for repairs and insurance. For non-domestic properties there have also been other methods of valuation (see Hepworth, 1984). Also there have been exemptions from rating for agricultural land and buildings, churches and charities. For the domestic sector the lack of rented

Rates and Spending: The Problem of Local Accountability 25

accommodation has made the resulting rateable values seem increasingly arbitrary.

The liability to rates has been the rateable value multiplied by the local rate poundage. This rate poundage has been lower for the domestic sector since the introduction of a grant called the domestic element in 1966 paid to rating authorities to cover a reduction in the domestic poundage, which by 1981, amounted to 18.5p per property in England and 36p in Wales.

In England and Wales the rate was collected by the district council (metropolitan, non-metropolitan, and London Boroughs) to cover the revenue spending net of grants and other income, of the district and the county and other upper tier authorities. Upper tier demands were called precepts and levied uniformly as rate poundages upon each constituent district. Within districts there were also sometimes variations in rate poundages to pay for expenditure by parish councils.

The overall aggregate structure of the grant system was very similar both under the separate needs and resources element based system in operation between 1974 and 1981, and the basic system after 1981 where the composite block grant replaced the separate elements. The first aggregate involved in each annual Rate Support Grant Settlement was the aggregate provision for local government's relevant expenditure made in the public expenditure plans. This latter comprised current expenditure plus the other items to be financed from revenue accounts - namely revenue contributions to capital, rate fund contributions to housing revenue accounts (HRAs) and loan charges. The Settlement announced how much Aggregate Exchequer Grant would be provided in support of relevant expenditure stating it as a proportion. Then the first call on aggregate grant was the estimated payments of Specific & Supplementary Grants. This left the rate support grant proper - the equalisation grants plus the grant for domestic element. Until 1982/83 the Settlement was made at price levels ruling in November prior to the financial year, with increases in grant provided later to compensate for actual cost increases, although from 1977 onwards cash limits were placed on the amount of such increases. The relative aggregates for 1980/81 are shown for England and Wales in Table 2A.1 (p.26).

The needs and resources elements were separate grants designed to compensate for differences in spending needs and resources between areas. Needs had been measured since 1974 by the Assessed Spending Needs (ASNs). Resources were measured by rateable value per head

Table 2A.1: Rate Support Grant Aggregates: England and Wales 1980/81

	£m
Current Expenditure	16132
Revenue Contributions to Capital Outlay	858
Loan Charges	1702
Rate Fund Contributions to HRAs	432
Interest Receipts	-275
Relevant Expenditure	18849
Aggregate Exchequer Grant:	11083
Specific & Supplementary Grants	1807
Domestic Element	700
Resources Element	2788
Needs Element	5788

Source: ACC (annual, 1981 edition)

and resources equalisation prior to 1981 had worked by supplementing the tax bases of all authorities with lower resources than the "national standard rateable value" (NSRV), with the amount of tax base sufficient to bring them up to the NSRV, which was set at £178 per head in 1980/81 and at similar values throughout the late 1970s. Thus an authority where average rateable value per head was £100 received an additional "ghost" or notional tax base of £78 per head. With an effective tax base of £178 per head each additional £1 per head of spending increased the local tax rate by £(1/178) = 0.5618p. Resources element was thus a constant matching grant given at a rate of £[(NSRV - ORV)/NSRV], where ORV was the authority's own average rateable value. For example, where ORV was £89 per head, the grant would be given at the rate of 50p on every £1 of expenditure.

The matching resources element ensured the same rate poundage price for each £1 per head of expenditure. The lump sum needs element then ensured that, for all areas receiving resources element, the same rate poundage could be charged for spending at ASN. The level of the common rate poundage for spending at ASN depended upon the difference between the national aggregate of ASNs and the aggegate amount of needs element provided. Needs element compensated fully for differences in ASNs (measured only for the main spending tiers). Thus, if authority A had an ASN £100 per head greater than authority B, it received £100 per head more than B in needs element grant. Needs element was a lump sum grant which did not vary with expenditure. Needs element amounted to 52.2% of Aggregate Exchequer Grant in England and Wales in 1980/81 - more than double the amount allocated to resources element. This was, in fact, far more than necessary to achieve full needs equalisation, leaving a substantial part to be paid simply on the basis of an equal amount per head of population. This part was thus a straightforward substitution of central funding for local taxation.

In 1980/81 authorities receiving resources element spending at ASN were left to raise £212 per head in rates. This meant that, with their effective tax bases equal to the NSRV of £178 per head, a rate poundage of £(212/178) = 119p was required. Given also that in these authorities each extra £1 per head of spending had the same rate poundage price, this meant that there was a common relationship between rate poundage and spending levels, measured by £ per head differences from ASN. This is shown in Figure 2A.1 (p.28) by the line A.

However, a few authorities had rateable values greater than the NSRV. In London there were a number of boroughs with "excess" resources, particularly the City, Camden, Kensington & Chelsea and Westminster. Their large rateable value made them able to charge much lower rate poundages for spending at ASN. However, the position of all London authorities was considerably modified by:

– a redistribution of the resources advantage within London by transfers of grant, and contributions from the non-domestic ratepayers of the City and Westminster, to the other London boroughs;

– a deduction from London's total entitlement of needs element to offset, but not eliminate, the resources advantage of London.

This meant that all London authorities had some rate poundage advantage for spending at ASN - either through having effective tax bases larger than the NSRV and/or some receipt of intra-London grant payments - which enabled rate bills to be closer to those in lower rateable value areas. An important point to note is that authorities with rateable values above NSRV could finance extra expenditure at a lower rate poundage cost. Thus an authority with a tax base of £250 per head needed to increase its rate poundage by only £(1/250) = 0.4p.

In Figure 2A.1, B represents a London authority receiving zero resources element, able to charge a lower rate poundage at ASN and to finance additions to expenditure at a lower rate poundage price.

The block grant system which replaced the separate needs element and resources element in December 1980 for the financial year 1981/82 (Department of the Environment, 1980) was a composite grant,

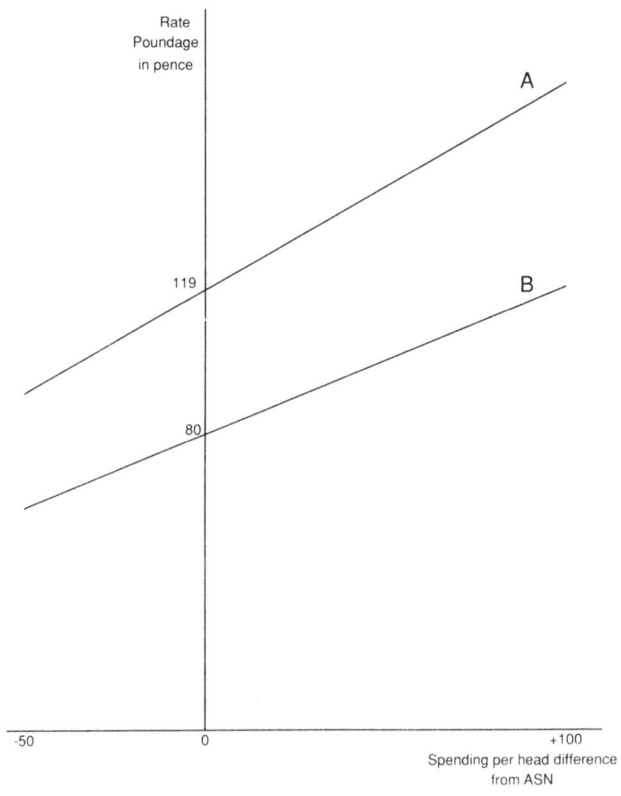

Figure 2A.1: Rate Poundage Functions 1980/81

Rates and Spending: The Problem of Local Accountability

which applied separately to England and Wales. It was similar to the previous system, but was now able to fully achieve rate poundage equalisation between areas - that was a common rate poundage for the provision of the same standard of service, with the standard of service measured by spending in relation to the new measure of the cost of providing a standard level of services: Grant Related Expenditure (GRE).

The basic block grant system was expressed by a two stage formula. First, the block grant claim of any local authority was to be the difference between its 'total expenditure' i.e.all spending left to be met on revenue account after receipt of other grants, and an amount it was deemed to raise by applying a standard tax effort function to its property tax base. This function, called grant related poundage (GRP) was an increasing function of total expenditure standardised in terms of absolute spending per head in relation to spending needs (GRE). The two stage formula was as follows:

$$BG_i = TE_i - GRP_i.GRV_i.M_i \tag{1}$$

and

$$GRP_i = GRP^* + 0.5618 \frac{(TE_i - GRE_i)}{POP_i} \tag{2a}$$

when expenditure was below threshold and

$$GRP_i = GRP^* + 0.5618 \frac{(TR_i - GRE_i)}{POP_i} + 0.7023 \frac{(TE_i - TR_i)}{POP_i} \tag{2b}$$

when expenditure was above threshold.

Where BG_i is the block grant claim of local authority i;

TE_i is the total expenditure of local authority i;

GRV_i is the gross rateable value of local authority i;

M_i is the multiplier for local authority i;

GRP_i is the grant related poundage (in pence) of local authority i;

GRP^* is the GRP for spending at GRE;

POP_i is the population of local authority i;

TR_i is the threshold of local authority i.

The potential full equalisation properties of the basic block grant was represented by the common rate poundage function at ratepayer level for expenditure in relation to the measure of expenditure needs, GRE, i.e. the sum of the GRP* and threshold of all tiers summed to the same total throughout England. The division of ratepayer GRP* and threshold between tiers was determined separately for each type of area - metropolitan, non-metropolitan, Inner and Outer London - on the basis of class shares of aggregate GRE within the area.

However, the potential full equalisation property given by a common GRP function at ratepayer level throughout England was modified by setting multipliers below unity for a number of authorities. The reasons for this were (1) to limit year-on-year grant losses and grant gains to individual authorities (in this comparatively rare case multipliers were set above unity) and (2) to replicate the resources advantage of London authorities obtained under the previous system. The London adjustment was quantitatively much the more important (and the more permanent) of the two uses of multipliers. Thus, the resources protection adjustment alone reduced each Inner London Borough's multiplier to 0.703757 in 1984/85 - a 29.6% rate poundage discount and each Outer London Borough's multiplier to 0.827949 - a 17.2% rate poundage discount.

The structure of grant received by each local authority as a function of its expenditure in relation to 'need' could be separated into an implicit lump sum component i.e. not varying with expenditure, and a matching component i.e. varying with expenditure. This aids comparison with the previous system with its explicit lump sum and matching grants.

The variable element of grant depended on the level of expenditure and the marginal rate of grant. The marginal rate of grant, resulting from the 1981/82 RSG settlement, on each £1 per head of expenditure was:

$$1 - \frac{\Delta GRP.GRV_i.M_i}{POP_i} \qquad (3)$$

where ΔGRP initially was 0.5618p below threshold and 0.7023p above threshold. This marginal rate could, unlike under resources element, be negative. Thus, for example, in an authority with a rateable value of £200 per head the marginal rate of grant was (assuming the multiplier was set at its neutral value of one) $(1 - 0.05618 \times 200) = -12.36p$. With the initial GRP slopes the marginal rate of grant on expenditure below threshold was negative for those authorities where $GRV_i.M_i$ was greater than £178 per head and on expenditure above threshold for those authorities where $GRV_i.M_i$ was greater than £142.4 per head.

The implicit lump-sum component was called 'fixed element' in Society of County Treasurers (1981) and found by substituting for $GRP_i = 0$ in the GRP formula and solving for TE_i:

$$\text{Fixed Element} = \frac{GRE_i - GRP^*.POP_i}{.005618} \quad \text{(in £s)} \quad (4)$$

The level of GRP* depended upon the aggregate amount of block grant available nationally and the pattern of local authority spending. From 1981 onwards the aggregate level of grant was reduced as a proportion of planned relevant expenditure - from 59.1% in 1981/82 to 48.7% in 1985/86 and from 54.9% to 46.6% as a proportion of actual outturn relevant expenditure. Thus compared to its implicit level of 119p in 1980/81 the rate poundage for spending at GRE increased fairly rapidly (by 59.3%) to 189.6p by 1985/86. Threshold was set throughout at 10% above the national average GRE, and the slope of the basic GRP function was fairly stable - after an increase to .6p and .75p in June 1981 it was unchanged until 1985/86 when slopes were increased to .69p and .8625p.

A crucial factor in the new grant system were the new GRE measures of spending need which strongly influenced how much grant each authority received. The ASNs had been much criticised for the attempt to relate needs to past expenditure by regression based methods which had resulted in considerable weight being given to proxy indicators, such as numbers of single parent families - rather than direct measures of identifiable "client groups". This had swung grant towards the urban areas and London, and was felt to encourage and validate high levels of spending. The process of calculating GREs was different in a number of ways - the two major changes being: (a) GREs were aggregated from service and sub-service GREs; (b) much greater reliance was placed on identifying numbers of direct clients and the unit or average costs of provision. The bulk of the national expenditure provision for a service was then distributed pro-rata to the number of clients in each local authority.

The new arrangements involved 64 indicators, compared to the 26 indicators (in London boroughs) and 23 indicators (in metropolitan districts and non-metropolitan counties) that had been used in the 1980/81 formula for measuring needs. Furthermore a number of indicators were themselves composites of complicated formulae involving additional factors, and several indicators were used in more than one service formulae. In other words, GRE calculations were lengthy and complex.

The expected initial shift in assessments back to the shire areas was rather small - although there were some big intial changes at individual authority level - and during the rest of the 1980s tended to be less than the relative shift of population.

In addition the block grant was supplemented by special expenditure targets with grant penalties on spending above targets which were achieved by additions to the GRP function. These penalties provided a relatively heavy disincentive to spending above targets and resulted in much larger negative marginal rates of grant than any arising from the basic GRP schedule, especially as they increased in severity after 1982/83 (for full details see ACC, Annual, 1985 edition). There were numerous problems associated with targets. Targets were more heavily influenced by past spending than GREs, and there was a tendency for high (low) spending local authorities to receive targets above (below) GRE. This was felt to be unfair by local authorities which were penalised even on spending below GRE. The use of past expenditure in constructing targets also gave rise to large opportunities for "creative accountancy" to boost targets and avoid grant penalties (Gibson and Travers, 1986; Audit Commission, 1984; Smith, 1987).

The pressures from lower spending councils led to the scrapping of targets and grant penalties in 1986/87, to be replaced by much stiffer basic block grant mechanisms, with the GRP slopes increased markedly - to 1.1p below threshold and 1.5p above. This was the basic system which the poll tax replaced and it is helpful to understand the marginal rate of grant in this system. Substituting in the formula for the marginal rate of grant for an authority with a rateable value per head of £200 per head gives the marginal rate of grant of (1 -0.011 x 200) = -120p on expenditure below threshold.

Notes

1. Longer term analyses are given in Richards (1988), Foster, Jackman, and Perlman (1980), and Travers (1986).

2. Relevant expenditure includes nearly all net expenditure to be met either from by the sum of grants given in the Rate Support Grant (known as Aggregate Exchequer Grant) or from local rates.

3. There had been a long sustained period of growth in local government spending in the 1960s, which actually gathered momentum in the early 1970s. There was in the early 1970s an expectation that this real growth would continue and this expectation was reflected in many of the official planning exercises undertaken in these years. For example, in 1973 local authorities, acting under DHSS guide-lines, prepared 10-year social services plans which would have required an increase in manpower over the 10-year period from 90,000 to 230,000.

4. This point is, I have found, fairly obvious to those with actual experience of local government, but is in any case backed by well established theory (Wilde, 1968) and empirical analyses of local authorities' expenditure (Bennett, 1982; Foster, Jackman, and Perlman, 1980).

5. The Financial Secretary to the Treasury, Leon Brittan, had warned the Society of Local Authority Chief Executives in July 1982 that local government overspending was the cause of the worsening relations between central and local government:

> ... we are concerned to ensure that our policies designed to improve the health of the national economy are not frustrated by the actions of local authorities. This necessarily means that we are concerned to influence their decisions about spending and the level of rates. ... Persistent spending above targets jeopardizes the whole balance which the Government and only the government must determine between spending, borrowing and taxation ...

and he had already delivered what can be seen as a last warning to local government:

> ... a failure to overcome the problem of overspending is bound to lead ultimately to developments which the friends of local government will find extremely unwelcome. It is bound to cause central government to intervene ever more obtrusively and seek ever greater powers over local authority finances ...

6. In Scotland the Scottish Office had had, and used, rate limitation powers earlier in the 1980s - see Midwinter (1984).

7. Direct control was also being achieved over the joint boards created by the abolition of the Metropolitan Counties and the Greater London Council, which themselves would have their expenditure and rate levels set for three years.

3.
THE GOVERNMENT'S ANALYSIS

In this chapter we will recall the main arguments for reforms given in the January 1986 Green Paper[1] 'Paying for Local Government'. We will mainly refrain from analysis and evaluation of the arguments which will be the main purpose of Chapters 8 and 9. The one exception though is that we will deal with the fundamental voting assertions which provide a major part of the basic argument for introducing the poll tax.

The first thing the Green Paper attempted to define (p. vii) was the relative roles of central and local government. For central government:

> The main task ... is to establish national policies and priorities for defence foreign affairs and the economy as well as for public services - such as education - which are provided locally but where there is a national interest in standards.

and for local government:

> Within this overall national framework the main role of local government is to provide services in a way which properly reflects differences in local circumstances and local choice.[2]

The Government diagnosed three problem areas as leading to a weakness in local accountability (Department of the Environment, 1986a, pp. 5-7):

- the extent to which local authorities' marginal spending is funded by non-domestic ratepayers;
- the mismatch between those who are entitled to vote in local elections, those who benefit from local authority services, and those who pay domestic rates;
- the operation of the grant system,

and proceeded to discuss the way that each contributed to the local accountability problem.

(i) The contribution from non-domestic rates

In England in 1984/85 54% of rate borne expenditure was met by non-domestic rates, with the domestic sector contributing 36% and a further 10% met by rebates. The Green Paper argued that the significance of this contribution by the non-domestic sector was in its impact on the marginal contribution of the domestic sector. On average this was less than half the local tax bill for any increase in spending.[3] Worse still there were local authorities where the non-domestic sector met more than this average - up to three quarters. The conclusion drawn was that "Authorities therefore find themselves in a position to increase spending on services for the voting domestic ratepayer largely at the expense of the non-voting, non-domestic ratepayer" (Department of the Environment, 1986a, para. 1.35).

(ii) Those who vote and those who pay

Extending this line of argument the Green Paper then stated that the poor linkage between those who vote and those who pay was exacerbated by the fact that many of those entitled to vote either do not pay rates at all, or do not pay full rates. This was the literal truth: in England in 1984/85 out of over 35 million electors only 18 million were liable to pay rates (ie received a rate bill). In addition of the 18 million receiving rate bills 3 million received partial rebates and a further 3 million full rebates. It was argued that although many not billed would be spouses, because they did not directly make any payment to their local authority they would not have much appreciation of the cost of local services, and this would be even more strongly true of other adult members of households.

(iii) The grant system

The grant system was perceived as giving rise to a number of problems. The first of these arose because the grant received by each local authority was variable - it varied not just with its own spending but with the expenditure of other local authorities,[4] and also through changes in the aggregate grant provision in each successive grant settlement. In addition there were fluctuations caused by changes in the method of assessing the cost of providing a similar standard of service in each area. For local authorities most affected this meant that there might be rate changes which were unrelated to changes in expenditure.

A worse problem arose, however, as a result of "resources equalisation". Without this there would be very large differences in the amount domestic ratepayers paid to provide similar standards of service, because of the large variation between areas in the number of offices, shops and factories, and, in addition, in the variation in the rateable values of domestic properties. Grant was paid to achieve full compensation for differences in rateable value per head in order to obtain equal rate poundages for equal standards of service (measured by £'s per head spending in relation to GRE).[5] This full equalisation of rate poundages meant, first, that rate bills in different areas varied for the same standard of service, and second, that increases in rate bills varied for the same increase in standard of service. Households living in areas where houses were much more expensive would therefore tend to have higher rate bills because the rateable value of their house would be more than that of an equivalent house in a cheaper area. The problem this caused was illustrated by the different bills in Carlisle and Luton (see Table 3.1). Rate bills were £175 (80%) higher in Luton than Carlisle for spending at GRE (ie the Government's assessment of the cost of providing a similar standard of service).

Table 3.1: **Rate poundages and rate bills in Carlisle and Luton 1984/85**

	Average domestic rateable value £ per *hereditament*	Rate poundage		Average rate bill	
		For spending at level of GRE p	Actual poundage levied p	For spending at level of GRE £	Actual average rate bill £
Carlisle	136	168.5	171.5	229	233
Luton	240	168.5	152.7	404	366

Source: *Department of the Environment, 1986a, p.7.*

Possible Directions for Reform

The Government then considered three possible directions for reform:
- changing the structure of local government;
- imposing much greater central control over local authorities;
- financial reform designed to improve local accountability.

However, the first two were briefly dismissed. Changing the structure of local government would do nothing to deal with the weaknesses in local accountability. Increasing central control had three variants - (1) putting a general limit on rates, (2) funding one or more of the main services entirely, with the budget set by central government, or (3) taking responsibility for a major part of spending, such as teachers' salaries, to the centre. All three variants were strongly rejected as they would need large increases in central manpower and the latter two an increase in national taxation. The Government argued strongly for making local authorities more accountable within the present structure of local government (Department of the Environment, 1986a, p.9)[6] because:

> It guarantees the continued existence of a healthy democratic system of local government. It should reduce the tension between central Government and local authorities. In the longer term it should help to ensure that services are provided more efficiently. And it strengthens the link between the local authority and those who live in its area. For the vast majority of people, this is the preferable way forward.

The Green Paper saw three main elements in a new finance system based on improved local accountability:

> - better arrangements for taxation of non-domestic taxpayers, so that the payments they make towards local services do not conceal from local voters the true costs of increased spending;
>
> - a more direct and fairer link between voting and paying, with more local voters contributing towards the cost of providing local authority services;
>
> - clearer grant arrangements, so that the consequences of increase or reductions in spending are felt directly and straightforwardly by local domestic taxpayers

Three separate chapters then dealt at greater length with the perceived problems and deficiencies of local non-domestic taxes, local domestic taxes and grants to local authorities.

Local non-domestic taxes

As well as the deleterious effects on local accountability caused by non-domestic rates there were a number of additional problems. Business representatives had expressed concern about the real increase in the level of non-domestic rates particularly in the early 1980s (Birdseye and Webb, 1981). The yield of rates paid by industry, commerce and public utilities in the UK had increased from £1.8 billion in 1975/76 to £6.2 billion in 1984/85.

In addition there had been a problem caused by the sometimes erratic year to year changes in rate demands, and the large differences in rate poundages between locations. The variation between rate poundages in 1984/85 was from 137p in Croydon to 291.8p in Newcastle-upon-

Tyne. In fact the range of rate poundages had widened since 1978/79 when the ratio of maximum to minimum poundage was 1.77 to 2.26 in 1985/86 (Bennett, 1986). The Government argued that the effect of recent experience of non-domestic rates was a reduction in efficiency and competitiveness. This was likely to have affected the level of employment and higher rate poundages in some high spending urban areas and also to have lead to distortion in location and other investment decisions as well as placing unfair burdens on those businesses which are tied to a particular area.

The problems of variable and uncertain non-domestic rates were additional to accountability considerations. In fact it was argued that non-domestic rates failed the normal criterion for a desirable local tax. This was because, ultimately, they would be paid either by consumers, the workforce, shareholders, or land and property owners who would not perceive any link with the spending behaviour of the local authority, and these ultimate taxpayers could bring little influence to bear on the particular authority.

The Green Paper rejected the possibility of abolishing non-domestic rates because of the difficulty of replacing this source of revenue, and regarded as unworkable the restoration of the business vote. Instead it argued that the tax could only be improved by converting it from a tax levied at variable rates by different local authorities according to their spending levels, into a nationally uniform tax set by central government, with the proceeds distributed to local authorities on an equal amount per adult basis. This would remove the differences in rate poundages between areas. Greater stability in the year-on-year changes in non-domestic rates was also to be achieved by placing a limit on annual increases to the level of increase in the RPI.

Local domestic taxes

Local domestic taxes were judged according to three criteria (1) technical adequacy (2) fairness and (3) contribution to local democratic accountability - but of these three it was stated that the Government saw that the third criteria "is now of crucial importance".

Rates failed the fairness test under both the "beneficial principle" and the "redistributive principle". With respect to the latter those groups with the lowest incomes paid a much higher proportion of their income in rates, although this was largely offset by rebates. In any case there were wide variations between rateable values within income groups, which made them a poor measure of ability to pay.

With respect to benefits, domestic rates did not properly reflect the use of local services by a household. This was because the balance of local services had now "swung heavily to more personal services", with education, personal social services and libraries alone accounting for more than 60% of local authority current expenditure.

Under what was now the overriding criterion of local democratic accountability, with two sub-criteria of (a) spreading the burden widely and (b) providing a clear link between changes in expenditure and changes in the local tax bill, the Green Paper evaluated domestic rates and two other alternatives, a local sales tax and a local income tax.

Domestic rates failed because, even after the reform - which the Government had already decided to introduce, in April 1988 - of making all rebate recipients liable to meet 20% of their rate bill, they left nearly half of all adults not directly liable to pay rates, and rates were "much less perceptible to those who are not directly liable for rates such as spouses and adult children living at home …". Rates also required revaluations and if infrequent, the large changes that took place were "one of the main reasons for the unpopularity of rates". Frequent revaluations, on the other hand, would mean changes in household tax bills often unrelated to changes in local expenditure.

Local sales taxes failed the accountability test because they were not directly perceptible and would often fall on non-residents. There were a number of objections to local income tax. First, they would be counter to the Government's objective of reducing direct taxation - an average rate of $4^1/_2$p in the pound would be needed to replace the net yield of domestic rates. Second, they would still only fall directly on 57% of the local electorate. Finally, as a buoyant tax, local authorities would use it to expand services without due regard to the economic benefits of reducing the overall burden of direct taxation.

The Green Paper argued that the best local tax was one which would "promote the efficient provision of services to the levels desired by most members of the community". The Government proposed that a new flat rate charge - a community charge - payable at the same rate by all adult residents of a local authority would "provide a closer reflection of the benefit from modern people-based services than a property tax". With respect to ability to pay, it said that at the lowest income levels, householders would face lower bills with a full community charge than with rates, and that overall the community charge would be no worse than rates. Annex F of the Green Paper also discussed the issue of the relative relationship to ability to pay of rates and the community charge. We will consider this in Chapter 5, but meanwhile note that the Green Paper maintained that the bulk of local authority services would continue to be funded from national taxes and the non-domestic rates. This meant that those with higher incomes, who pay proportionately more in national taxes and who bear more of the cost of non-domestic rates would continue to pay, directly or indirectly, a larger amount than those with lower incomes.

Grants to local authorities

Grants were used to compensate for differences in expenditure needs and taxable resources and also to support through central taxation a further portion of local expenditure. This latter was felt to be necessary because rates were only weakly related to ability to pay. This need would obviously continue under community charge.

The equalisation objective under the block grant system was designed to enable local taxpayers in all areas to finance similar standards of service, measured by expenditure per head in relation GRE - at the same rate poundage.[7] This required the block grant to be used to compensate fully for differences in rateable values per head - resources equalisation - and also to compensate fully for differences in GREs per head - needs equalisation. Resources equalisation was achieved by different rates of grant support on increments in expenditure, with the rate depending on the rateable value per head of each authority. This made grant levels depend on expenditure and contributed to the complexity of the grant system.

The Green Paper stated that although resources equalisation could be justified under the rating system, it resulted in subsidising the cost of local services to domestic ratepayers in local authorities where domestic rateable values were low. This was unfair according to the Government because domestic rateable values had no consistent relationship to ability to pay. This was also damaging to local accountability because "people whose bills for local authority services are being substantially subsidised, especially at the margin, have less incentive to be concerned about how much their local authority spends and whether services are provided efficiently" (Department of the Environment, 1986a, para. 4.25).

The GREs, although introduced by the Conservatives themselves in 1981, were criticised as damaging to accountability because they were too complex to be understood by local councillors or electors. They were lengthy because they were built up on a service-by-service basis and included additional refinements introduced in attempts to reflect special higher-cost factors. Changes in the GRE formula which had occurred were also thought to have lead to instability because they had "a powerful impact upon on the grant of individual authorities that are most affected ...". This again hindered local accountability because it produced "... significant changes in the amounts which ... (local authorities) ... need to raise from rates which are unrelated to changes in their expenditure" (Department of the Environment, 1986a para. 1.40).

The Green Paper saw two main reforms as desirable in a grant system which would be within a new framework based on a community charge and a national non-domestic rate. First, the need for resources equalisation would disappear, by definition, because each area would have the same domestic tax base per adult. Second, it wished to see greater simplicity and stability in GREs and intended to review the system to achieve a reduction in both the number of services for which separate assessments were made, and in the number of indicators used.

Needs grant would be paid as a lump sum compensating fully for each £ per adult difference in the cost of meeting local needs compared to minimum needs, with the remainder of grant, called standard grant,[8] being paid on a neutral equal amount per adult resident basis. So grant, like the proceeds of the national non-domestic rate, would be a fixed sum paid at the start of the year leaving all marginal expenditure to be financed by local domestic taxpayers.

Figure 3.1 illustrates the simplicity of the new system with a hypothetical numerical example, and the four separate sources of finance for revenue expenditure (after subtraction of specific grants)

- national non-domestic rate (NNDR): lump sum (at £150 per adult)
- standard grant: lump sum (at £100 per adult)
- needs grant: lump sum (amount per adult varying with assessed needs per adult)
- community charge (CC) (amount varying £-for-£ with spending)

All authorities receive grants and national non-domestic rates to enable them to finance spending at GRE at £120 per adult. Thus because B has needs £50 per adult larger than A, it receives £50 more needs grant per adult than A. Authority C has the same level of needs as B, but spends £60 per adult more than B, and therefore it has a community charge £60 per adult higher.

Notice that the community charge per adult at GRE will vary directly with the amount of aggregate external finance - an extra £10 per adult in grant (approximately £350 million in 1984/85) would mean an equivalent reduction in the community charge at GRE. Needs grant for each local authority[9] is a residual equal to the difference between GRE and receipt of the nationally fixed amounts of standard grant[10] and national non-domestic rates.

Comparison with Foster and Jackman, and Layfield

These then were the perceived defects and problems of the present system and the reforms to be introduced. The Green Paper can be

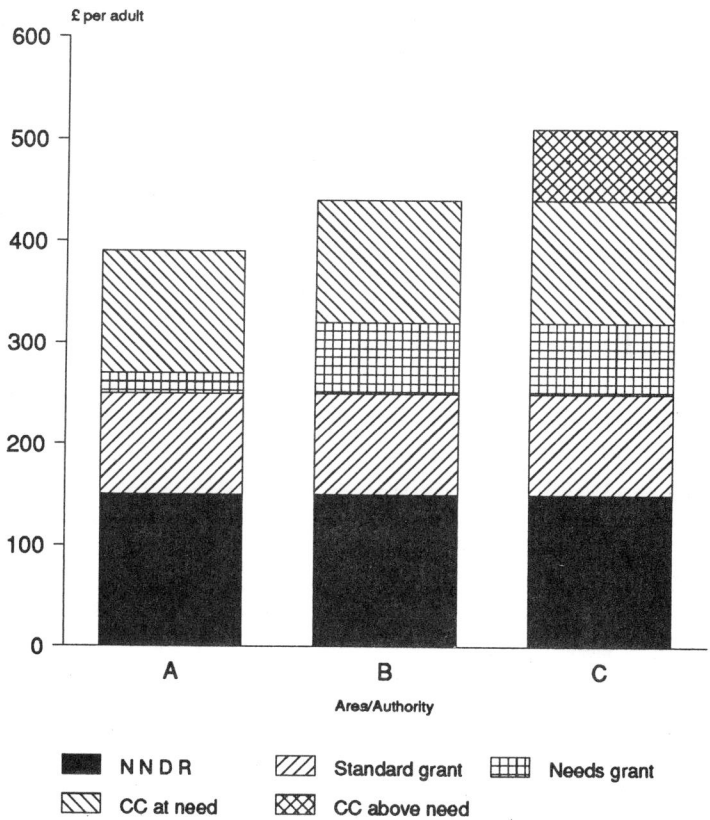

Figure 3.1: New Local Finance System – simple hypothetical example

interpreted as taking the earlier analysis of Foster and Jackman of discrepancies between the marginal cost of services provided and the cost of or benefits received from services,[11] to domestic ratepayers at the aggregate local authority level, and at household level, to its logical conclusion. Fundamentally it was such discrepancies which led to weaknesses in local accountability according to both Foster and Jackman and the Green Paper. Their solutions, to the weakness in local accountability, were similar to those which were presented four years later in the Green Paper.

Thus Foster and Jackman and the Green Paper have the same standardisation and nationalisation of the business rate; placing all local authorities on a full marginal cost basis by ending the matching component in the grant system. However, there is one crucial difference in the solutions: Foster and Jackman argued for retention of domestic rates or the introduction of a local income tax. There was no poll tax.[12]

In contrast the accountability problem in Layfield did not hinge on the fact that a particular group or majority of local electors were not paying a large enough share of local taxes, and thereby generating increases in expenditure by voting for councillors advocating expansions in services. The Layfield Committee was, of course, aware that there were large discrepancies between the payments made for services and the benefits received. However, in contrast to the analyses of Foster and Jackman and the Green Paper, it didn't regard this as a problem. The Layfield Report stated (p. 50):

> local authorities have to spend some people's money for the benefit of others. Many of those who benefit from local services do not pay much tax - while not all taxpayers enjoy the benefit of every service. Those who benefit from services and those who pay for them have different interests at different times. These conflicting interests can only satisfactorily be reconciled if whoever is responsible for deciding whether to spend more or less money on providing a service is also responsible for deciding whether to raise more or less taxation.

We will postpone a fuller evaluation of the debate over the reforms until Chapters 8 and 9. There is however one aspect of the argument which it is best to deal with straightaway. This is what I call the "fundamental voting assertions".

The fundamental voting assertions

The Green Paper is guilty of making assertions about voting behaviour and presenting them as truths. They are assertions because they relate to the characteristics of those who vote in local elections and as we shall see the Government admitted in answer to a parliamentary question that it had no relevant evidence on this matter. The assertions amount to maintaining both (i) that non-ratepayers are at least as, and probably more, active voters in local elections as full ratepayers and (ii) that the 60% of the local electorate who literally make no direct rate payment put much greater emphasis on their zero direct payment of a rates bill than on the rate bill paid in their household. For all these electors, as long as some benefits are received from local government services there is held to be an incentive to support further increases in expenditure. This is the logic of the fundamental voting assertions in the Green Paper. However, even in its own terms it cannot be regarded as a satisfactorily specified model because it does not indicate the determinants of actual chosen spending levels. If literal interpretation is fashionable, it is difficult to understand what puts a ceiling on local authorities' expenditure in the Government's model!

(i) Relative voting propensities of ratepayers and non-ratepayers

The extent of the Government's real evidence on this matter was shown when Barney Hayhoe asked in the House of Commons whether the minister would publish any statistical or survey evidence available to him on any correlation between the incidence of paying local taxes and voting at local elections in the United Kingdom or in any other country. The Minister's reply in a written answer on 24 July 1987 was "I am not aware of any research into this topic".[13]

Miller (1988, p. 232) has argued that "the whole accumulated wisdom of political science would imply exactly the opposite bias. Almost universally it is rich taxpayers who turn out to vote more readily than poor non-taxpayers". However, there is no direct evidence on turn-outs in local elections, although the data exists in the form of marked electoral registers.[14]

Miller conducted a panel survey of 745 local electors in May 1986. His findings were that turn-out bias was very small either toward left or right, council tenant or home owner, rich or poor. More pertinently there seemed to be if anything a hint of higher turn-out amongst ratepayers than non-ratepayers. Indeed, given the markedly higher turn-out rates in local elections frequently observed in affluent wards, this lack of turn-out bias, in favour of the rich and full ratepayers, in his survey results is very surprising.

(ii) Tax psychology of non-direct ratepayers

There seem to be some crucial weaknesses in the Government's assertion that non-direct ratepayers when they do vote also think only of their literal zero tax cost as opposed to the tax cost borne by the household as a whole. Accepting such an assertion also implies that with respect to the use of household goods which are paid via one household bill, such as gas, electric, and telephone, there will be large differences between the bill payer and other household members in their attitude to their use. It implies a great deal of policing is necessary, and/or conflict, within households over the use of such utilities.

Miller concluded from his survey that ratepaying was a psychologically meaningless variable because almost everyone regarded themselves as a ratepayer, irrespective of whether they were a spouse of a ratepayer or a ratepayer themselves, and irrespective of whether they enjoyed rate rebates.

Consideration of the above arguments and evidence leads to a complete rejection of this part of the Government's analysis. Given the lack of disunity between individual household members, in the later evaluation we will regard the household as a much more appropriate unit of analysis, when we further explore the relationship between economic efficiency and the Government's reforms in Chapter 8.

However, before this further analysis we will describe and explain the redistribution of local tax burdens which the reforms will bring. There are three reasons for doing this. First, it is essential to understand the redistribution to analyse the likely effects of the reforms. Second, there is a legitimate interest in the redistribution for its own sake. Third, consideration of the redistribution is important in assessing one of the Government's official reasons for introducing the poll tax and scrapping domestic rates - namely that retention of domestic rates would have necessitated a rating revaluation with its associated unacceptable consequences.

Notes

1. Although green and therefore, in principle, containing alternative proposals upon which decisions would be made only after the weight of evidence in responses obtained during the consultation period, there was, in fact, no viable alternative according to the paper and there can be little doubt that the Government's main decisions had already been made.

2. It can be argued that this is a narrow definition, which completely neglects the political rationale for local government. See Young (1988) and Jones and Stewart (1983).

3. Although this is literally true, this statement probably gave the misleading impression to non-specialist readers that on the average the domestic sector paid only 36p for each extra £1 of council spending. In fact it is much larger than this in nearly all local authorities, because of grant losses suffered on marginal expenditure, as we shall show in the next chapter.

4. This was the problem arising if the sum of grant entitlement claims differed from the total of block grant available, then a new grant related poundage schedule had to be introduced to make the sum of claims equal to the total available. This new schedule would then, of course, change the grant entitlement of local authorities. After the Government was embarrassed in 1986/87 by the need for a large mid-year redistribution (known as flowback) caused by losses in grant entitlement through the new stiffer basic block grant mechanisms, the block grant aggregate was made open ended and no further adjustments were made to the grant related poundage schedule after the Settlement. This, of course, ended the interdependence between authorities' grant entitlements.

5. See the appendix to Chapter 2 and also Chapter 4.

6. I must stress I am repeating the arguments of the Green Paper. Belief in the sincerity of the Government regarding its stated desire for strong local accountability is not compulsory.

7. Within London the effective rate poundage at GRE was lower: by a minimum of 29.3% in Inner London and 19.2% in Outer London in 1987/88. This reflected a political judgment that rate bills in London would be unfairly high if they were based on the national standard rate poundage schedule applied to London's higher domestic rateable values.

8. This distinction between the needs grant and the remainder, standard grant, whose purpose was simple substitution of national for local taxation, was later removed and the two grants became implicit within the overall grant payment.

9. The later introduction of area collection funds meant that any grant payments to upper tier authorities were paid to constituent collection funds pro-rata to relevant population.

10. See footnote 8.

11. This has to be stated carefully because as our analysis shows in Chapter 8 we should expect local authorities to supply services close to the level at which the value of the benefits received by the median or decisive voter is equal to the tax cost to this voter - whatever the relation between this internal marginal tax cost and the full real marginal cost.

12. The two authors even in 1982 had taken rather different positions on poll tax. Thus Jackman, 1982, in his written evidence to the Environment Committee Enquiry into Methods of Financing Local Government wrote: "The poll tax scarcely merits serious consideration". Foster, 1982, however, considered the poll tax among a credible inner circle of alternatives to domestic rates.

13. House of Commons, Parliamentary Debates (Hansard), Written Answers 24 July 1987. This reply does not sit easily with the claimed knowledge on voting behaviour contained in Ministerial speeches. Thus Michael Howard, the Minister given special responsibility for explaining the reforms asserted "In Liverpool only one voter in four pays rates directly and in full. In Manchester the proportion may be slightly lower".

14. The only published study using marked electoral registers by Dyer and Jordan (1985) covered turnout in Aberdeen in the 1979 General Election. They found that occupiers had a turnout a few percentage points higher than council house tenants.

4.
THE REDISTRIBUTION OF THE TAX BURDEN BETWEEN AREAS

Introduction

The reform of the system of local government finance will bring a large scale redistribution of the local tax burden. This and the next three chapters will analyse different aspects of this redistribution.

There are two separate reasons for devoting considerable attention to the redistribution. First, the redistribution of local taxation is, to the Government, the essential means for securing its objective of stronger local accountability and reductions in local authorities' expenditure. The basic idea of the reforms is that the redistribution of the tax burden will bring electors' tax costs more closely into line with benefits received, involving a sharp increase in local tax payments for many individuals and households and persuade them to demand reductions in local spending and/or better value for money from local authorities.

The second reason is simply that redistribution has (predictably) been the aspect of the reforms of most public interest. Attention to redistribution, for its own sake, is thought by some to be undesirable. Thus, Sir Christopher Foster, an adviser to the Government in its local government finance studies before 1986 hoped that attention would not focus on the redistribution, because this would be distracting from the potential efficiency gains the reforms would bring, and destructive because it would lead to the adoption of fixed party political stances (Foster, 1986).

Whether Foster was right or wrong to wish for public attention not to focus on the redistribution, the wish was absolutely certain to be unfulfilled. Redistribution matters for its own sake and a high proportion of the vast newspaper coverage of the reforms has focussed on general and particular aspects of the redistribution. Public reaction has been aroused far more by issues of redistribution than over the question of whether the reforms will bring an improvement in local accountability.[1] As another eminent economist, Karl Brunner (1978) has stated "The essence of politics is redistribution and political conflicts centre on matters of redistribution" and in a democracy any significant redistribution is bound to lead to much political controversy. The British are not peculiar in this respect - indeed other recent attempted reforms of local taxation in Europe have foundered due to political controversy caused by potential losing groups.[2]

Although it is an oversimplification we distinguish three types of redistribution which will concern us in this and the following three chapters - that between areas, that between households, and that between non-domestic ratepayers.[3,4] The first two redistributions are complicated. The reason for this is that they can only be fully understood if we explain the operation of the replaced block grant system, particularly a number of surprising or quirky features of that system. These quirks are important and bring some of the heaviest redistributions. First, however let us derive a basic general principle of the redistribution of local domestic taxation.

Redistribution of local domestic taxation: a general principle

The tax base is changing from rateable value to adult heads and the extent of the change in local tax bill in a local tax area, which we will label 'a' here, depends on the size of (i) the present rate bill:

$$DRP_a \times RV_a \tag{4.1}$$

and (ii) the poll tax bill:

$$CC_a \times A_a \tag{4.2}$$

where DRP_a is the domestic rate poundage in area a,

CC_a is the community charge in area a,

RV_a is the rateable value of property in area a

A_a is the number of adults in area a.

Now the area domestic sector's tax bill will be higher (lower) under poll tax than under domestic rates as ($CC_a \times A_a$) is larger (smaller) than ($DRP_a \times RV_a$). Dividing each term by ($DRP_a \times A_a$), this can be restated as:

The Redistribution of the Tax Burden between Areas 51

the area poll tax bill is higher (lower) than area domestic rates bill as (CC_a/DRP_a) is greater (smaller) than (RV_a/A_a).

Thus, whether the domestic tax bill falls or rises depends on the relative size of rateable value per adult and the ratio of community charge to domestic rate poundage. For example if the relevant poll tax is £300 per adult and domestic rate poundage is 200p, then the area will gain (lose) from the introduction of poll tax according to the extent to which domestic rateable value is greater (lower) than £150 per adult. Areas where rateable values per adult are high will tend to do better from the new system than areas where rateable values per adult are low. The same principle - the same equation - determines the redistribution at area level and household level. All that alters is the actual values of the number of adults and the rateable value of property.

Table 4.1: Ratio of poll tax to domestic rate poundage English tax areas, 1987/88 based data (Number of authorities)

Type of area	50-74	75-84	85-89	90-94	95-99	100-104	105-109	110-119	120-129	130-149	150-199	200-299	300 and above
Inner London	-	-	-	-	-	-	-	-	-	-	-	9	4
Outer London	-	-	-	-	-	-	1	11	6	2	-	-	-
Metropolitan	-	7	12	9	6	1	-	-	-	-	-	-	-
Non-metropolitan	1	39	128	94	22	8	2	2	-	1	-	-	-

Source: Author's computations

However, this is only a tendency, not an iron rule, because there are large variations between areas in the ratio of the community charge to domestic rate poundage. As we can see from Table 4.1, at 1987/88 spending levels, households in Inner London needed a rateable value per adult of more than double that in nearly all households outside London to make equivalent gains or losses.

The variation in ratio of community charge to domestic rate poundage is partly caused by differences in spending in relation to GRE (community charge rises faster with expenditure than does rate poundage), but it is also caused by the quirks in the operation of the replaced block grant system. We will explain these in the course of examining first, in this chapter, the redistribution of domestic tax burdens at authority/tax area level, then in the next chapter we will consider redistribution at household level.

The area level redistribution

The change in the domestic tax base from rateable values to adults, combined with the change in non-domestic rates from a local discretionary source of finance into a centrally fixed assigned revenue and the switch to fixed grants brings in a very different structure of finance. This results in some large changes in the domestic sector's total local tax contribution in the 366 different tax areas in England,[5] at present levels of spending, with the largest increases in some of the cities, especially in Labour controlled parts of inner London.

In the Green Paper the Government stated that it intended to impose "safety nets" in order to minimise the change in average bills at local authority level. These safety nets were then to be phased out over a period of four years. In this chapter we will concentrate mainly on the ultimate changes in bills which are implied by the new system because they better describe the long term changes in incentives facing local authorities.

The actual changes depend on the expenditure levels of local authorities and the precise form of the block grant system operating in the year used for comparisons. Each year since the first exemplifications were produced, based on 1984/85 data, has seen some changes in the results. However, we will concentrate in this chapter on 1987/88 based data, reserving for the last part of the book discussion of the further changes in the results for redistribution since 1987/88. The reasons for concentrating on 1987/88 are that they were of particular significance - they were the ones in front of Ministers, MPs, and in the public domain during the period when the Local Government Finance Bill was proceeding through Parliament.[6] They thus embodied the redistributions which would occur unless there were changes in the spending levels of local authorities or changes in functional responsibilities or financial arrangements. There were some changes on the horizon in 1987, namely the ring-fencing of housing revenue accounts and the proposals that willing inner London boroughs could request permission to take over education, within their boundaries, from ILEA. This latter was changed in 1988 to abolition of ILEA. Both the housing and ILEA proposals would have important effects and we will discuss these later after explaining the basic results.

A hypothetical example

Before facing the real complications of the English redistribution, let us give a hypothetical example, using the main 1987/88 parameters, to demonstrate the principle of area redistribution when the domestic tax base is changed from rateable values to number of adults. Under the rates system the block grant has operated to give equal rate poundages for equivalent standards of service in all areas (with both minor and important exceptions discussed later in this chapter) - under poll tax grant is paid as the difference between assessed needs (now called Standard Spending Assessment) and the proceeds of the national non-domestic rate to ensure equal poll tax bills for spending at needs. Let us take this latter figure as £178 per adult and examine the redistribution for two areas. (We assume simply for ease of exposition that areas are single tier local authorities). A has a low average domestic rateable value of £60 per adult (£48 per head) and B has a high average domestic rateable value of £150 per adult (£120 per head). In this example we set the parameters close to the 1987/88 actual levels under the block grant/domestic rates system, with the rate poundage for spending at GRE/needs set at 200p with a 1.1p per £ per head of spending rate poundage "price" below threshold, and 1.5p above threshold, with the latter set at £50 per head above GRE. We can see immediately that if the authorities spend at GRE the average domestic rates bill in A will be £120 per adult (i.e. the average domestic rateable value £60 multiplied by 200p) and in B it will be £300. In addition the rate poundage parameters determine that the marginal domestic tax contributions per £1 of expenditure will be 53p in A and £1.32p in B, below threshold, and 72p in A and £1.80p in B, above threshold.[7] We draw the relationship between local tax bills per adult and spending in relation to GRE in Figure 4.1 (p.54). A and B had very different local tax - expenditure relationships under rates. A's relationship is lower and much flatter than B's. In contrast, there is a common function for poll tax, applying to both A and B, with a local tax bill of £178 per adult at GRE and a slope of £1 per £1 of change in expenditure. Comparing poll tax and domestic rates we can see not only that if the areas were spending at GRE there is on average a reduction in the local tax bill per adult of £128 (43%) in B and a rise in A of £58 (48%), but that the difference - that is, cash gain per adult in A and cash loss per adult in B - gets larger at higher levels of spending. High domestic rateable value areas secure extra gains from higher spending.

Notice that this explanation of gains and losses to the domestic sector has been made without reference to the separate receipts of grant and

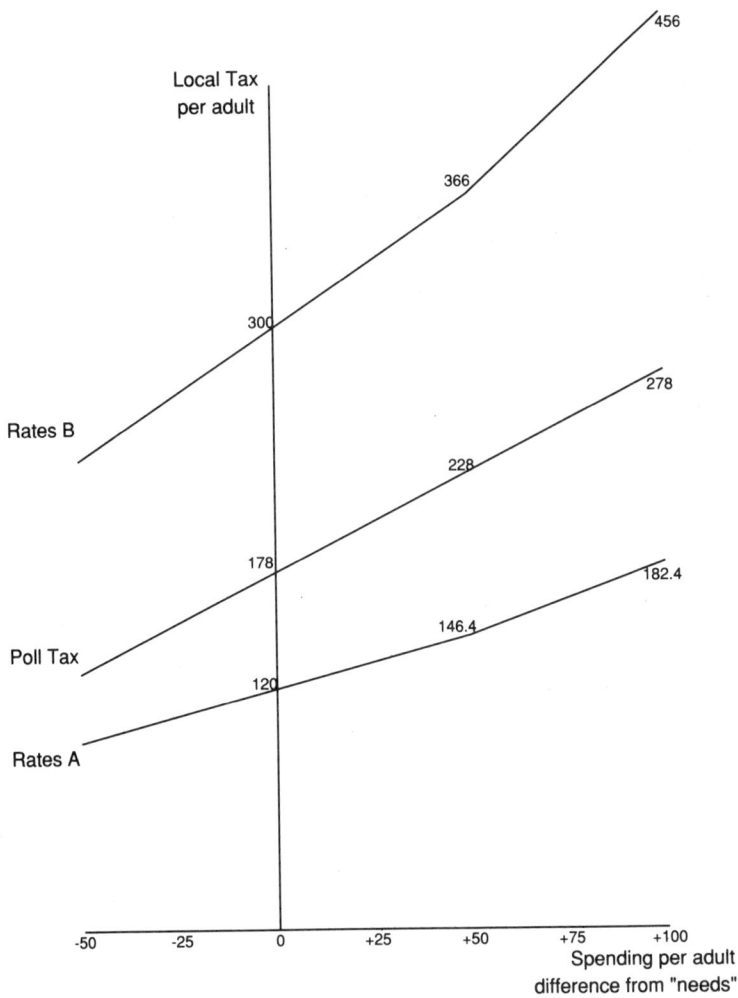

Figure 4.1: Redistribution between areas and spending in relation to "needs" – Poll Tax versus Domestic Rates

non-domestic rates. This is because in over 95% of tax areas there is a 'swings and roundabouts' relationship between the two - losses (gains) in non-domestic rates are offset by gains (losses) in grant, sufficient to bring all tax areas onto the common national poll tax function. For more explanation of this point see Appendix 4.1.

The Redistribution of the Tax Burden between Areas 55

However, as we shall see there are very few authorities where the marginal tax cost to the domestic sector is higher under rates than under poll tax. The necessary effective rateable value for the marginal domestic tax cost under rates to exceed £1 is £90 per head, and outside London there are few areas where this applies. In London, as we shall see later, special factors reduced marginal domestic tax costs under the rating system. For most areas the poll tax system increases the rate at which local tax bills increase as expenditure rises, providing an additional structural incentive for local electors or politicians to choose lower levels of expenditure. Let us now examine the data.

Table 4.2: Impact on average domestic tax bills of switch from domestic rates to poll tax, England 1987/88 (£ per year)

	Average rate bill per household £	Basic poll tax £	Spending above GRE per adult £	Poll tax per adult £	% change in bill between average rate bill and poll tax for two adults %
England	440	178	46	224	+ 1.8
Main areas:					
Shires	419	178	14	192	- 8.3
Metropolitan	424	178	53	231	+ 9.0
Inner London	594	178	399	577	+ 94.3
Outer London	517	178	48	226	- 12.6

Source: Parliamentary Written Answer, 29 June 1987 and author's computations.

Table 4.2 compares average rate bills per household by the main area subdivisions of local authorities for the 1987/88 pattern of local expenditure and aggregate grant totals. The poll tax in each area in England would have been £178 per adult for spending at GRE. However, we can see that the average level of poll tax would have been £224 per adult, because the average level of spending was £46 per adult above GRE. The average poll tax would have been much larger in inner London - £577 - than elsewhere: over double the metropolitan average and three times the shire average (£192), reflecting the average level of spending above GRE in the different areas. Although rate bills were higher in London the difference was much lower than that for poll tax and this shows in the calculated figures for changes in bills for two adult households with average rate bills and poll taxes for their areas. These fell by 8.3% in the shires and by 12.6% in outer London, and rose by 9.0% in the metropolitan areas and by 94.3% in Inner London.

Table 4.3: Impact on average domestic tax bills of switch from domestic rates to poll tax - English regions, 1987/88 based data (£ per year)

	Average rate bill per household £	Average poll tax per two adult household £	% change bill between average rate and poll tax for two adults %
North	390	512	+31
Yorkshire & Humberside	354	466	+32
North West	426	446	+5
East Midlands	398	412	+4
West Midlands	442	366	-17
East Anglia	382	344	-10
Greater London	546	696	+28
South East	479	368	-23
South West	389	372	-4

Source: Parliamentary written answer

Table 4.3 shows the broad regional effects of the switch in local tax. Three regions - the South East, East Anglia, and the West Midlands - gain from the change - and six regions lose with the biggest losses in Greater London, the North and Yorkshire & Humberside.

However, these figures mask much larger variations at tax collection area level. These variations are summarised in Table 4.4 showing percentage changes in bills and in Table 4.5 (p.58) showing cash changes in bills.

It can be seen that the shire tax areas in the south-east do markedly well from the change - in 91 of the 98 shire districts in the south-east there are gains, and in 56 of these the reduction in the domestic sector tax contribution is more than 20%. The largest tax increases are concentrated in Inner London, with 8 of the 9 tax areas where the domestic sector's tax contribution rises by more than 75%. The tables also show the sum of the adult population in each category of gain or loss. This shows an important feature - geographically the losses are relatively concentrated and the gains are more widely dispersed, with 20.8 million adults living in gaining areas compared to 15.2 million adults living in losing areas.

Table 4.4: Percentages changes in domestic sector tax contributions, English tax areas, 1987/88 (number of authorities and adult population)

Change in bills %	Inner London	Outer London	Metropolitan	Non-Metropolitan		Number of Adults
				Other	South-East	
below −40	-	-	-	1	5	344.3
−39.9 - −30	-	-	1	7	20	2380.4
−29.9 - −20	1	2	3	9	31	4860.2
−19.9 - −10	-	8	4	28	24	6148.6
−9.9 - − 0	2	5	5	55	11	7002.6
0.1 - 10	-	4	1	29	7	3323.7
10.1 - 20	-	1	6	30	-	3966.2
20.1 - 30	-	-	6	18	-	2792.3
30.1 - 50	-	-	7	12	-	2394.6
50.1 - 75	2	-	3	9	-	1299.7
75.1 - 100	3	-	-	1	-	583.4
100 and over	5	-	-	-	-	767.6

Source: Author's computations see Table 4.6 below

Table 4.5: Changes in average adult domestic tax contributions, English tax areas, 1987/88 (number of authorities and adult population)

Change in bills	Inner London	Outer London	Metropolitan	Non-Metropolitan		Number of Adults
				Other	South-East	
£ per year						
below −150	-	-	-	-	2	118.2
−149.9 - −100	1	-	-	-	8	782.2
−99.9 - −75	-	-	1	7	16	1992.4
−74.9 - −50	-	2	3	9	1	3844.0
−49.9 - −25	-	9	4	22	27	6146.5
−24.9 - 0	2	4	5	62	17	7852.8
0.1 - 25	-	5	2	42	7	4353.0
25.1 - 50	-	-	8	31	-	4605.9
50.1 - 75	-	-	5	14	-	2420.1
75.1 - 100	-	-	7	10	-	2048.8
100.1 - 150	-	-	1	2	-	242.3
150.1 - 200	-	-	-	-	-	-
200.1 - 250	3	-	-	-	-	458.6
250.1 - 300	3	-	-	-	-	497.0
300.1 - 350	2	-	-	-	-	290.3
above 350	2	-	-	-	-	311.5

Source: Author's computations: see Table 4.6 below

Table 4.6 (p.61) gives more detail for the figures for individual tax areas. We give the figures for the percentage change in the domestic sector's tax contribution and the change in cash in the average adult bill for actual spending levels - columns (9) and (10) - and if all local authorities in each area were spending at GRE - columns (4) and (5).

The Redistribution of the Tax Burden between Areas

Following our earlier hypothetical example we can make some generalisations for areas outside inner London (the latter is different enough to require a separate discussion). For these areas the gains reflect the interaction of (1) domestic rateable values per adult and (2) spending in relation to GRE. Again we will look at it in two components - the changes if all local authorities spent at GRE, and the additional changes caused by differences between actual spending and GRE.[8]

At GRE the size of the domestic sector's contribution under rates increases with the domestic rateable value per adult given that the standard rate poundage - reflecting the rate poundage equalisation of the present system - is in the 200p region. (The use of multipliers in the block grant formula for individual authorities is the most common reason why rate poundage equalisation is not precise - areas containing local authorities given lower multipliers had lower rate poundages for spending at GRE). Thus for St. Albans in Hertfordshire the average rate bill per adult at GRE is £261.8 (197.52p multiplied by an average rateable value per adult of £132.6) whereas for Boothferry in Humberside it is £139.1 (202.42p multiplied by an average rateable value per adult of £68.7). Given that the poll tax at GRE is £178 per adult we can see that there is a substantial loss to low rateable value areas like Boothferry and gains to high rateable value areas like St. Albans.

However, further changes are caused by spending differences from GRE - but again the important point is the additional changes are of a different magnitude, and can even be in a different direction. In low rateable value areas there are additional cash losses from overspending and for high rateable value areas additional cash gains from overspending. Thus the present rate bill cost of Boothferry's overspend of £46 per adult is only just over half at £25 per adult [Column (8) minus Column (3)] leading to additional cash losses of £21, whereas the rate bill cost of St. Albans £26 per adult overspend is £27. Again this reflects rate poundage equalisation - the rate poundage cost of a £1 per head change in expenditure is the same and the rate bill cost increases with domestic rateable value per head, and for St. Albans the domestic sector pays more than a £1 in rates to finance an extra £1 in services whereas in Boothferry the equivalent cost is less than 60p.

So we can see the importance of considering the interaction of the two factors - rateable values and spending.

A significant majority of areas gain if they spend at GRE, with the largest gains for the areas of highest domestic rateable values. The "break-even" domestic rateable value is £89 per adult when rate poundage at GRE is 200p - and nearly all the metropolitan districts in the north and most of the county districts north of the river Trent are below this level, and here average bills increase, even for spending at GRE.

The additional gains or losses from spending above GRE also depend on domestic rateable values and authorities with the highest effective domestic rateable values make additional gains - but the "break-even" domestic rateable value is higher than for the "at GRE" comparision with effective domestic rateable value having to be greater than about £118 per adult before additional gains are made from spending above GRE (the marginal cost to the domestic sector only exceeds £1 above a domestic rateable value of £90.9 per head - £118 per adult at the average ratio of population to adults - and this is necessary before extra spending costs more to the domestic sector in the block grant system than in the £-for-£ poll tax system). However, most authorities are below this level and make losses on additional spending and the rate of loss increases inversely with the size of domestic rateable value per adult. This is a reflection of the increase in the disincentives to extra spending in the new system.

(The assiduous reader will have noticed that Table 4.6 shows some irregularities which do not seem to fit with the above exposition - for example Brentwood in Essex with a very high domestic rateable value of £151 per adult suffers losses from poll tax at GRE, and additional losses from its overspend. The reason for this is that it had a multiplier in its block grant formula set at the extremely low value of 0.22, thus reducing the domestic marginal tax cost on district expenditure nearly fivefold below that implied by rateable value. As noted above, multipliers below unity were very common in the block grant system in the late 1980s. There were also other irregularities.[9])

The Redistribution of the Tax Burden between Areas

Table 4.6: Changes in local tax bills, English Tax Areas, 1987/88 based data

	(1)	(2)	(3)	(4)	(5)	(6)	(7)	(8)	(9)	(10)	(11)
	SPENDING AT GRE					ACTUAL SPENDING					
	Domestic Rate Poundage	Domestic Rateable Value per adult	Average Rate bill per adult	Change in local tax bill per adult		Over-spend per adult	Poll tax per adult	Average Rate bill per adult	Change in local tax bill per adult		Change in local tax bill per adult on difference from GRE
	p	£'s	£'s	%	£'s	£'s	£'s	£'s	%	£'s	£'s
LONDON											
Inner London											
City of London	75.04	354.4	265.9	-33.1	-87.9	278	456	465.3	-2.0	-9.3	78.6
Camden	124.52	185.6	231.2	-23.0	-53.2	604	782	429.9	81.9	352.1	405.3
Greenwich	94.14	109.5	103.1	72.6	74.9	430	608	247.7	145.5	360.3	285.5
Hackney	97.44	143.6	139.9	27.2	38.1	513	691	398.7	73.3	292.3	254.2
Hammersmith & Fulham	103.18	134.4	138.7	28.4	39.3	287	465	215.8	115.5	249.2	209.9
Islington	106.46	159.1	169.4	5.1	8.6	305	483	280.9	72.0	202.1	193.5
Kensington & Chelsea	107.74	329.4	354.9	-49.8	-176.9	192	370	371.3	-0.3	-1.3	175.7
Lambeth	103.21	134.5	138.9	28.2	39.1	369	547	288.5	89.6	258.5	219.4
Lewisham	100.68	122.6	123.4	44.2	54.6	499	677	356.9	89.7	320.1	265.5
Southwark	96.63	125.7	121.5	46.5	56.5	392	570	273.2	108.7	296.8	240.3
Tower Hamlets	83.21	141.2	117.5	51.5	60.5	461	639	291.5	119.2	347.5	287.1
Wandsworth	116.26	129.4	150.4	18.3	27.6	257	435	204.0	113.2	231.0	203.4
Westminster	104.98	352.6	370.2	-51.9	-192.2	218	396	514.2	-23.0	-118.2	74.0
Outer London											
Barking & Dagenham	156.82	107.7	168.9	5.4	9.1	43	221	199.8	10.6	21.2	12.1
Barnet	152.48	172.1	262.3	-32.2	-84.3	44	222	291.9	-23.9	-69.9	14.5
Bexley	153.52	116.4	178.7	-0.4	-0.7	33	211	204.0	3.4	7.0	7.7
Brent	157.80	129.4	204.2	-12.8	-26.2	105	283	310.2	-8.8	-27.2	-0.9
Bromley	149.46	146.1	218.4	-18.5	-40.4	-5	173	212.6	-18.6	-39.6	0.7
Croydon	156.56	147.3	230.7	-22.8	-52.7	-20	158	210.1	-24.8	-52.1	0.6
Ealing	153.34	127.3	195.1	-8.8	-17.1	100	278	291.5	-4.6	-13.5	3.7
Enfield	154.61	130.1	201.1	-11.5	-23.1	21	199	218.6	-9.0	-19.6	3.5
Haringey	139.11	130.1	181.0	-1.7	-3.0	151	329	324.8	1.3	4.2	7.2
Harrow	156.49	145.0	226.9	-21.5	-48.9	45	223	270.6	-17.6	-47.6	1.2
Havering	154.76	125.3	194.0	-8.2	-16.0	11	189	203.1	-6.9	-14.1	1.9
Hillingdon	150.29	130.3	195.8	-9.1	-17.8	43	221	231.8	-4.7	-10.8	7.0
Hounslow	153.68	132.3	203.3	-12.5	-25.3	-8	170	196.1	-13.3	-26.1	-0.8
Kingston-upon-Thames	148.01	144.2	213.4	-16.6	-35.4	34	212	245.3	-13.6	-33.3	2.1
Merton	153.81	140.9	216.7	-17.9	-38.7	-5	173	211.7	-18.3	-38.7	0.0
Newham	173.71	101.2	175.7	1.3	2.3	126	304	285.7	6.4	18.3	16.0
Redbridge	157.59	134.7	212.3	-16.1	-34.3	-7	171	204.6	-16.4	-33.6	0.7
Richmond-upon-Thames	146.95	154.0	226.2	-21.3	-48.2	55	233	281.8	-17.3	-48.8	-0.5
Sutton	157.92	134.6	212.6	-16.3	-34.6	46	224	254.5	-12.0	-30.5	4.1
Waltham Forest	148.00	115.1	170.3	4.5	7.7	187	365	340.1	7.3	24.9	17.2

62 The Politics and Economics of the Poll Tax

Table 4.6: Changes in local tax bills, English Tax Areas, 1987/88 based data (cont.)

	(1)	(2)	(3)	(4)	(5)	(6)	(7)	(8)	(9)	(10)	(11)
			SPENDING AT GRE					ACTUAL SPENDING			
	Domestic Rate Poundage	Domestic Rateable Value per adult	Average Rate bill per adult	Change in local tax bill		Overspend per adult	Poll tax per adult	Average Rate bill per adult	Change in local tax bill		Change in local tax bill per adult on difference from GRE
	p	£'s	£'s	%	£'s	£'s	£'s	£'s	%	£'s	£'s
METROPOLITAN AREAS											
Greater Manchester											
Bolton	210.83	83.5	176.0	1.1	2.0	24	202	193.0	4.7	9.0	7.1
Bury	210.76	93.0	195.9	-9.1	-17.9	66	244	247.7	-1.5	-3.7	14.2
Manchester	213.50	80.7	172.2	3.3	5.8	94	272	272.5	-0.2	-0.5	-6.2
Oldham	218.70	71.9	157.3	13.2	20.7	23	201	171.9	16.9	29.1	8.4
Rochdale	211.84	71.8	152.0	17.1	26.0	58	236	186.5	26.5	49.5	23.5
Salford	211.22	82.4	174.0	2.3	4.0	65	243	219.3	10.8	23.7	19.7
Stockport	207.14	110.1	228.0	-21.9	-50.0	5	183	233.8	-21.7	-50.8	-0.7
Tameside	219.15	71.9	157.6	13.0	20.4	55	233	192.0	21.3	41.0	20.5
Trafford	216.67	105.4	228.5	-22.1	-50.5	-22	156	208.8	-25.3	-52.8	-2.3
Wigan	213.93	75.8	162.3	9.7	15.7	67	245	204.9	19.5	40.1	24.3
Merseyside											
Knowsley	215.94	80.6	174.0	2.3	4.0	189	367	238.0	54.2	129.0	124.9
Liverpool	203.52	76.1	155.0	14.9	23.0	123	301	244.1	23.3	56.9	33.8
St Helens	213.36	76.9	164.0	8.5	14.0	65	243	210.2	15.6	32.8	18.8
Sefton	215.25	94.9	204.2	-12.8	-26.2	32	210	235.8	-10.9	-25.8	0.4
Wirral	209.52	101.1	211.7	-15.9	-33.7	68	246	274.5	-10.4	-28.5	5.3
South Yorkshire											
Barnsley	197.85	61.5	121.7	46.3	56.3	86	264	166.0	59.0	98.0	41.7
Doncaster	199.02	70.1	139.5	27.6	38.5	102	280	200.9	39.4	79.1	40.6
Rotherham	201.99	68.7	138.8	28.3	39.2	74	252	182.1	38.4	69.9	30.6
Sheffield	215.42	65.5	141.1	26.1	36.9	70	248	182.5	35.9	65.5	28.7
Tyne & Wear											
Gateshead	187.77	72.4	135.9	31.0	42.1	85	263	186.4	41.1	76.6	34.4
Newcastle upon Tyne	208.41	76.8	160.1	11.2	17.9	114	292	233.2	25.2	58.8	40.9
North Tyneside	202.72	82.2	166.6	6.8	11.4	87	265	229.7	15.4	35.3	23.9
South Tyneside	196.54	68.3	134.2	32.6	43.8	76	254	176.8	43.7	77.2	33.4
Sunderland	215.78	65.5	141.3	26.0	36.7	84	262	180.1	45.5	81.9	45.2
West Midlands											
Birmingham	240.29	96.4	231.7	-23.2	-53.7	8	186	239.2	-22.2	-53.2	0.5
Coventry	207.03	96.9	200.5	-11.2	-22.5	41	219	233.1	-6.1	-14.1	8.4
Dudley	209.97	104.2	218.9	-18.7	-40.9	25	203	240.2	-15.5	-37.2	3.7
Sandwell	213.19	89.5	190.8	-6.7	-12.8	-3	175	188.2	-7.0	-13.2	-0.4
Solihull	198.81	138.5	275.4	-35.4	-97.4	-15	163	258.5	-36.9	-95.5	1.9
Walsall	210.73	95.1	200.3	-11.1	-22.3	13	191	210.3	-9.2	-19.3	3.1
Wolverhampton	210.33	106.2	223.3	-20.3	-45.3	27	205	246.3	-16.8	-41.3	4.0
West Yorkshire											
Bradford	247.40	62.2	153.8	15.7	24.2	60	238	186.4	27.8	51.8	27.3
Calderdale	219.26	59.2	129.9	37.1	48.1	81	259	169.8	52.6	89.2	41.1
Kirklees	219.36	60.1	131.8	35.1	46.2	68	246	165.4	48.7	80.6	34.3
Leeds	215.95	72.9	157.3	13.1	20.7	26	204	172.9	18.0	31.1	10.4
Wakefield	211.71	70.1	148.8	19.9	29.6	57	235	191.0	23.0	44.0	14.4

The Redistribution of the Tax Burden between Areas

Table 4.6: Changes in local tax bills, English Tax Areas, 1987/88 based data (cont.)

	(1)	(2)	(3)	(4)	(5)	(6)	(7)	(8)	(9)	(10)	(11)
	___ SPENDING AT GRE ___					___ ACTUAL SPENDING ___					
	Domestic Rate Poundage	Domestic Rateable Value per adult	Average Rate bill per adult	Change in local tax bill		Over-spend per adult	Poll tax per adult	Average Rate bill per adult	Change in local tax bill		Change in local tax bill per adult on difference from GRE
	p	£'s	£'s	%	£'s	£'s	£'s	£'s	%	£'s	£'s
NON-METROPOLITAN AREAS											
Avon											
Bath	188.13	88.7	166.8	6.7	11.2	46	224	196.5	14.0	27.5	16.3
Bristol	203.83	83.0	169.3	5.2	8.7	59	237	210.7	12.5	26.3	17.6
Kingswood	207.85	90.6	188.3	-5.5	-10.3	28	206	209.5	-1.7	-3.5	6.7
Northavon	204.67	96.7	198.0	-10.1	-20.0	43	221	232.0	-4.7	-11.0	9.0
Wansdyke	202.83	96.6	195.8	-9.1	-17.8	26	204	218.6	-6.7	-14.6	3.2
Woodspring	204.12	101.5	207.2	-14.1	-29.2	41	219	241.9	-9.5	-22.9	6.3
Bedfordshire											
North Bedfordshire	193.03	105.3	203.2	-12.4	-25.2	63	241	253.0	-4.8	-12.0	13.2
Luton	195.41	117.8	230.2	-22.7	-52.2	61	239	284.6	-16.0	-45.6	6.6
Mid Bedfordshire	192.84	106.1	204.6	-13.0	-26.6	55	233	249.0	-6.4	-16.0	10.8
South Bedfordshire	190.63	120.9	230.5	-22.8	-52.5	58	236	283.7	-16.8	-47.7	4.8
Berkshire											
Bracknell	199.56	132.2	263.8	-32.5	-85.8	-34	144	228.9	-37.1	-84.9	0.9
Newbury	196.02	128.3	251.5	-29.2	-73.5	-27	151	225.4	-33.0	-74.4	-0.9
Reading	195.49	107.9	211.0	-15.6	-33.0	-10	168	200.8	-16.3	-32.8	0.2
Slough	192.96	112.4	216.9	-17.9	-38.9	-29	149	193.5	-23.0	-44.5	-5.6
Windsor & Maidenhead	190.16	145.5	276.7	-35.7	-98.7	-14	164	258.4	-36.5	-94.4	4.3
Wokingham	196.43	143.3	281.5	-36.8	-103.5	-29	149	250.0	-40.4	-101.0	2.5
Buckinghamshire											
Aylesbury Vale	199.71	112.8	225.2	-21.0	-47.2	13	191	236.5	-19.2	-45.5	1.7
South Bucks	191.60	176.6	338.3	-47.4	-160.3	28	206	378.6	-45.6	-172.6	-12.3
Chiltern	195.50	172.0	336.2	-47.1	-158.2	33	211	378.6	-44.3	-167.6	-9.4
Milton Keynes	195.07	119.9	233.9	-23.9	-55.9	43	221	271.4	-18.6	-50.4	5.6
Wycombe	196.21	147.1	288.6	-38.3	-110.6	23	201	320.3	-37.2	-119.3	-8.7
Cambridgeshire											
Cambridge	204.38	119.4	244.0	-27.1	-66.0	12	190	254.8	-25.4	-64.8	1.2
East Cambridgeshire	204.09	93.3	190.5	-6.5	-12.5	4	182	192.9	-5.7	-10.9	1.5
Fenland	204.79	84.8	173.7	2.5	4.3	7	185	178.5	3.7	6.5	2.3
Huntingdonshire	203.17	101.1	205.5	-13.4	-27.5	3	181	208.8	-13.3	-27.8	-0.3
Peterborough	201.72	94.0	189.6	-6.1	-11.6	36	214	217.4	-1.6	-3.4	8.2
South Cambridgeshire	203.31	127.5	259.2	-31.3	-81.2	-11	167	249.2	-33.0	-82.2	-1.0
Cheshire											
Chester	202.21	105.7	213.8	-16.8	-35.8	16	194	226.9	-14.5	-32.9	2.9
Congleton	203.36	100.4	204.1	-12.8	-26.1	9	187	211.0	-11.4	-24.0	2.2
Crewe & Nantwich	200.67	104.0	208.7	-14.7	-30.7	14	192	219.4	-12.5	-27.4	3.3
Ellesmere Port & Nes	200.18	102.6	205.4	-13.3	-27.4	38	216	229.2	-5.7	-13.2	14.2
Halton	204.99	87.7	179.8	-1.0	-1.8	16	194	190.7	1.7	3.3	5.1
Macclesfield	202.34	128.8	260.6	-31.7	-82.6	5	183	265.7	-31.1	-82.7	-0.1
Vale Royal	204.26	95.0	194.1	-8.3	-16.1	11	189	201.9	-6.4	-12.9	3.2
Warrington	206.23	89.0	183.4	-3.0	-5.4	14	192	193.7	-0.9	-1.7	3.7

The Politics and Economics of the Poll Tax

Table 4.6: Changes in local tax bills, English Tax Areas, 1987/88 based data (cont.)

	(1)	(2)	(3)	(4)	(5)	(6)	(7)	(8)	(9)	(10)	(11)
	SPENDING AT GRE					ACTUAL SPENDING					
	Domestic Rate Poundage	Domestic Rateable Value	Average Rate bill per adult	Change in local tax bill	Change in local tax bill per adult	Over-spend per adult	Poll tax per adult	Average Rate bill per adult	Change in local tax bill per adult	Change in local tax bill per adult	Change in local tax bill per adult on difference from GRE
	p	£'s	£'s	%	£'s	£'s	£'s	£'s	%	£'s	£'s
Cleveland											
Hartlepool	223.51	68.3	152.6	16.7	25.4	90	268	206.4	29.9	61.6	36.2
Langbaurgh	222.42	80.1	178.1	0.0	-0.1	92	270	241.4	11.9	28.6	28.7
Middlesbrough	221.40	78.0	172.7	3.1	5.3	99	277	237.4	16.7	39.6	34.3
Stockton-on-Tees	228.13	81.4	185.6	-4.1	-7.6	72	250	236.9	5.5	13.1	20.7
Cornwall											
Caradon	205.56	85.9	176.6	0.8	1.4	-20	158	162.2	-2.6	-4.2	-5.6
Carrick	204.60	86.7	177.3	0.4	0.7	-12	166	167.5	-0.9	-1.5	-2.1
Kerrier	209.21	73.5	153.9	15.7	24.1	-16	162	143.8	12.7	18.2	-5.9
North Cornwall	205.83	86.2	177.5	0.3	0.5	-16	162	165.6	-2.2	-3.6	-4.1
Penwith	205.43	83.7	171.9	3.6	6.1	-14	164	161.4	1.6	2.6	-3.6
Restormel	205.80	82.9	170.6	4.4	7.4	-17	161	158.3	1.7	2.7	-4.7
Cumbria											
Allerdale	199.78	62.8	125.4	41.9	52.6	74	252	164.4	53.3	87.6	35.0
Barrow-in-Furness	202.29	57.1	115.5	54.1	62.5	79	257	154.0	66.8	103.0	40.5
Carlisle	199.03	71.9	143.1	24.4	34.9	86	264	195.0	35.4	69.0	34.1
Copeland	196.57	64.9	127.6	39.5	50.4	80	258	169.9	51.8	88.1	37.7
Eden	200.40	66.9	134.1	32.7	43.9	65	243	171.7	41.5	71.3	27.5
South Lakeland	199.47	82.6	164.8	8.0	13.2	74	252	216.0	16.7	36.0	22.9
Derbyshire											
Amber Valley	222.68	77.3	172.1	3.4	5.9	59	237	203.8	16.3	33.2	27.3
Bolsover	221.81	65.0	144.2	23.5	33.8	88	266	187.9	41.5	78.1	44.2
Chesterfield	221.64	77.3	171.3	3.9	6.7	68	246	209.1	17.7	36.9	30.2
Derby	222.56	94.2	209.6	-15.1	-31.6	59	237	247.6	-4.3	-10.6	21.0
Erewash	222.83	80.5	179.5	-0.8	-1.5	59	237	212.7	11.4	24.3	25.7
High Peak	222.22	75.4	167.6	6.2	10.4	67	245	203.5	20.4	41.5	31.1
North East Derbyshire	221.51	80.2	177.7	0.2	0.3	74	252	220.8	14.1	31.2	30.9
South Derbyshire	224.15	85.5	191.7	-7.1	-13.7	54	232	223.5	3.8	8.5	22.2
Derbyshire Dales	221.74	88.4	195.9	-9.1	-17.9	58	236	231.0	2.1	5.0	22.9
Devon											
East Devon	201.09	100.1	201.3	-11.6	-23.3	-11	167	191.9	-13.0	-24.9	-1.6
Exeter	200.59	84.8	170.1	4.7	7.9	-19	159	158.0	0.6	1.0	-6.9
North Devon	200.67	73.7	148.0	20.3	30.0	-3	175	145.3	20.5	29.7	-0.3
Plymouth	206.61	87.0	179.8	-1.0	-1.8	-13	165	169.9	-2.9	-4.9	-3.1
South Hams	198.71	103.8	206.3	-13.7	-28.3	0	178	204.4	-12.9	-26.4	1.9
Teignbridge	199.56	92.9	185.3	-4.0	-7.3	-3	175	182.1	-3.9	-7.1	0.2
Mid Devon	201.05	77.8	156.4	13.8	21.6	-5	173	152.4	13.5	20.6	-1.0
Torbay	205.92	97.5	200.8	-11.4	-22.8	-1	177	200.0	-11.5	-23.0	-0.2
Torridge	199.95	66.9	133.7	33.2	44.3	2	180	133.7	34.7	46.3	2.0
West Devon	201.71	78.8	158.9	12.0	19.1	-10	168	152.3	10.3	15.7	-3.4

The Redistribution of the Tax Burden between Areas

Table 4.6: Changes in local tax bills, English Tax Areas, 1987/88 based data (cont.)

	(1)	(2)	(3)	(4)	(5)	(6)	(7)	(8)	(9)	(10)	(11)
	SPENDING AT GRE					ACTUAL SPENDING					
	Domestic Rate Poundage	Domestic Rateable Value per adult	Average Rate bill per adult	Change in local tax bill per adult		Over-spend per adult	Poll tax per adult	Average Rate bill per adult	Change in local tax bill per adult		Change in local tax bill per adult on difference from GRE
	p	£'s	£'s	%	£'s	£'s	£'s	£'s	%	£'s	£'s
Dorset											
Bournemouth	203.71	107.1	218.2	-18.4	-40.2	-13	165	206.5	-20.1	-41.5	-1.3
Christchurch	197.90	126.3	250.0	-28.8	-72.0	-12	166	236.5	-29.8	-70.5	1.6
North Dorset	201.51	94.1	189.6	-6.1	-11.6	-22	156	172.6	-9.6	-16.6	-4.9
Poole	200.45	128.5	257.6	-30.9	-79.6	-16	162	240.6	-32.7	-78.6	1.0
Purbeck	200.76	100.9	202.5	-12.1	-24.5	-24	154	182.5	-15.6	-28.5	-4.1
West Dorset	198.48	96.8	192.2	-7.4	-14.2	-21	157	176.1	-10.9	-19.1	-4.9
Weymouth & Portland	202.53	87.5	177.2	0.5	0.8	-13	165	167.6	-1.5	-2.6	-3.4
Wimborne	196.48	134.1	263.5	-32.4	-85.5	-5	173	254.8	-32.1	-81.8	3.6
Durham											
Chester-le-Street	210.98	71.6	151.1	17.8	26.9	36	214	173.5	23.3	40.5	13.6
Darlington	210.03	70.0	147.0	21.1	31.0	67	245	189.6	29.3	55.4	24.4
Derwentside	208.17	59.3	123.4	44.2	54.6	86	264	167.1	58.0	96.9	42.4
Durham	208.72	68.8	143.6	23.9	34.4	46	224	170.1	31.7	53.9	19.5
Easington	219.83	60.0	131.9	35.0	46.1	20	198	142.6	38.8	55.4	9.3
Sedgefield	205.92	61.4	126.5	40.7	51.5	75	253	161.6	56.6	91.4	39.9
Teesdale	208.65	59.0	123.0	44.7	55.0	16	194	131.1	47.9	62.9	7.9
Wear Valley	207.10	56.1	116.2	53.2	61.8	69	247	147.3	67.7	99.7	37.9
East Sussex											
Brighton	196.91	115.2	226.9	-21.6	-48.9	-2	176	221.2	-20.4	-45.2	3.7
Eastbourne	204.40	128.0	261.7	-32.0	-83.7	-5	173	255.7	-32.3	-82.7	1.0
Hastings	204.98	101.4	207.8	-14.3	-29.8	-9	169	199.5	-15.3	-30.5	-0.7
Hove	184.44	130.0	239.7	-25.8	-61.7	-4	174	228.3	-23.8	-54.3	7.5
Lewes	200.35	127.5	255.4	-30.3	-77.4	-6	172	247.1	-30.4	-75.1	2.4
Rother	198.95	132.4	263.3	-32.4	-85.3	-2	176	257.7	-31.7	-81.7	3.6
Wealden	201.81	112.9	227.7	-21.8	-49.7	-3	175	222.7	-21.4	-47.7	2.0
Essex											
Basildon	206.52	129.2	266.8	-33.3	-88.8	81	259	320.1	-19.1	-61.1	27.7
Braintree	203.49	105.5	214.7	-17.1	-36.7	-1	177	214.1	-17.3	-37.1	-0.5
Brentwood	186.76	151.3	282.6	-37.0	-104.6	161	339	349.3	-2.9	-10.3	94.4
Castle Point	201.21	124.8	251.2	-29.1	-73.2	8	186	257.9	-27.9	-71.9	1.3
Chelmsford	201.71	134.6	271.4	-34.4	-93.4	3	181	274.2	-34.0	-93.2	0.2
Colchester	206.35	106.5	219.7	-19.0	-41.7	-10	168	211.2	-20.5	-43.2	-1.5
Epping Forest	196.18	146.1	286.6	-37.9	-108.6	6	184	292.3	-37.1	-108.3	0.3
Harlow	207.19	115.5	239.3	-25.6	-61.3	137	315	312.9	0.7	2.1	63.5
Maldon	206.01	121.4	250.1	-28.8	-72.1	1	179	251.0	-28.7	-72.0	0.2
Rochford	202.79	131.0	265.7	-33.0	-87.7	-1	177	265.0	-33.2	-88.0	-0.3
Southend-on-Sea	202.59	130.4	264.1	-32.6	-86.1	6	184	269.9	-31.8	-85.9	0.2
Tendring	203.43	111.9	227.6	-21.8	-49.6	6	184	233.2	-21.1	-49.2	0.4
Thurrock	203.30	116.1	236.1	-24.6	-58.1	64	242	263.2	-8.1	-21.2	36.9
Uttlesford	200.89	129.0	259.1	-31.3	-81.1	5	183	263.9	-30.6	-80.9	0.3
Gloucestershire											
Cheltenham	203.96	108.5	221.2	-19.5	-43.2	2	180	223.0	-19.3	-43.0	0.3
Cotswold	202.00	109.6	221.3	-19.6	-43.3	2	180	223.3	-19.4	-43.3	0.1
Forest of Dean	202.20	73.8	149.2	19.3	28.8	13	191	156.2	22.2	34.8	6.0
Gloucester	206.25	83.8	172.9	3.0	5.1	5	183	176.1	3.9	6.9	1.8
Stroud	203.47	94.0	191.2	-6.9	-13.2	14	192	201.3	-4.6	-9.3	3.8
Tewkesbury	205.10	104.8	214.9	-17.2	-36.9	-5	173	210.6	-17.9	-37.6	-0.8

The Politics and Economics of the Poll Tax

Table 4.6: Changes in local tax bills, English Tax Areas, 1987/88 based data (cont.)

	(1)	(2)	(3)	(4)	(5)	(6)	(7)	(8)	(9)	(10)	(11)
		SPENDING AT GRE						ACTUAL SPENDING			
	Domestic Rate Poundage	Domestic Rateable Value per adult	Average Rate bill per adult	Change in local tax bill	Change in local tax bill	Over-spend per adult	Poll tax per adult	Average Rate bill per adult	Change in local tax bill	Change in local tax bill	Change in local tax bill per adult on difference from GRE
	p	£'s	£'s	%	£'s	£'s	£'s	£'s	%	£'s	£'s
Hampshire											
Basingstoke & Deane	193.39	115.2	222.8	-20.1	-44.8	-15	163	211.0	-22.8	-48.0	-3.2
East Hampshire	193.39	122.3	236.5	-24.7	-58.5	3	181	238.0	-24.0	-57.0	1.5
Eastleigh	195.17	116.6	227.5	-21.8	-49.5	-2	176	225.0	-21.8	-49.0	0.5
Fareham	195.89	121.4	237.9	-25.2	-59.9	1	179	238.5	-24.9	-59.5	0.4
Gosport	197.75	104.2	206.1	-13.6	-28.1	-9	169	198.7	-14.9	-29.7	-1.6
Hart	195.40	128.4	250.8	-29.0	-72.8	7	185	256.7	-27.9	-71.7	1.2
Havant	199.29	116.8	232.7	-23.5	-54.7	-10	168	223.3	-24.8	-55.3	-0.6
New Forest	193.32	111.0	214.6	-17.1	-36.6	3	181	216.2	-16.3	-35.2	1.4
Portsmouth	193.00	83.5	161.1	10.5	16.9	9	187	166.2	12.5	20.8	4.0
Rushmoor	194.31	96.0	186.5	-4.5	-8.5	4	182	187.9	-3.2	-5.9	2.5
Southampton	196.42	90.3	177.4	0.4	0.6	-2	176	175.3	0.4	0.7	0.0
Test Valley	194.59	108.4	210.9	-15.6	-32.9	-7	171	204.7	-16.5	-33.7	-0.8
Winchester	194.69	117.5	228.7	-22.2	-50.7	2	180	229.5	-21.6	-49.5	1.2
Hereford & Worcester											
Bromsgrove	205.58	122.2	251.3	-29.2	-73.3	-43	135	208.3	-35.2	-73.3	0.0
Hereford	204.39	86.0	175.9	1.2	2.1	-29	149	154.6	-3.6	-5.6	-7.7
Leominster	203.12	81.7	165.9	7.3	12.1	-32	146	143.7	1.6	2.3	-9.7
Malvern Hills	201.94	114.6	231.4	-23.1	-53.4	-28	150	203.1	-26.2	-53.1	0.3
Redditch	205.34	112.0	230.1	-22.6	-52.1	-25	153	206.3	-25.8	-53.3	-1.3
South Herefs.	204.08	86.6	176.6	0.8	1.4	-45	133	145.2	-8.4	-12.2	-13.6
Worcester	204.98	112.3	230.2	-22.7	-52.2	-28	150	203.2	-26.2	-53.2	-0.9
Wychavon	204.12	119.2	243.4	-26.9	-65.4	-28	150	214.7	-30.1	-64.7	0.7
Wyre Forest	201.03	102.8	206.7	-13.9	-28.7	-12	166	195.1	-14.9	-29.1	-0.4
Hertfordshire											
Broxbourne	200.12	114.5	229.1	-22.3	-51.1	16	194	243.0	-20.2	-49.0	2.1
Dacorum	197.77	134.1	265.1	-32.9	-87.1	20	198	285.9	-30.7	-87.9	-0.8
East Herts.	198.90	119.7	238.0	-25.2	-60.0	18	196	254.9	-23.1	-58.9	1.1
Hertsmere	198.04	131.2	259.8	-31.5	-81.8	34	212	293.3	-27.7	-81.3	0.5
North Herts.	198.81	125.0	248.4	-28.4	-70.4	19	197	267.2	-26.3	-70.2	0.3
St Albans	197.52	132.6	261.8	-32.0	-83.8	26	204	288.7	-29.3	-84.7	-0.9
Stevenage	202.23	118.5	239.6	-25.7	-61.6	55	233	277.8	-16.1	-44.8	16.8
Three Rivers	198.93	139.7	277.8	-35.9	-99.8	27	205	307.7	-33.4	-102.7	-2.9
Watford	197.73	116.0	229.3	-22.4	-51.3	28	206	254.9	-19.2	-48.9	2.4
Welwyn Hatfield	200.53	129.7	260.2	-31.6	-82.2	47	225	291.5	-22.8	-66.5	15.7
Humberside											
Beverley	203.49	101.2	206.0	-13.6	-28.0	41	219	239.2	-8.4	-20.2	7.8
Boothferry	202.42	68.7	139.1	28.0	38.9	46	224	164.1	36.5	59.9	21.0
Cleethorpes	201.21	81.4	163.7	8.7	14.3	51	229	196.7	16.4	32.3	18.0
Glanford	202.15	83.7	169.1	5.3	8.9	41	219	196.3	11.6	22.0	13.8
Great Grimsby	203.77	74.7	152.2	16.9	25.8	41	219	176.8	23.9	42.2	16.4
Holderness	204.24	82.2	167.9	6.0	10.1	37	215	192.3	11.8	22.7	12.6
Kingston-upon-Hull	204.60	64.4	131.7	35.2	46.3	70	248	171.0	45.1	77.0	30.7
East Yorkshire	203.68	71.9	146.4	21.6	31.6	52	230	177.4	29.6	52.6	20.9
Scunthorpe	195.52	83.7	163.7	8.7	14.3	83	261	210.4	24.0	50.6	36.3

The Redistribution of the Tax Burden between Areas

Table 4.6: Changes in local tax bills, English Tax Areas, 1987/88 based data (cont.)

	(1)	(2)	(3)	(4)	(5)	(6)	(7)	(8)	(9)	(10)	(11)
	SPENDING AT GRE					ACTUAL SPENDING					
	Domestic Rate Poundage	Domestic Rateable Value per adult	Average Rate bill per adult	Change in local tax bill per adult		Over-spend per adult	Poll tax per adult	Average Rate bill per adult	Change in local bill per adult		Change in local tax bill per adult on difference from GRE
	p	£'s	£'s	%	£'s	£'s	£'s	£'s	%	£'s	£'s
Isle of Wight											
Medina	191.87	89.6	171.8	3.6	6.2	31	209	193.6	8.0	15.4	9.2
South Wight	191.92	94.2	180.7	-1.5	-2.7	37	215	209.8	2.5	5.2	7.9
Kent											
Ashford	201.44	98.4	198.3	-10.2	-20.3	-30	148	173.5	-14.7	-25.5	-5.2
Canterbury	201.60	92.4	186.3	-4.4	-8.3	-26	152	165.7	-8.3	-13.7	-5.5
Dartford	196.66	87.0	171.0	4.1	7.0	-29	149	148.8	0.1	0.2	-6.8
Dover	201.65	84.3	170.0	4.7	8.0	-34	144	146.4	-1.6	-2.4	-10.4
Gillingham	185.73	100.0	185.7	-4.1	-7.7	-28	150	159.0	-5.6	-9.0	-1.3
Gravesham	200.81	97.8	196.3	-9.3	-18.3	-26	152	174.4	-12.8	-22.4	-4.0
Maidstone	201.16	96.3	193.8	-8.2	-15.8	-31	147	169.0	-13.0	-22.0	-6.1
Rochester upon Medway	201.52	92.4	186.2	-4.4	-8.2	-47	131	151.9	-13.8	-20.9	-12.7
Sevenoaks	201.00	103.6	208.2	-14.5	-30.2	-27	151	184.1	-18.0	-33.1	-3.0
Shepway	198.75	112.9	224.4	-20.7	-46.4	-18	160	206.1	-22.4	-46.1	0.3
Swale	201.97	79.6	160.8	10.7	17.2	-25	153	143.2	6.8	9.8	-7.4
Thanet	202.15	96.5	195.0	-8.7	-17.0	-24	154	175.5	-12.3	-21.5	-4.5
Tonbridge & Malling	201.62	92.1	185.7	-4.1	-7.7	-26	152	165.2	-8.0	-13.2	-5.5
Tunbridge Wells	200.51	97.6	195.7	-9.0	-17.7	-26	152	173.4	-12.4	-21.4	-3.7
Lancashire											
Blackburn	206.55	59.3	122.5	45.3	55.5	28	206	136.2	51.3	69.8	14.3
Blackpool	213.11	81.3	173.2	2.8	4.8	16	194	186.1	4.2	7.9	3.1
Burnley	203.38	52.8	107.5	65.6	70.5	61	239	133.3	79.3	105.7	35.2
Chorley	207.14	81.8	169.4	5.1	8.6	12	190	176.5	7.6	13.5	4.9
Fylde	207.84	96.3	200.2	-11.1	-22.2	11	189	208.2	-9.2	-19.2	2.9
Hyndburn	205.91	55.6	114.5	55.5	63.5	34	212	130.6	62.4	81.4	17.9
Lancaster	206.49	73.3	151.4	17.6	26.6	12	190	158.1	20.2	31.9	5.3
Pendle	206.03	53.7	110.5	61.0	67.5	34	212	126.1	68.1	85.9	18.4
Preston	206.72	75.4	155.8	14.2	22.2	23	201	170.3	18.0	30.7	8.6
Ribble Valley	203.22	80.9	164.4	8.3	13.6	21	199	176.6	12.7	22.4	8.8
Rossendale	204.03	62.5	127.6	39.5	50.4	50	228	152.4	49.6	75.6	25.2
South Ribble	207.76	77.8	161.7	10.1	16.3	11	189	168.5	12.2	20.5	4.2
West Lancashire	207.77	95.2	197.7	-10.0	-19.7	12	190	206.6	-8.1	-16.6	3.1
Wyre	204.40	89.1	182.1	-2.2	-4.1	11	189	189.3	-0.1	-0.3	3.8
Leicestershire											
Blaby	204.41	104.5	213.7	-16.7	-35.7	11	189	223.4	-15.4	-34.4	1.3
Charnwood	203.57	104.0	211.8	-16.0	-33.8	17	195	226.1	-13.8	-31.1	2.7
Harborough	204.18	106.3	217.1	-18.0	-39.1	18	196	232.7	-15.8	-36.7	2.4
Hinckley & Bosworth	207.16	97.4	201.8	-11.8	-23.8	7	185	207.1	-10.7	-22.1	1.7
Leicester	199.86	76.7	153.2	16.2	24.8	42	220	177.7	23.8	42.3	17.5
Melton	192.41	106.1	204.1	-12.8	-26.1	26	204	222.7	-8.4	-18.7	7.4
North West Leicester	203.47	91.8	186.8	-4.7	-8.8	32	210	210.4	-0.2	-0.4	8.4
Oadby & Wigston	203.44	103.5	210.5	-15.4	-32.5	16	194	224.3	-13.5	-30.3	2.2
Rutland	206.13	93.9	193.5	-8.0	-15.5	17	195	206.5	-5.6	-11.5	4.0

The Politics and Economics of the Poll Tax

Table 4.6: Changes in local tax bills, English Tax Areas, 1987/88 based data (cont.)

	(1)	(2)	(3)	(4)	(5)	(6)	(7)	(8)	(9)	(10)	(11)
	\multicolumn{5}{SPENDING AT GRE}			\multicolumn{4}{ACTUAL SPENDING}	
	Domestic Rate Poundage	Domestic Rateable Value per adult	Average Rate bill per adult	Change in local tax bill per adult		Over-spend per adult	Poll tax per adult	Average Rate bill per adult	Change in local tax bill per adult		Change in local tax bill per adult on difference from GRE
	p	£'s	£'s	%	£'s	£'s	£'s	£'s	%	£'s	£'s
Lincolnshire											
Boston	203.45	84.1	171.0	4.1	7.0	-26	152	152.7	-0.4	-0.7	-7.7
East Lindsey	204.62	83.4	170.7	4.2	7.3	-21	157	155.3	1.1	1.7	-5.6
Lincoln	205.13	77.1	158.2	12.5	19.8	-20	158	144.9	9.0	13.1	-6.7
North Kesteven	204.06	83.7	170.9	4.2	7.1	-23	155	154.0	0.6	1.0	-6.1
South Holland	203.69	82.1	167.3	6.4	10.7	-23	155	151.2	2.5	3.8	-6.9
South Kesteven	200.23	93.9	188.1	-5.4	-10.1	-24	154	168.7	-8.7	-14.7	-4.6
West Lindsey	203.19	79.3	161.0	10.5	17.0	-12	166	152.0	9.2	14.0	-3.0
Norfolk											
Breckland	203.71	91.1	185.6	-4.1	-7.6	-31	147	162.1	-9.3	-15.1	-7.4
Broadland	202.68	104.6	212.0	-16.0	-34.0	-26	152	188.7	-19.5	-36.7	-2.8
Great Yarmouth	202.30	88.5	179.0	-0.5	-1.0	-12	166	169.6	-2.1	-3.6	-2.6
North Norfolk	200.58	94.6	189.7	-6.2	-11.7	-26	152	169.1	-10.1	-17.1	-5.4
Norwich	200.91	90.5	181.9	-2.1	-3.9	-6	172	176.6	-2.6	-4.6	-0.8
South Norfolk	202.92	103.5	209.9	-15.2	-31.9	-29	149	185.4	-19.6	-36.4	-4.5
Kings Lynn & West No	201.89	83.8	169.2	5.2	8.8	-24	154	151.9	1.4	2.1	-6.6
Northamptonshire											
Corby	197.93	98.1	194.2	-8.3	-16.2	11	189	201.1	-6.0	-12.1	4.1
Daventry	202.15	111.2	224.8	-20.8	-46.8	54	232	256.3	-9.5	-24.3	22.5
East Northants.	203.44	91.5	186.2	-4.4	-8.2	-20	158	172.0	-8.2	-14.0	-5.8
Kettering	199.55	91.0	181.6	-2.0	-3.6	8	186	186.5	-0.3	-0.5	3.1
Northampton	204.41	102.7	210.0	-15.2	-32.0	10	188	218.0	-13.8	-30.0	2.0
S. Northants.	199.93	114.4	228.7	-22.2	-50.7	-7	171	223.4	-23.4	-52.4	-1.7
Welling-borough	199.09	96.9	193.0	-7.8	-15.0	2	180	194.5	-7.4	-14.5	0.5
Northumberland											
Alnwick	207.60	77.0	159.8	11.4	18.2	37	215	181.2	18.6	33.8	15.5
Berwick-upon-Tweed	210.21	77.8	163.6	8.8	14.4	28	206	181.0	13.8	25.0	10.6
Blyth Valley	209.88	78.0	163.7	8.8	14.3	74	252	211.3	19.3	40.7	26.4
Castle Morpeth	209.83	97.2	203.9	-12.7	-25.9	37	215	231.5	-7.1	-16.5	9.3
Tynedale	208.95	81.4	170.1	4.6	7.9	39	217	194.8	11.4	22.2	14.3
Wansbeck	208.83	66.5	139.0	28.1	39.0	73	251	178.5	40.6	72.5	33.5
North Yorkshire											
Craven	196.91	72.8	143.4	24.2	34.6	6	184	146.3	25.7	37.7	3.0
Hambleton	198.86	83.0	165.1	7.8	12.9	1	179	165.8	8.0	13.2	0.3
Harrogate	195.19	92.0	179.5	-0.9	-1.5	28	206	199.9	3.1	6.1	7.7
Richmondshire	198.48	70.6	140.2	27.0	37.8	6	184	143.1	28.6	40.9	3.1
Ryedale	198.42	77.9	154.6	15.2	23.4	3	181	156.2	15.9	24.8	1.4
Scarborough	196.87	74.8	147.3	20.8	30.7	14	192	155.4	23.5	36.6	5.9
Selby	198.31	79.3	157.2	13.2	20.8	22	200	165.0	21.2	35.0	14.2
York	197.87	70.7	140.0	27.2	38.0	-5	173	137.5	25.9	35.5	-2.5

The Redistribution of the Tax Burden between Areas

Table 4.6: Changes in local tax bills, English Tax Areas, 1987/88 based data (cont.)

	(1)	(2)	(3)	(4)	(5)	(6)	(7)	(8)	(9)	(10)	(11)
	SPENDING AT GRE					ACTUAL SPENDING					
	Domestic Rate Poundage	Domestic Rateable Value per adult	Average Rate bill per adult	Change in local tax bill per adult		Over-spend per adult	Poll tax per adult	Average Rate bill per adult	Change in local tax bill per adult		Change in local tax bill per adult on difference from GRE
	p	£'s	£'s	%	£'s	£'s	£'s	£'s	%	£'s	£'s
Nottinghamshire											
Ashfield	209.01	68.2	142.5	24.9	35.5	31	209	159.7	30.9	49.3	13.8
Bassetlaw	210.38	74.2	156.0	14.1	22.0	60	238	184.9	28.7	53.1	31.1
Broxtowe	207.30	85.8	177.8	0.1	0.2	24	202	195.1	3.5	6.9	6.7
Gedling	208.07	92.4	192.2	-7.4	-14.2	23	201	210.1	-4.3	-9.1	5.1
Mansfield	201.49	75.2	151.6	17.4	26.4	59	237	184.6	28.4	52.4	26.0
Newark & Sherwood	205.69	78.9	162.2	9.7	15.8	31	209	181.5	15.1	27.5	11.7
Nottingham	211.36	76.6	161.8	10.0	16.2	29	207	180.6	14.6	26.4	10.2
Rushcliffe	208.79	98.7	206.2	-13.7	-28.2	27	205	228.4	-10.2	-23.4	4.8
Oxfordshire											
Cherwell	198.76	102.0	202.7	-12.2	-24.7	23	201	220.6	-8.9	-19.6	5.1
Oxford	197.74	98.0	193.7	-8.1	-15.7	42	220	226.1	-2.7	-6.1	9.6
South Oxfordshire	197.75	117.3	231.9	-23.3	-53.9	24	202	253.7	-20.4	-51.7	2.3
Vale of White Horse	195.53	114.2	223.3	-20.3	-45.3	15	193	239.3	-19.3	-46.3	-0.9
West Oxfordshire	195.54	105.7	206.6	-13.9	-28.6	27	205	229.6	-10.7	-24.6	4.0
Shropshire											
Bridgnorth	205.66	90.5	186.1	-4.3	-8.1	-6	172	181.9	-5.5	-9.9	-1.9
North Shropshire	204.86	80.1	164.1	8.4	13.9	-1	177	163.4	8.3	13.6	-0.2
Oswestry	204.84	76.1	155.9	14.2	22.1	5	183	158.5	15.5	24.5	2.4
Shrewsbury & Atcham	203.86	95.8	195.2	-8.8	-17.2	10	188	201.9	-6.9	-13.9	3.3
South Shropshire	201.89	80.4	162.3	9.7	15.7	-2	176	161.4	9.0	14.6	-1.1
Wrekin	202.32	93.3	188.7	-5.7	-10.7	25	203	206.5	-1.7	-3.5	7.2
Somerset											
Mendip	199.31	91.5	182.4	-2.4	-4.4	0	178	182.2	-2.3	-4.2	0.2
Sedgemoor	196.58	93.9	184.6	-3.6	-6.6	13	191	193.2	-1.1	-2.2	4.5
Taunton Deane	196.33	94.1	184.7	-3.6	-6.7	3	181	186.9	-3.1	-5.9	0.8
West Somerset	199.25	96.9	193.1	-7.8	-15.1	3	181	195.4	-7.4	-14.4	0.7
South Somerset	199.96	91.8	183.6	-3.1	-5.6	0	178	183.8	-3.1	-5.8	-0.1
Staffordshire											
Cannock Chase	208.73	85.2	177.8	0.1	0.2	8	186	182.8	1.7	3.2	3.0
E. Staffordshire	207.65	85.3	177.1	0.5	0.9	-1	177	176.1	0.5	0.9	0.0
Lichfield	208.50	112.3	234.2	-24.0	-56.2	-4	174	230.5	-24.5	-56.5	-0.3
Newcastle-under-Lyme	207.64	86.9	180.5	-1.4	-2.5	8	186	185.4	0.3	0.6	3.0
S. Staffordshire	208.35	114.3	238.1	-25.2	-60.1	-6	172	233.0	-26.2	-61.0	-0.9
Stafford	207.30	97.8	202.8	-12.2	-24.8	-1	177	202.2	-12.5	-25.2	-0.4
Staffs Moorlands	207.12	87.1	180.4	-1.3	-2.4	6	184	184.3	-0.2	-0.3	2.1
Stoke-on-Trent	207.22	75.3	156.1	14.0	21.9	9	187	161.0	16.1	26.0	4.1
Tamworth	205.70	101.0	207.8	-14.3	-29.8	5	183	210.6	-13.1	-27.7	2.2

Table 4.6: Changes in local tax bills, English Tax Areas, 1987/88 based data (cont.)

	(1)	(2)	(3)	(4)	(5)	(6)	(7)	(8)	(9)	(10)	(11)
	SPENDING AT GRE					ACTUAL SPENDING					
	Domestic Rate Poundage	Domestic Rateable Value per adult	Average Rate bill per adult	Change in local tax bill	Change in local tax bill per adult	Over-spend per adult	Poll tax per adult	Average Rate bill per adult	Change in local tax bill	Change in local tax bill per adult	Change in local tax bill per adult on difference from GRE
	p	£'s	£'s	%	£'s	£'s	£'s	£'s	%	£'s	£'s
Suffolk											
Babergh	200.40	101.7	203.9	-12.7	-25.9	-5	173	199.0	-13.1	-26.0	-0.1
Forest Heath	199.21	86.8	172.9	3.0	5.1	-9	169	166.7	1.4	2.3	-2.8
Ipswich	202.94	96.8	196.5	-9.4	-18.5	14	192	210.0	-8.6	-18.0	0.5
Mid Suffolk	199.84	92.4	184.7	-3.6	-6.7	-1	177	182.9	-3.2	-5.9	0.8
St Edmundsbury	203.12	93.8	190.6	-6.6	-12.6	-17	161	178.2	-9.7	-17.2	-4.6
Suffolk Coastal	200.50	110.4	221.4	-19.6	-43.4	0	178	220.5	-19.3	-42.5	0.9
Waveney	200.06	95.5	191.1	-6.8	-13.1	-3	175	188.1	-7.0	-13.1	-0.1
Surrey											
Elmbridge	193.39	170.0	328.9	-45.9	-150.9	61	239	362.2	-34.0	-123.2	27.7
Epsom & Ewell	197.54	149.7	295.8	-39.8	-117.8	4	182	294.5	-38.2	-112.5	5.3
Guildford	195.23	133.7	261.1	-31.8	-83.1	-18	160	242.0	-33.9	-82.0	1.0
Mole Valley	194.40	132.4	257.3	-30.8	-79.3	-9	169	247.6	-31.7	-78.6	0.8
Reigate & B.	196.70	135.4	266.2	-33.1	-88.2	5	183	265.8	-31.2	-82.8	5.4
Runnymede	193.98	123.3	239.1	-25.6	-61.1	-27	151	213.1	-29.2	-62.1	-1.0
Spelthorne	179.12	127.2	227.9	-21.9	-49.9	1	179	223.2	-19.8	-44.2	5.7
Surrey Heath	193.69	149.1	288.7	-38.4	-110.7	-38	140	247.8	-43.5	-107.8	2.9
Tandridge	188.93	123.1	232.5	-23.4	-54.5	-5	173	227.1	-23.8	-54.1	0.4
Waverley	194.55	141.4	275.2	-35.3	-97.2	-4	174	270.1	-35.6	-96.1	1.1
Woking	190.98	145.9	278.6	-36.1	-100.6	-38	140	241.7	-42.1	-101.7	-1.1
Warwickshire											
N. Warks.	207.99	93.9	195.3	-8.9	-17.3	30	208	208.9	-0.4	-0.9	16.4
Nuneaton & B.	200.52	99.7	200.0	-11.0	-22.0	22	200	216.3	-7.5	-16.3	5.7
Rugby	202.72	107.8	218.6	-18.6	-40.6	2	180	218.8	-17.7	-38.8	1.8
Stratford-on-Avon	202.74	132.2	268.0	-33.6	-90.0	-4	174	263.3	-33.9	-89.3	0.7
Warwick	203.15	125.1	254.2	-30.0	-76.2	-2	176	251.2	-29.9	-75.2	1.0
West Sussex											
Adur	198.71	108.6	215.8	-17.5	-37.8	2	180	218.4	-17.6	-38.4	-0.6
Arun	198.53	117.4	233.1	-23.6	-55.1	-19	159	213.5	-25.5	-54.5	0.6
Chichester	198.15	117.2	232.3	-23.4	-54.3	-26	152	206.4	-26.4	-54.4	-0.1
Crawley	201.74	99.5	200.8	-11.4	-22.8	41	219	201.7	8.6	17.3	40.1
Horsham	198.51	118.7	235.6	-24.5	-57.6	-29	149	207.6	-28.2	-58.6	-1.0
Mid Sussex	199.85	120.8	241.5	-26.3	-63.5	-16	162	223.4	-27.5	-61.4	2.1
Worthing	199.02	113.5	225.8	-21.2	-47.8	-23	155	203.7	-23.9	-48.7	-0.9
Wiltshire											
Kennet	199.70	90.1	179.9	-1.0	-1.9	12	190	188.6	0.8	1.4	3.3
North Wiltshire	200.53	80.2	160.8	10.7	17.2	23	201	175.0	14.9	26.0	8.8
Salisbury	201.01	96.2	193.3	-7.9	-15.3	6	184	198.7	-7.4	-14.7	0.6
Thamesdown	196.70	84.4	166.1	7.2	11.9	60	238	205.1	16.1	32.9	21.0
West Wiltshire	201.56	85.9	173.1	2.8	4.9	8	186	178.6	4.1	7.4	2.5
Isles of Scilly	247.82	104.8	259.8	-31.5	-81.8	-85	93	170.8	-45.5	-77.8	4.0

Source: Author's computations

The Redistribution of the Tax Burden between Areas 71

We can reinforce this explanation and provide a key part of the reason why inner London is so atypical by now examining the cost to the domestic sector of an extra £1 of spending in a number of local authorities. This is shown in Table 4.7 (p.72) which in the first row registers the fact that under the poll tax system the domestic tax cost or saving of each £1 of spending difference from GRE is simply £1 because of the major structural simplification of converting grant and the proceeds of the non-domestic rates into lump sum form, fixed at the start of the financial year. Column (1) shows that under the block grant system (1987/88) for nearly all authorities in receipt of block grant an additional £1 in expenditure leads to losses in grant. This means that the cost to ratepayers as a whole (i.e. domestic plus non-domestic), shown in Column (2), of spending an extra £1 is greater than £1 - it is £1 plus the loss of block grant on each £1 of spending. The range of grant change is from an extra 3.2p for Kirklees with the low rateable values per head typical of West Yorkshire to a loss of 151p for Kensington & Chelsea. This variable change in grant in Column (1) reflects the resource equalisation properties of the present system, achieved by setting through the block grant formula a common rate poundage cost for an extra £1 per head of spending. The unique feature of the English (and Welsh) system has been that the differential variation in grant was nearly always negative, rather than positive, reflecting the Government's overriding objective of attempting to discourage expenditure whilst still retaining the resource equalisation properties of the system.

In contrast under the rates-block grant system the total cost of an extra £1 of spending shown in Column (2) must be borne by ratepayers and is shared between the domestic and non-domestic sectors according to their share of aggregate rateable value. The net result for the domestic sector is shown in Column (3) and for the non-domestic sector in Column (4). Column (3) shows that there is a substantial variation between authorities receiving block grant in the cost to domestic taxpayers of a £1 of spending under the present system from just over 50p in Kirklees with very low rateable values to £1.93p in Kensington & Chelsea with its high rateable values.

Now let us look at the inner London authorities, ILEA, Camden, and Westminster, which do not suffer any losses in block grant on marginal expenditure because they receive no block grant. The reason why these authorities do not receive any grant is because their rateable values are very high and their expenditure is more than sufficient to have exhausted their entitlement to grant. In fact, ILEA (rateable value

The Politics and Economics of the Poll Tax

Table 4.7: Cost to domestic sector of extra £1 of spending under the poll tax system and the domestic rate system (1987/88 data, in pence)

	(1) Change in block grant	(2) Total Extra cost to local taxpayers	(3) Extra cost to domestic taxpayers	(4) Extra cost to non-domestic taxpayers
Poll tax system				
All authorities	0.0	100.0	100.0	0.0
Domestic rate system				
Shire counties				
Buckinghamshire	-94.2	194.2	107.4	86.8
Cornwall	-24.0	124.0	71.2	52.8
Essex	-76.9	176.9	103.6	73.3
Northumberland	-19.6	119.6	64.4	55.2
Suffolk	-45.9	146.5	79.6	66.2
Warwickshire	-63.4	163.4	95.0	68.4
Shire districts				
Chelmsford	-55.2	155.2	86.4	68.8
Colchester	-52.4	152.4	85.7	66.7
Southend-on-Sea	-58.9	158.9	95.8	63.2
Blyth Valley	-12.1	112.1	71.5	40.6
Castle Morpeth	-58.0	158.0	87.6	70.4
Tynedale	-34.9	134.9	70.4	64.5
Metropolitan districts				
Oldham	-15.0	115.0	66.3	48.7
Liverpool	-79.8	179.8	91.1	88.7
Sheffield	-31.5	131.5	61.9	69.6
Newcastle-Upon-Tyne	-114.3	214.3	98.4	115.9
Birmingham	-97.8	197.8	98.9	98.9
Solihull	-66.8	166.8	105.5	61.2
Kirklees	3.2	96.8	50.0	46.8
Inner London:				
precepting				
ILEA	0.0	100.0	26.3	73.7
Boroughs				
Camden	0.0	100.0	24.7	75.3
Hackney	-64.2	164.2	75.0	89.2
Kensington & Chelsea	-251.5	351.5	193.2	158.3
Westminster	0.0	100.0	16.2	83.8
Outer London				
Barnet	-74.3	174.3	119.3	61.5
Bromley	-45.9	145.9	96.1	49.8
Newham	-116.4	216.4	96.0	10.8

Source: author's computations

£517 per head) loses all grant at an expenditure below its GRE and Westminster's huge rateable value per head (£1789) ensures that it receives no block grant whatever its level of expenditure.[10] With no grant penalties at the margin, the cost of an extra £1 of spending is simply £1 for these authorities. In addition because the non-domestic sector is such a large proportion of the total rateable value in these authorities, the end result is extremely low domestic ratepayer marginal costs: in ILEA and Camden it is in the 25p per £1 region - less than half the figure for the lowest rateable value authorities outside London. This helps explain the Government's particular concern about Labour controlled inner London authorities supporting what it regards as their excessive expenditure at very little expense to their domestic ratepayers and largely at the expense of the non-domestic ratepayer.

This change in the domestic marginal contribution on the very large overspend (£252 per adult) of ILEA is the main reason why the new system has by far the biggest impact in Inner London, with ILEA's overspend costing £1 per £1 under poll tax compared to 25p per £1 under the rating system. This is shown in column (11) of Table 4.6 by the large extra increase in bills on expenditure above GRE for all the Inner London tax areas.

The situation for all Inner London tax areas would be better if they were spending close to GRE. In fact, the domestic rateable values of The City, Camden, Kensington & Chelsea, and Westminster[11] are high enough to make them very large potential gainers at GRE (see Columns (3) and (4) of Table 4.6). This is despite the fact that the gains at GRE to inner London are less than would be expected from the high domestic rateable values because of the reduction in present rate poundages and rate bills effected through "resource protection" multipliers in the block grant system. This applies a basic multiplier of 0.707 to the amount to be raised from Inner London ratepayers (a similar effect reducing the gains from high domestic rateable values occurs to a lesser extent in outer London).[12] There have been some other significant changes in some authorities' positions since 1987/88 arising out of the ring-fencing of Housing Revenue Accounts and the scrapping of ILEA (this is briefly covered in Appendix 4.2).

Redistribution between non-domestic ratepayers

It was planned from the outset that two changes would affect non-domestic ratepayers. First, the standardisation of business rate poundages. Second, a revaluation of non-domestic properties to come into force on 1 April 1990, simultaneously with the introduction of the reformed system. A revaluation was long overdue and it would have been urgent even in an unreformed local government finance system. There were indications that it might have substantial redistributional effects, with rateable values probably climbing most steeply for modern retail premises in prime sites, offices, and warehouses in the more prosperous parts of the country and tending to fall for older industrial premises in the north and the midlands. The Green Paper showed the general shift in the non-domestic rates which would occur between the regions (see Table 4.8) based on 1984/85 data. On average non-domestic rates would fall by 18% in the northern region and by 12% in Yorkshire and Humberside and the North West, whereas they would rise by 11% in the South East and East Anglia. These regional figures reflected what many would see as a desirable side effect of the reforms given the relatively greater levels of unemployment in the north.

Table 4.8: Changes in non-domestic rate bills with a national non-domestic rate - English regions (1984/85 based data)

	Present non-domestic rate bill £m	Change: £m	%
North	367	-66	-18
Yorkshire & Humberside	530	-62	-12
North West	722	-88	-12
East Midlands	401	+1	+0[a]
West Midlands	532	+48	+9
East Anglia	187	+20	+11
Greater London	1995[b]	+6[b]	+0[ba]
South East	1077	+119	+11
South West	393	+23	+6

[a] 0= less than 1/2%
[b] Greater London actual bills reduced by large use of balances in 1984/85

Source: Department of the Environment (1986a, Figure D3, p. 96.)

The standardisation of business rate poundages appeared to indicate relatively minor shifts in many areas. Thus the Green Paper claimed that 60% of bills would change by less than 15% on the basis of 1984/85 data. In 1987/88 the uniform poundage would have been 224p and 227 rate poundages were in the 200p to 250p region. However, there were 28 of the metropolitan district where rate poundages were at or above 250p - ranging up to Manchester at 354.5p. In outer London 12 of the 20 boroughs had poundages below 200p, with business in Croydon (rate poundage 158p) facing a potential rise of over 40% in rate bills from standardisation. Worst hit potentially though were businesses in Kensington & Chelsea where the 1987/88 rate poundage was, at 117.4p, not much over half the uniform national rate. We shall return to the non-domestic rating revaluation later in this book and further discuss non-domestic rates in Chapter 8.

Final comments

Finally let us return to the impact of the poll tax on domestic taxpayers and attempt to put it into perspective. The doubling of average tax bills in some areas and its near halving in others (see Table 4.4) should be set against the fact that the largest year-on-year increase in average bills caused by shifts in block grant in the 1980s, was barely above 10% in real terms. Thus the impact of the reforms is dramatically larger than anything experienced in the 1980s through the block grant system or grant penalties between 1981 and 1986. Yet those lesser redistributions caused great controversy both in Parliament and in the media. This also shows that Foster's (1986) likening of the changes due to reform to the changes arising from an annual Rate Support Grant Settlement is at the least either complacent or extremely optimistic. One extremely important fact makes it extremely inaccurate however, and this is that the poll tax brings a redistribution between households, whereas a Rate Support Grant Settlement only brings shifts in grant between areas.[13]

However, we must in turn quickly put this large change in average bills at area level into perspective by giving some figures which show that the change between individual households is much greater than the change in local authority average bill. A Parliamentary written answer stated that 3 million households in England would face increases of more than 50% in their tax bills when poll tax replaces rates. This implies that 6 million households will face bill changes above 50% i.e. 35% of English households.[14] Compared to this the 1987/88 based

76 *The Politics and Economics of the Poll Tax*

figures showed only 19 areas (with 1.2 million households) out of 369 tax collection areas where the average bill change per adult would have been greater than 50%. The reason for this is that there is a much larger variation between individual households, than there is between local authorities' averages, in the relative amounts of the two factors which affect the distribution of tax bills under the present and new system: rateable values and the number of adults. It is this redistribution between households, caused by poll tax, to which we now turn in Chapter 5.

APPENDIX 4.1:
THE OFFSETTING EFFECTS OF CHANGES IN GRANT AND NON-DOMESTIC RATES

An example can demonstrate why it is generally misleading to focus attention separately on the role of changes in grant receipts or non-domestic rates as the cause of changes in the domestic sector tax contribution. In nearly all areas the change in the domestic sector's tax contribution is independent of non-domestic rateable value and is determined mostly by the effective rateable value. The proportions of previous receipts between grant and non-domestic rates are irrelevant.

All figures in this example are given in per adult terms. Let two authorities A and B have the same average domestic rateable value of £60 but let A have a non-domestic rateable value of £60 and B have a non-domestic rateable value of £140. Also let both have a GRE of £600 and assume that both spend at GRE. This gives them both a rate poundage of 200p under the rating system and an average domestic rates bill of £120. The remaining £480 is financed in A by £120 in non-domestic rates and £360 in block grant, whereas in B the respective sums are £280 and £200. Now under the poll tax system the poll tax in both A and B will be £178 per adult - both authorities lose: the domestic sector tax contribution rises by £58 per adult in both A and B and this is entirely determined by average domestic rateable values. We can now show that all that happens is a 'swings and roundabouts' relationship between grant and non-domestic rates, once the domestic sector change is determined.

There is a common amount of national non-domestic rates receipts - say £200, and grant will provide the difference between the poll tax for spending at GRE - say £178 - and national non-domestic rates.

Thus A and B will both receive £222 in needs grant. This shows the 'swings and roundabouts' relationship between grant and non-domestic rates: in A grant falls by £138 but is offset by an increase in non-domestic rates receipts of £80 to leave the predetermined domestic sector loss of £58, and in B grant rises by £22 and non-domestic rates fall by £80, to leave the same predetermined domestic sector loss.

APPENDIX 4.2

OTHER INTERACTING CHANGES: RINGFENCED HRAs AND THE SCRAPPING OF ILEA

The Government planned to ringfence HRAs from the rate fund from 1 April 1990 and this was likely to have major effects on poll tax levels in a number of authorities, especially in the inner cities. The size of the effect depends upon the extent to which the rate fund contribution to (or from) the HRA is greater than the GRE allowance for these contributions. At a national level the GRE for HRA contributions was £420 millions in 1987/88 which was heavily concentrated in inner London with much lesser amounts in the provincial cities, and the vast majority of areas had zero GREs.[15] Analysis in CIPFA (1988b) showed that the major effects were also concentrated in inner London with reductions in poll tax levels of £133 in Camden, £119 in Lambeth, £107 in Southwark, £96 in Hammersmith & Fulham. There were increases in poll tax levels of £63 in Wandsworth, £50 in Barking & Dagenham, and £47 in Tower Hamlets. Poll tax levels tended to fall in the provincial cities but generally by less than £20 per adult.

The Government's plans for ringfencing have been heavily criticised elsewhere but the main point here is that the concentration of poll tax reductions from this source markedly reduces the level of poll tax in some of the inner London boroughs. However, it must be remembered that where there are gains for the poll tax payers there is an equivalent loss of financial support from the rate fund borne by a relatively smaller number of tenants.

Finally we must mention the decision to scrap ILEA. This was also certain to have a major impact on the poll tax levels of the inner London boroughs. The gap between spending and GRE was £252 per adult in 1987/88 and an analysis by CIPFA showed that without spending cuts the overspend (and therefore poll tax per adult level) would rise in many of the more deprived inner London boroughs: by £11 in

Lambeth, £12 in Southwark, £26 in Lewisham, £34 in Tower Hamlets, £51 in Greenwich and £53 in Hackney.

Notes

1. My personal experience speaking to numerous groups on this subject, as disparate as Labour Party ward members and National Federation of Townswomens' Guilds suggests that newspapers have correctly guessed that it is redistribution of tax bills which a large number of their readers care about most.

2. See for example the description of recent attempts to introduce new local taxes in Italy (Fraschini, 1989).

3. Prest (1982a) reminds us that ultimately the burden of all taxes are borne by households. We do not deal with the, complicated, problem of the ultimate incidence of the tax burden arising from the reforms, instead we give our attention to the primary change in household and business tax bills.

4. One important point to be made is that although we make a broad distinction between the redistribution between tax areas and the redistribution between households there is no clean cut distinction between them. This is because, for example, the change brings a redistribution of the share of upper tiers' precepts between households living in different tax areas (districts or boroughs) - caused by the shift from equal rate poundage precepts between constituent districts/ boroughs to equal poll tax bills per adult precepts. This obviously combines what we will analyse in this chapter as redistribution between areas and redistribution between households. The most dramatic such effect is Inner London (see footnote 11).

5. The poll tax will, of course, be collected at district level and the change at this level will reflect the net changes on the local authorities and joint boards at each tier in each tax collection district.

6. The only later year for making a reasonably fair comparison is 1988/89, because for 1989/90 the grant system was an artificially fixed grant system, with fixed grant payments based on a Government predetermined notional level of expenditure for each local authority.

7. As shown in the Appendix to Chapter 2 each £1 per head of spending leads to an increase in the domestic sector's tax contribution of the rate poundage price multiplied by the domestic rateable value.

Thus in the case of A - with the change in GRP equal to £0.011 below threshold and an average domestic rateable value of £48 per head it is (in per head terms):

£0.011 × £48 = £0.53

8. There are some differences between these calculations and the Department of the Environment's figures. The most important is that in the Department's figures the aggregate level of domestic rates yield was increased by an amount reflecting the extent to which use of balances in 1987/88 reduced the aggregate yield of non-domestic rates. Also the figures at GRE differ from CIPFA (1987) figures because, rather than notionally constraining the yield of grant and non-domestic rates in the rating system calculations, they are here allowed to vary. This reduces the extent of the gains to local authorities for spending at GRE.

9. Also important is the actual non-neutrality in the block grant system arising from two sources: (1) where one tier is spending above threshold the notional redistribution of expenditure between actual overspend and the notional zero overspend at GRE brings larger rate poundage and rate bill changes than implied by domestic rateable values, and more significantly (2) different tiers' spending may have different domestic marginal costs in a tax area because of either (a) different multipliers in their block grant formula or (b) one tier not suffering marginal grant penalties because all block grant entitlement has been lost (this is important in inner London, as will be seen later).

10. In 1987/88 ILEA lost its entitlement at a level of expenditure below its GRE. See CIPFA (1988a).

11. The system of equal rate poundage precepts was a powerful engine of redistribution within inner London. Thus the ILEA precept in 1987/88 (adjusted for use of balances) which led to domestic rates bills ranging from £310 per adult in Westminster to £124 per adult in Tower Hamlets will now be shared between them as an equal amount per adult. The switch of this precept to an equal amount per adult basis obviously causes a large redistribution from poorer to richer boroughs. The scrapping of ILEA actually tends to reinforce this redistribution.

12. The outer London resource protection multiplier discounted 18% of rateable value.

13. Pedantically shifts between areas are shifts between households in different areas, but the point is substantially valid because successive

rate support grants in the 1980s did not alter tax shares between households within the same local authority.

14. Data given in Parliamentary Written Answer, 25 November 1987.

15. Political considerations, not logic, governed the decision made in 1982 and continued throughout the 1980s to allow authorities where the Department of the Environment identified potential HRA surpluses to have zero, rather than the computed negative GREs.

5.
REDISTRIBUTION BETWEEN HOUSEHOLDS

There are three separate aspects of the redistribution of the local domestic tax burden between individual households which we will consider in this and the next chapter. These are:

(1) Structural characteristics - that is the extent to which bills are redistributed according to the size of household;

(2) Regressivity/progessivity characteristics – that is the redistribution in relation to the income of households;

(3) Disturbance characteristics - that is the actual extent to which bills change, both absolutely and in relation to the present level of bills.

In addition we will, later in this chapter, consider spatial aspects of the redistribution between households - namely the "within-city" pattern of redistribution, which is pertinent given the Government's stated policy priority for the inner cities.

Safety nets and the area effects on redistribution between households

Although safety nets most obviously affect the inter-area and inter-regional redistribution they also to an extent modify the regressive nature of the switch in local taxation. Given that many of the official figures comparing the regressivity of poll tax and domestic rates have been based upon safety netted figures it is important to deal with this point first.

Safety nets bring a different redistribution for households because they alter the bills in tax areas, by an amount which varies according to the size of the change in the domestic sector tax contribution, and therefore alter the extent of the change in tax bills to all households. This different distribution with safety nets is not neutral because areas

82   *The Politics and Economics of the Poll Tax*

which gain from the fundamental long-term redistribution tend to have above average proportions of higher income groups and areas which lose tend to have above average proportions of lower income groups. Safety nets increase the bills in gaining areas and reduce them in losing areas, thus indirectly restraining the reduction in bills to high income groups in gaining areas and restraining the increase in bills to low income groups in losing areas.[1] This point is not easily demonstrated because income data at local authority level is not readily available,[2] but we can give one actual example here. A recent Parliamentary answer to a written question provided data on the proportion of households receiving rebates in each tax area. Table 5.1 shows these figures by tax areas grouped by change in domestic sector tax contribution in 1987/88. It can be seen that distribution of these rebates shows a notable skewness towards losing areas with nearly double the proportion of full rebate recipients in authorities where the domestic sector tax contribution rises by more than 50% compared to authorities where the domestic sector tax contribution falls by more than 20%. Although this skewness will be greatest for the lowest income groups represented by rebate receipients, there will obviously be a similar, if less emphatic, tendency towards skewness in the distribution of other income groups.

Table 5.1: Relationship between % change in area tax bills and the proportion of households receiving rebates

Tax areas with % change in bills in range:	Number of Households			Proportion of Households	
	All	receiving full rebates	receiving rebates	receiving full rebates	receiving rebates
below -40	168616	19614	42293	11.63	25.08
-39.9 - -30	1210305	130869	302157	10.81	24.97
-29.9 - -20	2490678	337575	701138	13.55	28.15
-19.9 - -10	3141920	410867	862466	13.08	27.45
- 9.9 - 0	3563010	552620	1129410	15.51	31.70
0.1 - 10	715407	240318	490605	14.01	28.60
10.1 - 20	2068754	403847	790266	19.52	38.20
20.1 - 30	1442227	269867	507824	18.71	35.21
30.1 - 50	1246935	222089	443468	17.81	35.56
50.1 - 75	681465	159469	297662	23.40	43.68
75.1 - 100	324252	76290	131032	23.53	40.41
over 100	423449	87275	148523	20.61	35.07

Source: Author's computations from Parliamentary Written Answer, 2 November 1987

Safety nets will, therefore, temporarily reduce the increase in bills for a majority of the lower income groups and vice-versa for high income groups. Thus as safety nets are removed bills will tend to rise for a majority of lower income groups and fall for a majority of high income groups. So the fundamental redistribution caused by the replacement of domestic rates by poll tax is more regressive than its initial impact. We will return to this point with more evidence later in this chapter.

Basic example of the redistribution between households

Before proceeding, let us look again at the nature of the redistribution caused by the change in the local tax base. The comparison is based on an approximation of the calculated unsafety netted data in Table 4.6 for Southampton in Hampshire in 1987/88, with a rate poundage of 194p and a poll tax of £176 per adult, and almost no change in the domestic sector tax contribution. The general principles applying to all households can be derived from this example. The nature of the redistribution can be demonstrated with the aid of Figure 5.1 (p.84) which compares rate bills and the poll tax bills of households with one, two, and three adults.

Domestic rateable value is measured along the horizontal axis and the size of local tax bill per household is measured along the vertical axis. The rate bill for each household is the sum of domestic rateable value multiplied by the rate poundage. Thus rate bills increase proportionately with rateable values, and this is shown by the line from the origin OR, with the slope of the line determined by the size of the rate poundage. Poll tax bills are simply either £176, £352, or £528 for one, two and three adult households respectively - these are shown by the lines Ss, Dd, and Tt. It can be seen that the break even points where local tax bills under the two systems are equal are at the rateable values £90.7 for a one adult household (point B1), at double this value, £181.4, for a two adult household (point B2), and at a further 50% higher, £272.2 for a three adult household (point B3).

We can show the potential variability between the same size households. Consider one adult households. They will have to occupy relatively low rateable value houses - under £90.7 (the average domestic rateable value per hereditament in Southampton in 1987 was £180.7) - to lose from the switch to poll tax. A one adult household occupying a house with a rateable value of £181.4 will have its local tax bill halved by the switch to poll tax. In contrast a three adult household would have their local tax bill trebled if they lived in a £90.7 rateable value house and increased by 50% if in a £181.4 rateable value house.

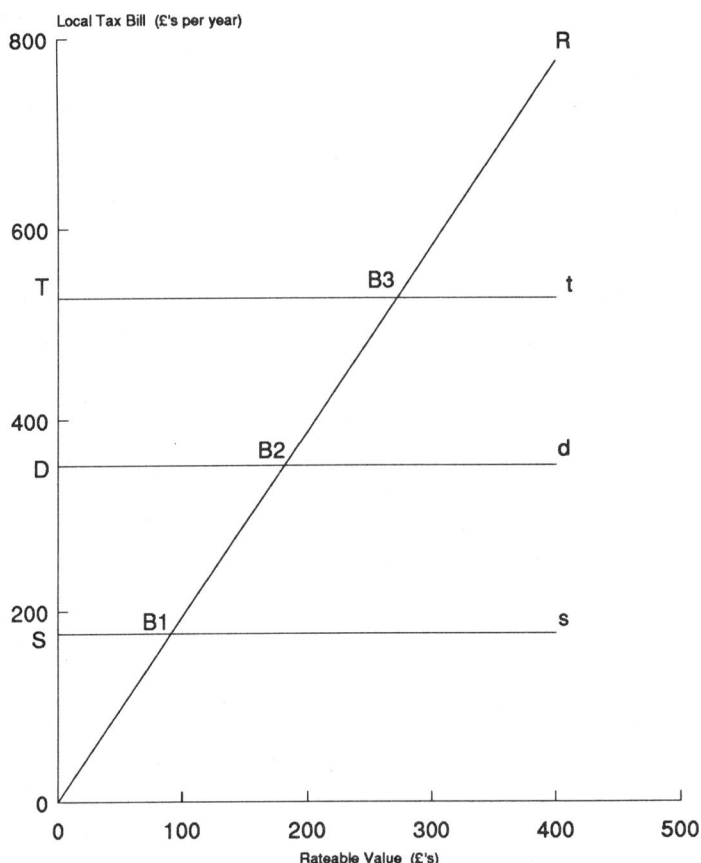

Figure 5.1: Comparative Local Tax Bills

The amount of variability between households of the same size will depend on the distribution of rateable values. There is no published data on this, but my own studies in County Durham showed that there was considerable dispersion. Thus for single adult households in Chester-le-Street, where there was an average rateable value per domestic hereditament of £148 in 1987, only 31% of two adult households lived in properties in the £126-£175 range - whereas 14% lived in properties below £75 in rateable value and 18% lived in properties above £200. Similar wide dispersions were exhibited by one and three adult households.

Structural characteristics

On average larger households occupy houses with higher rateable values, but the increase is less than proportional. Thus, Smith and Squire (1987), tabulated data from the 1984 Family Expenditive Survey which shows that the average rateable value of property occupied by two-adult households without children is only about 20% higher than for single-adult households without children. It is this less than proportional increase which causes a structural redistribution of tax bills.

Table 5.2 (p.86) shows the clear tendency for household local tax bills to fall under poll tax for single adult households and to rise for three adult households, with a more even pattern for two adult households. However, there is considerable variation within each household type and this is caused by the large differences in rateable values between households. Households with low rateable values (for their size of household) will, of course, tend to lose, and those with high rateable values (for their size of household) tend to gain, under poll tax.

The table shows that with safety nets a slight majority of households have increased bills, but this is reversed substantially when safety nets are removed, with 58% of households then having bill reductions. This reflects the fact, dealt with in Chapter 4, that a sizeable majority of adults and households live in tax areas where the domestic sector tax contribution falls and the losses are more concentrated than gains.

This data was provided by a Parliamentary written answer - given in Table 5.3 (p.87) - which also covered the distribution of changes in weekly household bills for households by the different English regions. This shows that after the removal of safety nets the number of losing households is more than double the number of gaining households in the Northern and Yorkshire & Humberside regions, whereas in the West Midlands and especially in the South East (outside Greater London) gainers are more than double losers. In fact in the South East 14.6% of households face bill reductions of more than £5 per week and only 1.9% face bill increases of more than £5 per week. In contrast the comparable figures in the Northern region are 3% £5+ gainers and 13.6% £5+ losers. This provides a useful lead into the regressivity section.

Regressivity/Progressivity

There is a common perception that a poll tax is a regressive tax - more regressive than domestic rates. Thus, the 1981 Green Paper, when

Table 5.2: Households (thousands) gaining and losing with full replacement of domestic rates by the poll tax, England, (£ per week, 1986/87 prices)

	Single Pensioner	Other single adult	Two adults	Three adults	All households
With safety nets					
Losers					
10 +	-	-	-	90	90
5 -10	-	-	100	645	740
2 - 5	10	70	1665	1010	2750
1 - 2	35	120	1445	275	1870
0 - 1	340	285	2950	195	3765
Total losers	380	475	6160	2215	9225
Gainers					
0 - 1	1330	695	2035	85	4145
1 - 2	240	275	975	50	1545
2 - 5	365	575	1320	90	2350
5 -10	160	165	510	40	880
10 +	15	20	130	15	185
Total gainers	2110	1740	4925	280	9105
With No Safety Nets					
Losers					
10 +	-	-	130	165	295
5 -10	0	35	355	600	990
2 - 5	25	115	1555	780	2470
1 - 2	60	105	1120	290	1570
0 - 1	410	295	2270	230	3205
Total losers	495	545	5425	2060	8525
Gainers					
0 - 1	1190	590	1850	135	3770
1 - 2	230	270	1205	90	1795
2 - 5	365	550	1735	125	2775
5 -10	185	225	735	60	1205
10 +	25	30	180	25	255
Total gainers	1995	1665	5705	435	9805

0=less than 12500
Numbers may not add due to rounding

Source: Parliamentary Written Answer, 13 January 1988

Table 5.3: Households (thousands) gaining and losing with full replacement of domestic rates by the poll tax, English regions (£ per week, 1986/87 prices)

	Northern	York & Humber- side	East Midlands	East Anglia	Greater London	South East	South Western	West Midlands	North Western
With No Safety Nets									
Losers									
10+	20	25	10	0	210	5	5	0	15
5 -10	160	220	70	15	215	70	50	40	150
2 - 5	295	445	270	75	305	300	220	190	365
1 - 2	135	250	160	55	215	265	150	130	210
0 - 1	305	495	295	160	375	495	300	315	470
Total losers	915	1440	805	305	1325	1130	720	680	1210
Gainers									
0 - 1	220	300	340	210	405	835	370	530	565
1 - 2	60	90	165	115	215	530	160	255	210
2 - 5	85	155	190	125	345	890	255	400	340
5 - 10	30	60	70	50	120	470	95	155	155
10+	10	10	15	5	35	110	15	30	25
Total gainers	405	615	775	505	1115	2835	895	1370	1290

0 = less than 12500

Numbers may not add due to rounding

Source: Parliamentary Written Answer, 13 January 1988

considering alternatives to domestic rates, had pointed out the notable regressive feature of poll tax (Department of the Environment, 1981, p.74):

> For any given household type ... the lower-income households would pay a higher proportion of their income in tax than the higher income households. Moreover, since domestic rate payments tend to increase with income - though less than proportionately - replacing rates by a poll tax will mean that higher-income households gain more or lose less (in pounds per week) than the lower-income households of the same type.

Given this common perception and the emphatic official statement above it might seem unnecessary to examine the relative regressivity of poll tax and domestic rates. However, from the outset in 1986 the Government have been keen to deny that domestic rates have any better relationship to ability to pay than the poll tax. Thus the 1986 Green Paper actually states (para. 3.37) that "at the lowest income levels, householders would face lower average bills with a full community charge than with domestic rates. Overall a community charge would perform no worse than the rates." Bramley (1987b, p.189) commented that this statement was "rather surprising" and also disingenuous because annex F clearly showed that domestic rates were more closely related to household equivalent net income - that is income after making allowance for the number of dependents. Comparisons made on the basis of raw net incomes are misleading because they ignore household commitments. A single adult household with income of £50 a week obviously has a higher standard of living than a two adult household with the same net income. The result for the lowest raw net income group arises from the household size effect and it was noted in Annex F of the Green Paper that 95% of households with net incomes below £50 per week in 1984/85 and 61% of the next income band were single adult households.

The relative regressivity of poll tax and domestic rates is therefore shown here (in Table 5.4) by the relationship between tax bills and equivalent net household income. The bottom row shows how net bills rise for the lowest income groups, apart from the very lowest, but then fall for those groups above £200 per week by increasing amounts as income increases. For the very highest income group (over £500 per week) there are gains of nearly £7 per week. Figure 5.2 (p.89) shows visually how strikingly more regressive the poll tax is compared to domestic rates.

Table 5.4: Relationship of rates and poll tax to net household income - average local tax bill (England 1986/87 prices)

	Ranges of equivalent net household income (£ per week)											
	Under 50	50-75	75-100	100-150	150-200	200-250	250-300	300-350	350-400	400-500	500+	All
Gross:												
Rates	6.07	6.17	6.72	7.32	7.95	8.31	8.72	9.27	9.95	10.54	13.64	7.40
Poll tax	6.00	6.36	7.27	8.03	8.12	8.01	7.59	7.36	7.09	7.42	7.00	7.41
Net:												
Rates	1.64	3.04	5.94	7.18	7.90	8.29	8.71	9.27	9.95	10.50	13.62	6.37
Poll tax	1.63	3.13	6.31	7.64	7.91	7.89	7.52	7.31	7.03	7.34	6.89	6.25
Difference	-.01	.09	.37	.46	.01	-.40	-1.19	-1.96	-2.92	-3.16	-6.73	-.12

Source: Parliamentary Written Answer, 25 January 1988

This heavy redistribution towards the three highest income groups is the key to the political problems caused by the poll tax, an issue that is discussed in more detail in Chapter 11. The Parliamentary answer which provided the data for Table 5.4 also gives the average proportion of equivalent net income paid in both domestic rates and poll tax. This

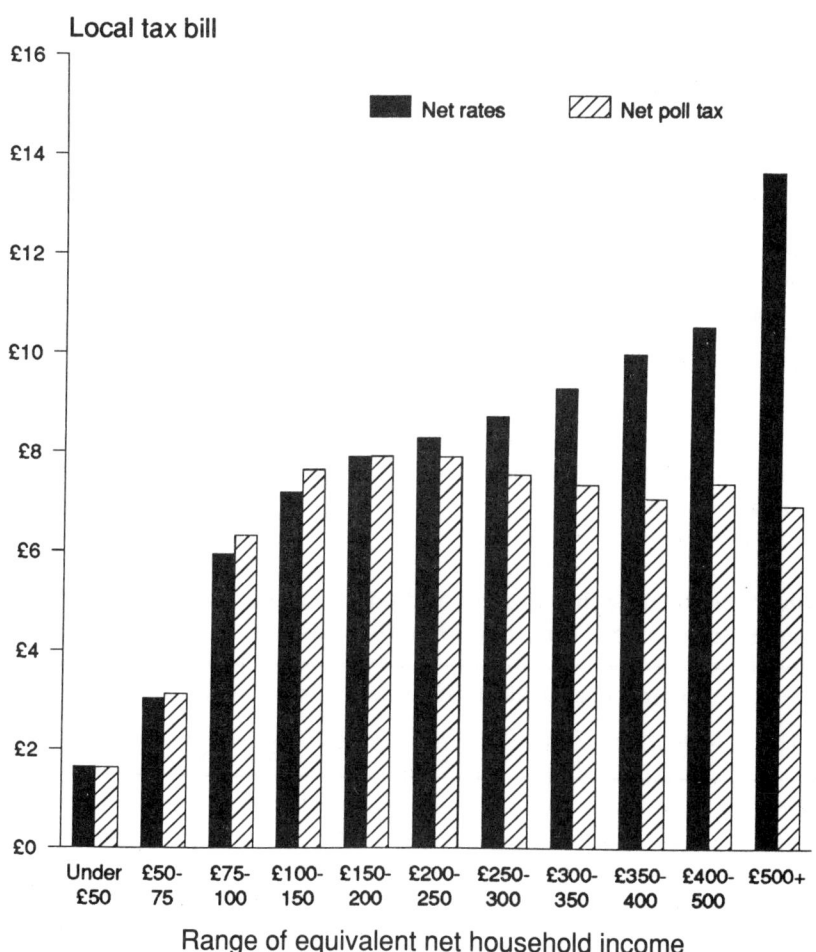

Figure 5.2: Net Rates and Net Poll Tax – relationship to income (England 1986/87 prices – £ per week)

is given in Table 5.5 and shows that both taxes are regressive above an income of £100 per week, but poll tax substantially more so, especially at the highest income levels.

Table 5.5: Relationship of rates and poll tax to net household income - average local tax bill as % of income (England 1986/87 prices)

	Ranges of equivalent net household income (£ per week)										
	Under 50	50-75	75-100	100-150	150-200	200-250	250-300	300-350	350-400	400-500	500+	All
Gross:												
Rates	11.0	7.7	5.3	3.8	3.2	2.9	2.7	2.6	2.5	2.3	2.1	3.8
Poll tax	10.8	8.0	5.7	4.2	3.3	2.8	2.3	2.1	1.8	1.6	1.1	3.8
Net:												
Rates	3.0	3.8	4.7	3.8	3.2	2.9	2.7	2.6	2.5	2.3	2.1	3.3
Poll tax	2.9	3.9	5.0	4.0	3.2	2.7	2.3	2.1	1.8	1.6	1.1	3.2

Source: Parliamentary Written Answer, 25 January 1988

Another approach is through figures for a particular structure of household. Some data (given in Table 12.4 on p.197) on this was produced by the Grants Working Group in 1986 by given type of household for two broad income groups. These groups are those with net incomes under £200 per week and those with incomes £200 per week and over. The data emphatically shows the inherent greater regressivity of the poll tax compared to domestic rates. The ratio of gainers to losers from poll tax is 40:60 for the below £200 a week group but 64:36 for the high income group.

Having established the quite substantial greater regressivity of poll tax, let us finally note the extra regressivity caused by the removal of safety nets. In Table 5.6 the bills for two adult households, both with and without safety nets, are shown. Data is given by only four broad income groups. However, it shows that with safety nets gross bills rise slightly by income range, whereas when safety nets are withdrawn the trend is reversed. The removal of safety nets increases average gross bills in the £50-£100 income group by 4%, whereas it reduces them for the £300+ income group by 8%. The percentage of net income paid in poll tax after receipt of rebates falls from a peak of 5.1% for the £100-£200 income group to 2.2% for the £300+ income group.

Table 5.6: Relationship of poll tax to net household income - average local tax bill: with and without safety nets (England 1988/89 prices)

	Ranges of net household income (£ per week)					
	Under 50	50-100	100-200	200-300	300+	All
Gross:						
With safety nets	*	9.14	9.20	9.32	9.70	9.31
No safety nets	*	9.52	9.34	9.15	9.03	9.26
Net:						
With safety nets	*	3.35	7.64	9.18	9.66	7.87
No safety nets	*	3.43	7.62	9.00	9.00	7.71
Net bills as a % of net income						
With safety nets	*	3.9	5.1	3.8	2.3	3.7
No safety nets	*	4.0	5.1	3.7	2.2	3.6

* = No reliable figures available

Source: Parliamentary written answer, 11 January 1989

Rebates

An important aspect of all these official figures is the level of rebates for lower income groups. The Government's plan to place a maximum on rate rebates was formed before the publication of the January 1986 Green Paper. The Green Paper 'Reform of Social Security' (Department of the Health and Social Security, 1985) published in June 1985 announced that it had been decided to impose a maximum level of support for rates at less than 100%, and indicated that the Government had in mind a figure of the order of 80%.

The proposals were subject to widespread criticism of the likely effects of the 20% contribution on the poor, and the Government gave an undertaking before the 1987 General Election that there would be compensation for the average 20% contribution through inclusion of an extra amount in the income support scales. There was intense suspicion in some quarters[3] about the sincerity of the Government's intention to pay full compensation. A major problem is that the compensatory element in the income support scales is not a separate identifiable allowance. Thus it is included within the scales and Esam and Oppenheim (1989) state that in both April 1988 and April 1989 the income support rates were not increased even in line with inflation. This did not inspire confidence that the level of rebates would ever be increased in line with average poll tax bills. In fact the Government's intention since 1987 has always been that the compensation amount would be equivalent to what it estimated as the average poll tax bill based on local government meeting the Government's spending provision. Thus on the 1987/88 data even if compensation were based on the average poll tax level in England of £226 per adult, those on income support in authorities such as Camden would have to meet an extra 20% of the near £550 per adult difference in the local poll tax - an amount over £2 a week. In fact the real situation is rather worse for rebate recipients because of the large gap between actual average poll tax levels and the Government's planned average which are included in the uprating of scales in advance of poll tax levels being known. In Scotland in 1989/90, its first year of poll tax, this gap was £75 per adult.

Finally, it should be pointed out that the official figures on net tax bills under poll tax are unrealistic and rather "utopian", because they are based on a 100% take-up of entitlement to rebates. In 1984 it was estimated that the take-up rate for housing benefit was 77%, with over 1.9 million eligible failing to claim £500 million in benefit. Poll tax rebates expand the net of potential claimants especially among non-householders, and the evidence is that take-up rates are lowest amongst this group (Fry and Stark, 1987). Despite this, the official figures on net poll tax bills have shown a rapidly rising level of notional rebates. Thus whereas in the 1984/85 based figures in the Green Paper poll tax rebates averaged 97p per household[4] (10p more than the figure given for domestic rates) by the time figures for 1988/89 were released they had grown to £1.80 per week (a full 50p more than the figure for rate rebates). These figures aroused suspicion and a sharp exchange of letters between the Labour shadow Environment Minister and the Secretary of State.[5]

The "within-city" pattern of redistribution

Not surprisingly the greater regressivity of the poll tax is mirrored in the pattern of redistribution of local tax burdens within the cities, with households in deprived inner city wards faring much worse than those in the suburbs. Let us take Birmingham as an example. Table 5.7 (p.94) gives the data at ward level for Birmingham, based on a comparison between a domestic rate poundage of 242.3p and a safety netted poll tax of £249.50, for its 1987/88 spending, a level at which there is very little change in average household bill at local authority level. This gives a fairly clear picture of the quite dramatic contrast between inner city wards with core area definitions, especially those including priority areas, and the outer wards, with very large gains in all three wards of Sutton Coldfield and in Edgbaston. There is some ambiguity, however, because wards such as Edgbaston combine the most luxurious private housing areas with small pockets of multi-occupied run down housing. Thus the table also includes data on the Conservative proportion of the Conservative plus Labour vote in the 1988 local elections and this shows a strong trend towards wards where the Conservatives are strong (the linear correlation coefficient between poll tax gains and the Conservative share of the vote is .78). Other local authorities with inner city areas have also carried out the same type of study and have found similar results.[6]

There is also a tendency for ethnic minority households to fare much worse than the average. This is because on average they have households with relatively high numbers of adults compared to the rateable value of property occupied. A recent survey (Brown, 1984) estimated that 17% of Afro-Caribbeans and 22% of Asians lived in households with more than three adults, compared to 6% for white people. A study conducted by Newcastle upon Tyne found that a much higher proprtion (78%) of households with Asian heads were losers compared to those with UK heads (56%). Also, as Table 5.8 (p.95) shows, there was an even greater relative disparity towards heavy losses.

Closing Comments

This chapter has demonstrated the substantially greater regressivity of poll tax compared to domestic rates, and also that this greater regressivity is underestimated in official figures because (1) they are based on an overoptimistic view of the take-up for poll tax rebates, and (2) they do not include the additional redistribution in favour of higher income households which will follow the removal of safety nets.

The greater regressivity of poll tax compared to domestic rates has implications for the effects of the poll tax on the economic and political activity of the electorate, as well as central government and local authorities, and this will be dealt with in Chapters 8 and 9.

Table 5.7: Impact on average household domestic tax bills of switch from domestic rates to poll tax - Birmingham by ward level (£ per year)

	Average gain/loss per household	Percentage of households gaining	Ward characteristics: Conservative share of Con. plus Labour vote (1988 local elections)	Inner area definition
Sutton Four Oaks	348.5	86.5	88.1	-
Edgbaston	239.5	79.2	60.8	P (part)
Sutton Vesey	191.3	78.0	82.2	-
Sutton New Hall	125.6	74.8	77.4	-
Quinton	78.7	67.3	60.3	-
Kings Norton	61.9	62.2	36.2	-
Hall Green	56.5	64.9	75.0	P
Weoley	44.9	62.2	45.1	-
Harborne	42.3	57.0	59.8	-
Moseley	25.8	54.8	41.9	P (part)
Brandwood	15.7	59.2	49.1	-
Erdington	14.4	57.9	47.5	P
Northfield	10.7	58.1	55.8	-
Kingsbury	9.4	61.7	28.3	P
Bartley Green	7.5	59.3	51.3	-
Shard End	1.3	50.8	29.8	P
Billesley	-1.9	50.8	42.1	P (part)
Bournville	-2.1	51.1	48.5	-
Ladywood	-3.4	56.9	25.9	C & Pr.
Hodge Hill	-6.4	47.9	44.9	P
Longbridge	-6.9	52.0	38.0	-
Sheldon	-17.7	47.3	50.3	P
Sandwell	-21.2	55.3	45.2	P & Pr.
Yardley	28.3	83.2	48.4	P
Perry Barr	-41.4	36.4	54.1	P
Oscott	-44.6	40.9	50.4	P
Aston	-46.5	49.6	12.6	C & Pr.
Selly Oak	-55.6	40.4	47.5	-
Stockland Green	-58.7	51.4	36.7	P & C (part)
Fox Hollies	-70.3	45.5	32.4	P & C (part)
Kingstanding	-76.2	41.4	29.8	P
Acocks Green	-88.0	38.2	42.5	P & C (part)
Nechells	-94.4	43.9	18.3	C & Pr.
Handsworth	-97.5	44.3	18.1	C & Pr.
Washwood Heath	-104.7	35.0	21.7	C
Sparkhill	-115.3	49.5	28.4	C & P (part)
Soho	-126.0	35.9	13.3	C & Pr.
Sparkbrook	-153.5	31.0	15.8	C & Pr.
Small Heath	-197.4	22.4	32.6	C
Birmingham average			44.6	

Key: P: Partnership area - area for economic regeneration
C: Core area - high levels of economic, physical and social deprivation
Pr: Priority ring where the greatest concentration of deprivation exists

Source: Birmingham City Council, (1988a)

Table 5.8: Poll Tax Impact: Ethnic Minorities - Newcastle upon Tyne
(£ per year)

	Households with UK born heads %	Households with Asian born heads %
Gainers	44	28
Losers	56	72
Loss under £100	16	12
Loss £100 - £250	18	19
Loss more than £250	20	41

Source: *Newcastle upon Tyne City Council, (1988)*

Notes

1. As Oates (1972) has pointed out using grants to local authorities is a much less efficient way of helping those on low incomes than direct transfers, because the grants reduce the required local tax rate for both high and low income groups.

2. Recently data has been published at county level - see HM Treasury (monthly).

3. Thus *The Guardian*, 23 September 1987 reported the Scottish Association of Directors of Social Work as saying that civil servants had informed the Association that the 'compensation' would be temporary and would be withdrawn "... by not increasing benefits fully in line with inflation in future years".

4. The 1986 Green Paper estimated that there would be an increase in caseload in Great Britain of approximately 18% but an increase in rebates paid of only 4%.

5. In this correspondence the Secretary of State revealed that due to improved modelling facilities it had been possible to include, for the first time, an extra £150 million per year of community charge rebates, reflecting the absence, under the new system, of non-dependant deductions.

6. See Birmingham City Council, (1988b).

6.
THE COMPARATIVE IMPACT OF POLL TAX AND RATING REVALUATIONS

Introduction

In Chapter 1 I tried to show that there were great difficulties in accepting at face value the Green Paper's explanation of the reason for the Government's drive for reform in terms of the perception of weaknesses in local accountability. My own opinion has always been that the political problems caused by the rating revaluation in Scotland in 1985 provided at least 75% of the impetus for reform. These were not reforms based on courage and high principle. According to Dowle (1987) the Scottish Secretary of State, George Younger, must take much of the credit for the introduction of the poll tax, the merits of which were not immediately apparent to either the Treasury, the Department of the Environment, or the Home Office. The Treasury was worried that the emphasis on voter accountability with no specific expenditure controls might not be sufficient to restrain local government spending. Inside the Department of the Environment there were many with grave doubts about the practicality of the poll tax and the impact on lower-income families. Younger succeeded, against earlier resistance by the DOE in his push for earlier, separate legislation for Scotland. Other accounts (Insight Team, 1990; MacGregor, 1988), stress the determination of Mrs Thatcher to abolish domestic rates and avoid a politically damaging revaluation in England, and the failure of the strong opposition of the Chancellor of the Exchequer, Nigel Lawson, to the introduction of the poll tax and the decision to bring it in without phasing - the so-called "big bang" approach.[1]

Midwinter, Mair and Ford (1987) have described the Scottish rating revaluation as a "catalyst for change" and state that "although much was made in the media of widespread public dissatisfaction, in our view the pressure was confined to a small but vociferous and active number of pressure groups, both of the ratepayer and business variety". The particular problem of the 1985 revaluation was that, on average, it increased most the rateable values of properties occupied by those whom the Conservatives regarded as their natural supporters. Thus owner occupiers' rateable values rose three times on average compared to 2.6 for all domestic property and 2.3 for all rateable values in Scotland.

The importance of the Scottish revaluation has, I think, been either much underestimated or forgotten. Certainly revaluation has featured largely in Ministerial speeches on the reforms, including a number of replies by the Prime Minister to questions in the House of Commons. In this and the next chapter we deal with the subject of revaluation. - in this chapter presenting a study of comparative disruption effects with the introduction of poll tax, and in the next presenting official figures on the effects of a rating revaluation based on capital values.

A comparative study of poll tax and rating revaluation

[The contents of following study completed for Durham County must have been familiar to Ministers,[2] and I think they were very foolish to ignore these findings and continue upon their chosen route of introducing a poll tax. The report was written in 1987 and the tenses have been left unchanged].

The findings of this study could be described as dramatic. The results strongly point to the necessity of withdrawing the poll tax proposal if the government wishes to avoid a level of disruption in household finances which is much greater than levels of disruption which it itself has recently described as unacceptable or extremely undesirable. The first criterion was presented by the Government in the Green Paper 'Paying for Local Government'. The second was presented by the Secretary of State for the Environment in a major speech in May 1986 to the Association of Metropolitan Authorities (AMA) one-day conference on the Green Paper.

The necessity for withdrawal follows in an entirely reasonable way from the demonstration that the poll tax offends Ministers' own criteria for unacceptability. Presumably Ministers were not aware of this and we are pleased to be able to bring these findings to light before the legislation reaches the statute book. There exist a number of precedents for withdrawal of legislation in this field - most notably the Local

The Comparative Impact of Poll Tax and Rating Revaluations 99

Government Finance Bill of 1981, when it emerged that the proposed budgetary referendums would unexpectedly apply to a number of southern shire districts.

First, we must describe the criterion of unacceptable developed in the Green Paper and then compare the results of this study with the criterion - this will quickly show that the poll tax will be exceedingly more disruptive than the Government's own Green Paper criterion for unacceptable disruption. Second, we will describe Mr Baker's criterion - and again we will show that the poll tax implies much more severe changes than that which Mr Baker publicly presented as extremely undesirable at the AMA conference.

It is important to emphasise, however, that the results and the conclusions which follow from the results are not confined to residents of County Durham. Under the actual path of implementation proposed in the Green Paper it can be confidently stated that the disruption shown will apply to households throughout the country to, more or less, the same degree: residents of Kent, Barnet, Cambridgeshire, Dyfed, Grampian - any area one cares to mention - will also experience a level of disruption far in excess of that which the Government itself described as unacceptable.

The Green Paper Criterion

First, the criterion of unacceptable disruption is to be discovered in the Green Paper in the chapter on Scotland. There, in discussing Scotland's rating revaluation, the Green Paper [para. 8.17, page 61] states that based on this experience:

> ... an unacceptable price has to be paid in the disruption faced by ratepayers following any revaluation

and later on the same page [para. 8.20, page 61] makes it clear that the "unacceptable price" occurred because:

> ... over 100,000 householders in Scotland have faced increase of more than one third in their rate bills between 1984/85 and 1985/86

This certainly seems to be very disruptive for an extremely large number of households. But let us analyse the figures further - the necessary data for an objective analysis is provided in the Green Paper itself:

(1) Figure C1 on page 92 of the Green Paper shows that there are approximately 1,900,000 households in Scotland. Thus 100,000 households is less than 6% of Scottish households (5.26% to be exact).

(2) Figure C7 on page 93 of the Green Paper shows that there was an average increase in domestic rates in Scotland in 1985 (1985/86) compared to 1984 (1984/85) of 14%. This was the result of inflation and grant loss rather than the tax change and therefore the one-third increase referred to above measures a deviation from a trend of 19-20% as the criterion for unacceptable.

So in the context of a "straightforward" substitution of one tax (domestic rate) for another (community charge), with no change in the aggregate national domestic tax bill the Green Paper's criterion of unacceptable disruption is presumably when *more than 5.26% of households experience an increase in their tax bill of more than 20%*.

The results compared to the Green Paper Criterion

We now present the results of a comparison between existing domestic rate bills of individual households and the poll tax bills which they

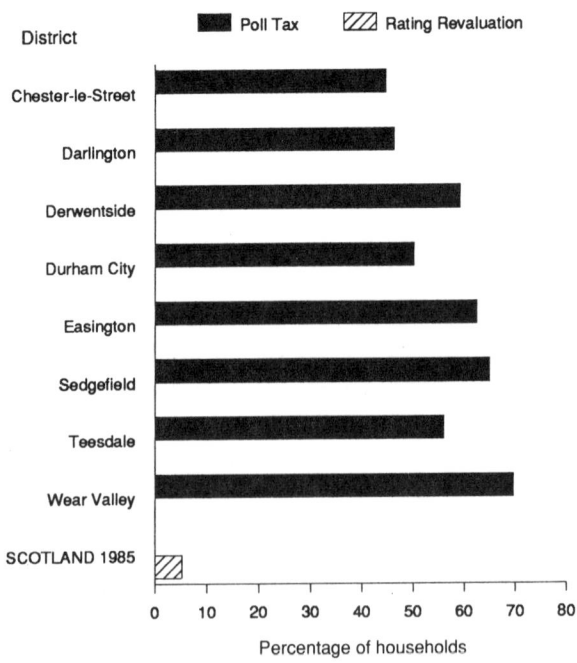

Figure 6.1: % of households with more than 20% bill increases under poll tax (County Durham – without safety nets)

The Comparative Impact of Poll Tax and Rating Revaluations 101

would have to pay. This analysis has been completed for over 160 thousand households (160,562 to be exact) living in County Durham. [A note on the research method is given in the appendix]. The bills are those which apply for 1984/85 spending levels - as were tables in the Green Paper which showed the incidence effects of the new tax. Two sets of figures are compared with the Government's criterion. First, there are those figures which apply if the poll tax is introduced without special "safety-net" payments to compensate local authorities for changes in grant and non-domestic rate income. These are, in fact, the figures associated with a system where the underlying objective of equal poll tax levels per adult in all areas for equal standards of service.

(a) Without safety nets

So in this case does the percentage of households who suffer bill increases of greater than 20% exceed the Government's unacceptable criterion - the critical 5.26%? Yes it does and it is not just marginally above the (already) unacceptable 5.2% of households. The percentage of households with bill increases greater than 20% is:

>44.68% in Chester-le-street
>46.30% in Darlington
>59.19% in Derwentside
>50.21% in Durham City
>62.49% in Easington
>64.94% in Sedgefield
>56.05% in Teesdale
>69.56% in Wear Valley

The results are shown graphically in Figure 6.1.

On the basis of these figures Durham county alone would have more households suffering 20% increases than in the whole of Scotland in 1985.

(b) With safety nets

A possible response to these figures is to say that the Government will actually be making "safety-net" payments to all local authorities to control for changes in grant and non-domestic rate income which would otherwise occur under the switch from the existing finance system to the proposed one. The broad principles of safety-nets are described in Chapter 5 of the Green Paper. A recent exemplification by the Department of the Environment does, in fact, show that even after safety netting there are some slight changes in average bills, but for purposes of simplicity we have calculated households tax bills on the basis of average domestic rate bills being set equal to average poll tax bills in each district.

There is in fact no need to quibble about a few percentage points of approximation here and there, because again, when we ask whether the percentage of households whose bill increases exceed 20% is greater than the (already) unacceptable 5.26%, we find that there is still a massive excess. Naturally the figures now narrow in range - but the range is centred around 35%.

32.80% in Chester-le-street
36.16% in Darlington
35.93% in Derwentside
33.65% in Durham City
31.30% in Easington
33.7% in Sedgefield
37.51% in Teesdale
40.11% in Wear Valley
and the county average is 34.69%.

The results are shown graphically in Figure 6.2.

Thus even with safety netting the poll tax will cause a level of disruption to over 30% of households, which is described as unacceptable in the Green Paper when it applies to 5.26% of households.

The immediate implications of the results

It is the safety net results which carry immediate, and important, implications for the country as a whole. Basically safety nets put all local authorities in a situation where average domestic tax bills are unchanged (or very little changed) for present levels of spending by each local authority.[3] Of course there is a large scale redistribution of tax burdens between households, within authorities, but the average change is close to zero. Thus given that we have found that (say) 35% of households in County Durham have bill increases greater than 20% we can be certain that similar percentages of households will be affected in all other areas. Although safety nets provide protection, albeit temporary, for local authorities, it does not provide protection for households for the switch from domestic rates to poll tax.

This was a slight, but necessary, digression from our analysis of Government criteria. Now that the point has been made that our safety net results have "iron like" nationwide implications, we can move on to consider Mr Baker's criterion.

Mr Baker's criterion

On 20 May 1986, the Secretary of State for the Environment Kenneth Baker made a speech to the AMA conference on the Government's Green Paper the full text of which was attached to a Department of the Environment news release under the title 'Local Income Tax - recipe for conflict says Kenneth Baker'.

In this speech Mr Baker discussed in the context of the option of retaining domestic rates the fact that it would urgently require a revaluation and that a revaluation based on capital values, favoured by many, would mean that:

> Over a million households in England would see increases of 80% or more in their rate bills.

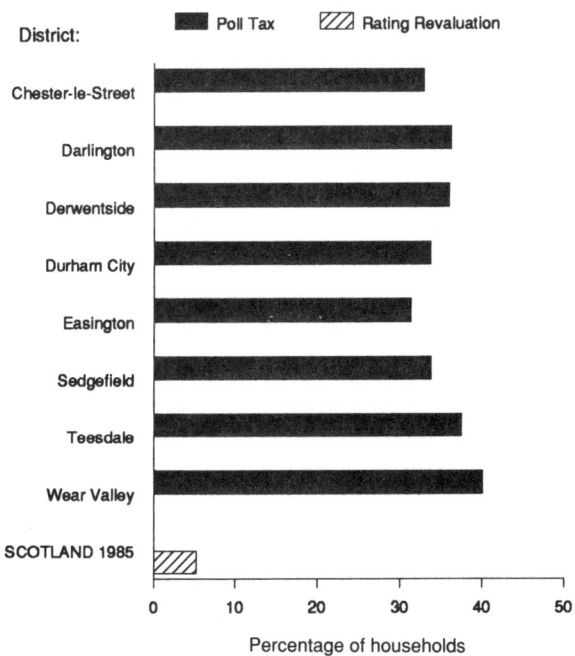

Figure 6.2: % of households with more than 20% bill increases under poll tax (County Durham – with safety nets)

and further asserted that:

> Half of these would be owners of modest terrace houses - many of them first-time buyers.

Again it is useful that the Secretary of State has presented a criterion against which to measure the community charge. Once again the Government has presented data for the purpose of discrediting a rival to its own proposals. It provides a useful chance to place the spotlight upon their own proposals. First let us examine Mr Baker's criterion in more detail. The vital question is what percentage of English households is 1 million households? Here we can turn again to information provided in the Green Paper itself:

(1) In Figure C1 on page 92 we can see that there are approximately 17,650,000 households in England, and therefore:

(2) 1,000,000 households facing bill increases of 80% or more, under domestic rates with a revaluation based on capital values, represents 5.66% of English households.

The results compared to Mr Baker's criterion

We return to the analysis based on the rating register and electoral register. Again we ask, does the percentage of households who suffer bill increases of 80% or more under poll tax exceed Mr Baker's figure for the percentage of households who would suffer such bill increases under domestic rates with a revaluation based on capital values - does it exceed 5.66% of households? In this case, however, we will simply give safety net results because they are the results which carry the nationwide implications. The percentage of households with bill increases of 80% or more under community charge is:

> 14.66% in Chester-le-street
> 17.67% in Darlington
> 16.05% in Derwentside
> 14.37% in Durham City
> 10.11% in Easington
> 16.95% in Sedgefield
> 19.34% in Teesdale
> 19.52% in Wear Valley
> and the county average is 15.47%

The results are shown graphically in Figure 6.3.

Once again it is true that a Government presentation of the figures designed to show that revaluation is extremely unpleasant or unacceptable has been confronted with the important further fact that the poll tax is much worse. The poll tax leads to bill increases of 80% or more for nearly three times as many households than domestic rates with a revaluation.[4]

Households in "modest terrace houses" under the poll tax

As we saw above, the Secretary of State himself introduced the phenomenon of "modest terrace houses" into the debate. Apparently he had the knowledge that half of the households who would suffer increases in bills of 80% or more under a revaluation live in modest terraced houses. That is half of the 5.66% of households i.e. 2.8% of households affected have the joint characteristics –

(1) living in a modest terraced house, and

(2) suffering a bill increase of 80% or more.

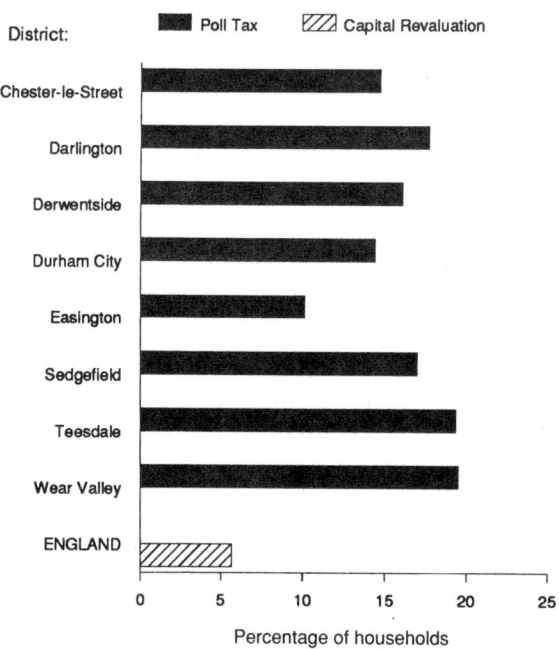

Figure 6.3: % of households with more than 80% bill increases under poll tax (County Durham – with safety nets)

Let us examine the data for one district - Darlington - and compare the effects of introduction a poll tax with a revaluation using Mr Baker's criterion. As we saw above, on the basis of our sample, 17.67% of households in Darlington (that is 4,643 households) suffer bill increases of more than 80% under poll tax. For convenience let us call these households "heavy losers".

Let us assume that the most modest houses in Darlington are those with the lowest rateable values. Our data shows that the worst effected households are overwhelmingly concentrated in such properties. Thus out of 4,643 heavy losers 3,566 live in properties with rateable values of £100 or less and 4,323 live in properties with rateable values of £150 or less. Only 23 live in properties with rateable values of over £200.

Even if we confine the category "modest terrace houses" to properties with a rateable value of £100 or less we can still produce, under poll tax, over five times the proportion of households with Mr Baker's dreaded joint characteristics, as Mr Baker could produce under a rating revaluation.

To round off the comparison though we can examine the type of property occupied by those households who would experience reductions in bills of more than 40%. There are 4,682 such households. Let us call them "heavy gainers". 3,537 heavy gainers live in properties with rateable values greater than £150, none live in properties with rateable values of £100 or under. Out of 332 properties with a rateable value above £400 there are 280 occupied by households who would be heavy gainers under poll tax. The skewing of benefits towards occupiers of higher value properties under poll tax is clear.

Conclusions

This report has provided results which cure a deficiency in the Government's presentation of the distruption effects of the poll tax compared to the major alternative of retaining domestic rates. Thus the Green Paper only presented figures on the disruption effects of the Scottish rating revaluation, without giving a comparison with the effects of the poll tax. Mr Baker likewise omitted any comparative poll tax figures in presenting the potential disruptive effects of a revaluation in England. Also the Government chose to present the absolute figures on the percentage of households with bill increases above the quoted figures rather than the percentage of households so affected. We have demonstrated that in terms of percentages of households affected poll tax is many times more disruptive than revaluation. We have also demonstrated how poll tax is directed against those living in low rateable value properties, and favours those living in high rateable value properties. Compared to this a rating revaluation is relatively neutral.

Given that we have presented percentage figures in this report, but that the Government prefers to present absolute figures, we will summarise our main conclusions in absolute terms. The implications of the County Durham safety netted results for Great Britain are:

(1) Under poll tax over 7 million (over one in three) households will face local tax increases of more than 20%

(2) Under poll tax over 3 million (over one in seven) households will face local tax increases of more than 80% - under the alternative of a rating revaluation it is less than one million

(3) This disruption is not only many times more severe than a fair comparison with a rating revaluation but it also hits poorer households, whereas the Scottish revaluation did not disadvantage poorer households.

APPENDIX 6A:

NOTE ON RESEARCH METHOD

The study compares the rate bill and poll tax of each household given 1984/85 spending levels by the county and the appropriate district. The households data was obtained by a comparison of the rating register and the electoral register both of which are on the County's mainframe computer. The first stage was the application of district level figures for domestic rate poundages (to compute household rate bills) and poll tax per adult (to compute household poll taxes) and these were derived from a national level model of the system. In fact the unsafety netted model results used give average increases slightly below comparable figures from those in a 1984/85 model run by the Department of the Environment - thus we cannot be accused of exaggeration. To reinforce this point not all the records could be matched (see columns 1 and 3 of Table 6A.1, p.108) and the resulting sample results dampen further the average increases in bills compared to the actual average in seven of the eight districts (compare columns 4 and 5 of Table 6A.1).

Table 6A.1: Details of the Durham study

Rating Authority	Number of records		Average % change in bills per household		
	On rating register	matched	Sample rate %	Actual	Sample
(1)	(2)	(3)	(4)	(5)	(6)
Chester-le-street	19945	13836	69.37	17.54	17.89
Darlington	37868	26273	69.38	25.64	12.98
Derwentside	34105	20404	59.83	47.65	39.79
Durham City	31223	21608	69.21	25.13	21.25
Easington	37945	30620	80.70	46.57	44.79
Sedgefield	34532	24919	72.16	56.13	52.98
Teesdale	9787	4860	49.66	31.76	30.45
Wear Valley	24923	18042	72.39	63.73	61.07

Notes

1. The Green Paper originally suggested that poll tax should gradually be phased in and domestic rates phased out, over a period of 3 years in Scotland and up to 10 years in those areas of England where rate bills were largest. This was known as 'Transitional Arrangements' and was regarded as important by the then Secretary of State, Kenneth Baker. Not important enough, however, for him to have succeeded in warning of the dangers of scrapping the Transitional Arrangements, in response to great enthusiasm from the floor for the "big bang" at the 1987 Conservative Party Conference. In Scotland it had been decided earlier in 1987 to drop the Transitional Arrangements.

2. Copies of the original research report were sent to the Department of the Environment. In addition the contents formed the basis of a speech at a conference on the reform of local government finance at the Association of District Councils in September 1987. This followed a speech by the Minister, Michael Howard, who, apologised that he would have to depart urgently to continue his tour "round the country to explain why the time is ripe for reform", but stated that "I shall ask [my official] to stay and report to me on your discussions".

3. The Green Paper is incorrect when it claims that "the arrangement would generally provide local domestic taxpayers with full protection from the distribution effects of the grant and non-domestic rate proposals in the first year of the new system". This is misleading, as it is only local authorities' aggregate domestic tax bills which are being protected, and within this overall tax take there is a redistribution of the tax burden between households, as our results below show.

4. We can look at the results in another way. Let us ask what is the percentage change in bills suffered by the worst affected 5.66% of households in County Durham under a safety net regime for the introduction of poll tax? In this case we find that these households suffer increases in bills of 140% or more.

7.
THE REVALUATION ALTERNATIVE

Introduction - a populist argument

This is a brief chapter on the subject of rating based on capital values. The issue of the administration of the tax and the basis for valuation is not dealt with - it is effectively covered by Foster, Jackman, and Perlman (1980, Pt. 3 Ch. 2). In any case it is self evident that such a local tax would be far easier and cheaper to administer than the poll tax. It would also have the merit that the basis of valuation would be feasible to undertake and more acceptable and more understandable than the previous notional rental values base. (Crawford and Davidson, 1982).

The Layfield Committee had recommended the replacement of rating based on notional rental values by valuations based on capital values. This had been accepted by the Labour Government in its 1977 Green Paper and the intention was to introduce capital valuation for the next revaluation in 1982. This revaluation was postponed in 1979 by the new Conservative Government. Foster, Jackman, and Perlman (1980) gave strong support to the introduction of capital valuation arguing (p. 411) that the case for it was "overwhelming if rates are to be a credible 'ad valorem' property tax". It was also well understood during the earlier debate that capital valuation would provide a rather more progressive tax.

The Conservative Government have used populist arguments against capital value rating. An often repeated example is the case of a single old lady paying the same bill as, say, 5 income earners living next door. This is held to be sufficient to demonstrate the unfairness of the rating system. However, there is an alternative way of looking at this example. The houses, given that there are 5 earners in one of them, are likely to be owner occupied, in which case the old lady possesses 5 times the net capital assets (in housing) per head as the average adult in the house next door - even more if there are also children and a mortgage is being paid. Mrs Thatcher herself was not averse to using this logic, when there was controversy about reductions in housing benefit in the spring of 1988, arguing that the elderly with any consequent financial difficulties could ease their problem by realising some of the equity tied up in their houses.

In the context of the reform of local government finance the approach has been very different and the Government has made large efforts to rubbish capital valuation. The interpretation of some official data is a particularly bizarre example of this.

Official Information - a Government interpretation

The statement by the Secretary of State for the Environment to the AMA conference highlighted in the previous chapter meant that Mr Baker claimed to have knowledge on the effects of a rating revaluation based on capital values. In fact a note on the effects had been placed in the library in July 1986. A later Parliamentary question by the shadow Environment secretary Dr John Cunningham asked for details of more recent work on the alternative of applying to domestic properties valuation for rating purposes based on capital values.

The answer was given by Mr Ridley on 2 November 1987 and he informed the house that he had placed new information in the library and presented the following conclusions:

(i) "Because house prices vary more widely between regions than either existing rateable values or incomes, rates based on capital values would be even less well related to ability to pay."

(ii) "The effects would be different for different types of housing. Terraced houses on average would face increases everywhere except the Midlands and the North West. There would be 30% increases on average, for detached houses in the South East."

(iii) "Some individual occupiers would face very large changes in liability. Nearly 15% of households would have had an increase of more than 50%, and 5% would have had bills which more than doubled had the change taken place at the end of 1986."

He also stated that there are large changes in relative capital values on a cyclical basis so that were there to be regular revaluations on a capital basis, there would also be periodic large changes in rate bills.

His overall conclusion was that capital value rates would, therefore, be more unfair, and more unstable than the present rating system.

In addition he stated that they would lead to large changes in household bills unrelated to the use of local services or ability to pay. They would do nothing to alter the fundamental weaknesses of accountability which existed under the rating system and which he claimed the Government's proposals specifically addressed.

Table 7.1: Capital value, rateable value (RV) and income by region compared to England averages

Region	(1) Average net household income	(2) Average domestic RV per household	(3) Average house price
Northern	89	73	66
Yorks & Humberside	90	71	68
East Midlands	95	87	76
East Anglia	94	94	96
Greater London	111	130	145
South East	113	118	129
South West	97	92	102
West Midlands	94	104	76
North West	95	91	73
England	100	100	100

Notes: Sources of data are:
Col (1); the Family Expenditure Survey 1981-84 repriced to 1985-86 prices
Col (2); data from the Family Expenditure Survey 1981-84
Col (3); Survey of Building Society Mortgages 1986

Source: Parliamentary written answer, 2 Nov. 1987

Alternative conclusions

The data upon which Mr Ridley based most of his conclusions is shown in Tables 7.1 and 7.2 (p.114). Table 7.2 shows the greater general progressivity of capital value rates. Over the country as a whole occupiers of detached houses would pay a greater share of domestic rates, with an average increase of 13%, and this would apply within each region. In contrast the payments by occupiers of flats would fall by 9%, and their share of domestic rates would fall in every region. To many these would not seem to be undesirable redistributions of the local tax burden.

Table 7.2: Average changes in rate bills for each house type in each region in England resulting from a capital revaluation in 1986

	Flats		Terraced		Semis		Detached		All	
	% change	Nos of households	% change	Nos of households	% change	Nos of households	% change	Nos of households	% change	Nos of households
Northern	-27	150	+3	450	-15	400	-4	250	-12	1150
Yorkshire & Humberside	-31	50	+4	750	-20	600	-4	400	-7	1850
East Midlands	-45	0	-12	450	-25	500	-8	450	-15	1450
East Anglia	-11	50	+7	200	-5	200	+9	300	+3	750
Greater London	-3	1200	+12	850	+16	450	+37	150	+11	2650
South East	-5	550	+12	1300	+14	1000	+33	950	+16	3800
South West	-1	150	+12	600	+7	450	+37	450	+15	1700
West Midlands	-46	100	-30	500	-37	750	-18	500	-29	1900
North West	-39	100	-14	900	-25	850	-9	550	-21	2400
ENGLAND	-9	2050	+4	6050	-7	5350	+13	4200	0	17650

Notes:
(1) Numbers rounded to nearest 50,000.
(2) The % changes and numbers in each region and house type were calculated from different sources and so may not be consistent when aggregated.

Source: Parliamentary written answer, 2 Nov. 1987

The data provide a good opportunity to make a fair comparison between the disruption caused by introducing capital value rating and the poll tax, based on the safety netted data[1] considered in Chapter 6, with both unameliorated by transitional domestic relief. The results in Figure 7.1 show clearly the relatively much greater proportions of households experiencing either bills which more than double - 13.5% under poll tax compared to 4.7% under capital values - or bills which fall by more than a half - 10.4% under poll tax compared to 5.2% under capital values.

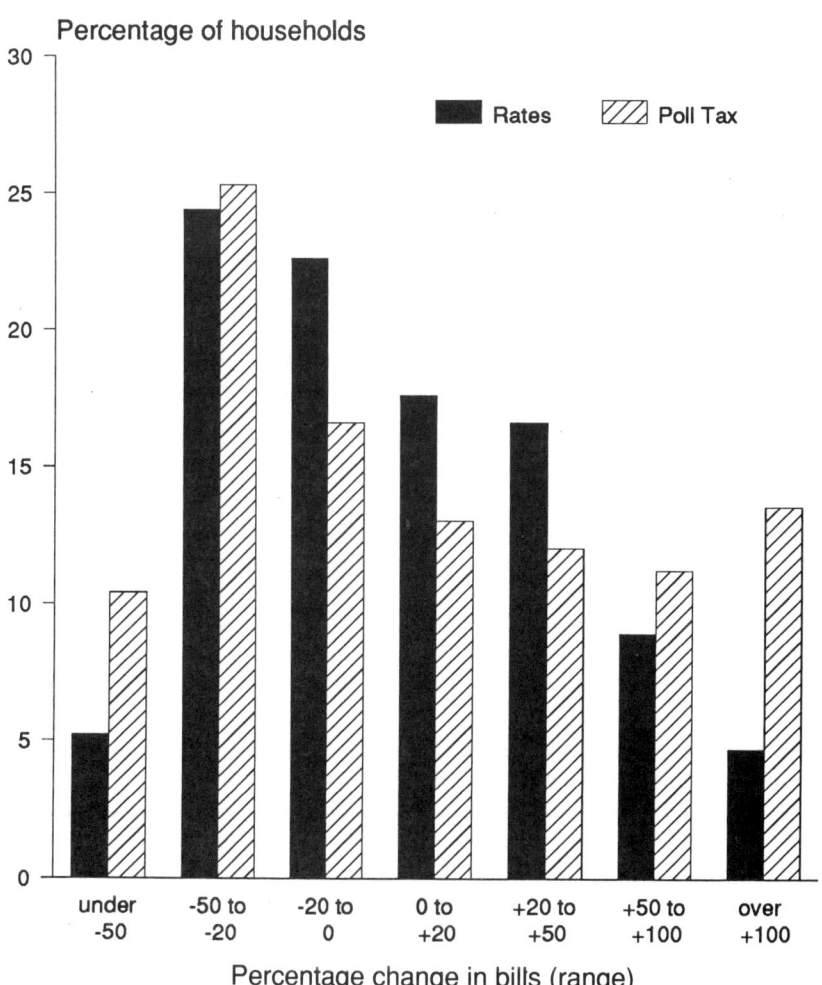

Figure 7.1: Comparative Disruption –
Poll Tax and Capital Value Rates

Concluding comments

There are, of course, some pertinent and difficult issues which arise in the operation of rating based on capital values, such as how to deal with regional differences in house prices. However, as we have seen in Chapter 2, Foster and Jackman (1982) have proposed an acceptable solution to this problem – basing equalisation grants on local income levels. Capital values then form the basis of "within-area" local tax shares. It is shown in the next chapter that there are strong arguments for preferring these tax shares to those arising from the poll tax. One very important fact which the data and analysis in this chapter has shown is that Government ministers have been guilty of highly misleading presentations.[2] The subject of presentation will be dealt with more fully in Chapter 12.

Notes

1. There are no safety nets for rating based on capital values, so the poll tax has been given a head start in these figures.

2. At the time of writing in the spring of 1990 there is no sign of Ministers being able to kick the habit.

8.
ACCOUNTABILITY AND EFFICIENCY

In this and the next chapter we will examine the likely effects of the reforms to local government finance, and evaluate the extent to which they will secure the Government's stated objectives. For this purpose we will examine the relationship between economic efficiency, the level of spending and local accountability using first a simple economic model, and then move on to consider the, somewhat idealised, median voter version model of collective decision making.[1] This provides us with an interesting basis for comparing the effects of poll tax with the present system of domestic rates, and also with possible alternative local tax systems within a reformed grant and non-domestic rates structure. We will then, in the next chapter, introduce some limitations in this economic approach to modelling the behaviour of all the main actors - electors, local government employees, and central government - which are relevant to the choice of local tax. This leads to an effort to extend the model, using a public choice approach, to a fuller political-economic model of real electors and central and local politicians (especially central) in the British setting. This will finally enable us to evaluate the extent to which the Government's reforms will deliver an improvement in efficiency and local accountability.

In the 1986 Green Paper and in subsequent Ministerial speeches the main emphasis in the Government's case for reform has been largely a negative one, with discussion literally confined to the existing weaknesses in local accountability or the unacceptable effects of a rating revaluation. There has been very little in the way of direct statement of what constitutes strong local accountability. However, the Government's ideas can be discerned by placing together two statements made in the Green Paper. First, when it was argued (para. 3.31, p.24) that the best local tax was one which would:

> promote the efficient provision of services to the levels desired by most members of the community.

Second, it was its view (para. 1.43, p.8) that the present arrangements resulted in a pattern of local domestic tax prices and tax shares which ensured that:

> ... electors are either indifferent to the level of expenditure adopted by their local council or are encouraged to vote for higher service standards than they would be prepared to finance if they bore the full marginal cost themselves.

This shows that there is a strong link in the Government's view between economic efficiency and satisfactory local accountability. An important implication, however, is that the Government's model assumes a responsiveness to the wishes of the electorate in the present system, in that local authorities supply the levels of service demanded by a majority of voters.[2]

However, this responsiveness by local authorities does not represent satisfactory local accountability. This is because the demands they are responding to are inappropriate (although the Government's emphasis has always been on demands being too high) because they are based on inappropriate tax prices. Tax prices are inappropriate in three ways:

(1) the burden of local taxation is placed on too few shoulders, given that nearly half of the local electorate do not receive direct local tax bills, and a further one-sixth receive local tax rebates.

(2) there is a substantial general subsidy in the marginal tax price facing the domestic sector as a whole in most local authorities, with particularly large marginal subsidies in local authorities where the non-domestic sector is a substantial share of rateable value.

(3) tax prices facing households and individuals under domestic rates are not, and cannot be, even if the marginal subsidy from non-domestic rates is removed, related either to the costs of, or benefits received from, services consumed. This is referred to as the absence of the "beneficial principle" in local taxation.

Let us deal with the first two points before moving on to the analysis proper. We have already discussed the first alleged source of weakness in the latter part of Chapter 3. There we rejected the idea that a majority of those who have not received direct rate demands act (vote) on the assumption that expenditure by local authorities have zero cost to themselves. It seems totally unreasonable to believe that spouses have been (a) unaware of rate bills received by their households - absurd surely to pretend that the recipients haven't mentioned rate bills to their spouses, and, perhaps, complained about their level, and (b) have been unconcerned about the effect of higher rate demands upon household finances. Thus the validity of the "literally zero" idea in the Government's analysis is rejected and no further discussion of this point will be made here.

In contrast with respect to the second point, the facts - shown in Table 8.1 - support the Government's case. Nearly 60% of local government expenditure is by authorities where the gross marginal tax cost is less than 80p per £, and there is a wide variation in the level of marginal contribution. This is further reinforced when we remember that this is the gross domestic tax cost - the domestic sector's net tax cost after receipt of rebates is usually less than 80% of the gross tax cost.

Table 8.1: Gross Tax Contribution of Domestic ratepayers to finance of an extra £1 of expenditure, English local authorities, 1987/88 (spending below threshold)

Range	Number of local authorities	Total expenditure of authorities in each range £m.	Cumulative Percentage of Total expenditure of authorities by each range %
less than 10p	1	71.8	0.3
10 - 19.99p	4	114.8	0.7
20 - 29.99p	3	1205.6	5.4
30 - 39.99p	14	246.2	6.3
40 - 49.99p	33	619.3	8.7
50 - 59.99p	71	2546.1	18.6
60 - 69.99p	96	4601.5	36.4
70 - 79.99p	89	5990.0	59.5
80 - 89.99p	60	5134.1	79.4
90 - 99.99p	34	2554.9	89.3
100 - 109.99p	19	2587.4	99.3
110 - 119.99p	1	134.3	99.8
more than 120p	1	51.0	100.0

Source: author's computations

120 The Politics and Economics of the Poll Tax

The third point relating to the benefit principle is more complicated and we will postpone further consideration until later. Let us first show the basic economic reasoning behind the linking of the marginal subsidy to the idea that local authorities' spending is too high. First we start with a consumer purchasing a private service freely in the market as shown in Figure 8.1. Let the real marginal cost of providing the service X be OC. The demand curve of the consumer is shown by BD and registers the value of the benefits of each successive unit of X to the consumer. If the price per unit facing the consumer is OC, the quantity purchased will be OE and this is the most efficient choice because the marginal benefits to the consumer of the OEth unit (OR) are equal to its marginal cost (OC). The marginal cost represents the opportunity cost or alternative benefits available from the resources used in providing the OEth unit. At this output the net benefits, that is the difference between the consumption value of X, trapezium OBRE and its costs, OCRE, are maximised. If instead the price facing the consumer were OS, then OF would be chosen and the benefits of the extra units consumed, RVFE, are less than the real costs of the resources consumed, RWFE, by the amount, RWF.

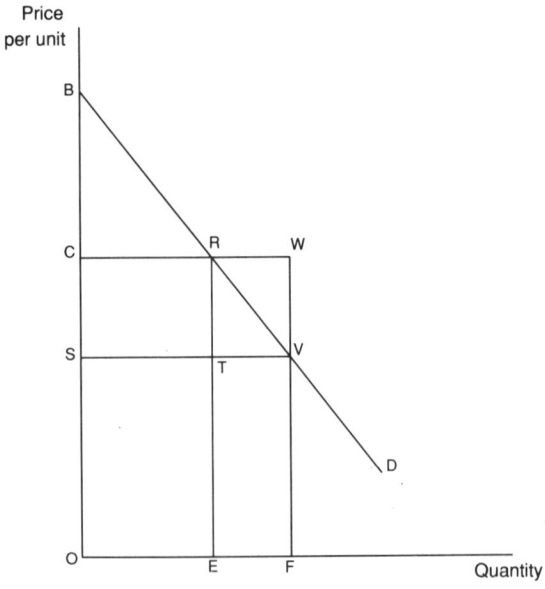

Figure 8.1: Marginal subsidy and inefficiency

Accountability and Efficiency

Given the extent of the subsidy to the domestic sector in many local authorities, then the structural change in local government finance, which in most areas results in an increase in the marginal tax cost to the domestic sector, should be helpful to economic efficiency, especially where the marginal subsidy in the block grant system has been greatest. However, two linked questions arise:

(1) Is it justifiable to remove entirely - as opposed to partially - the marginal contribution of non-domestic rates to the marginal expenditure of local authorities?

(2) Which local tax is best guaranteed to deliver economic efficiency and local accountability?

To some extent these questions cannot be answered independently – the choice of local tax may interact with the necessary supporting structure of local government finance. Let us deal with the local tax first and start by reminding ourselves about the Government's analysis. In the Green Paper it is stated that the search for the best local tax has been an attempt to reconcile the conflicting objectives of having a tax related to both the "beneficial principle" - that is the benefits received from local services - and the "redistributive principle" - that is to ability to pay. It further maintains that domestic rates perform no better than poll tax on the ability to pay criterion, but that a poll tax is much more closely related to benefits received than domestic rates. The reason given for this important conclusion is that the "use of local authority services ... now more closely reflects the number of people in a household than the value of the property occupied." (Department of the Environment, 1986a, para. 3.34) This is therefore the best local tax - the local tax which makes local authorities accountable and "promotes the efficient provision of services to the levels desired by most members of the community".

There is an implicit economic model of efficient collective choice here. This model shows that collective choice will tend to be more efficient when the tax prices facing different groups are in the line with the benefits they receive from services.

Collective decision making

Assume that it has been decided that a certain good or service, X, is to be provided, and consumed collectively - that is that a certain quantity will be provided and consumed equally by all residents.[3,4] The main difference from the market model is that consumers cannot

122   *The Politics and Economics of the Poll Tax*

directly purchase and consume their preferred quantities. Instead all residents will - given the structure of tax prices facing them as a requirement of paying for collective provision - have their preferred quantities[5] and these will usually be different, but only one option can be chosen. First it is necessary to map the preferred demands of residents for the collectively provided service. The essential problem can be shown by a 3-residents model.

Let residents L, M, and H have the demand curves Dl, Dm, and Dh, shown in Figure 8.2, respectively. In the case of collective consumption the total value of each extra unit is the sum of the residents marginal values (willingness to pay) for that unit, which is shown by their demand curves. Following Samuelson (1954) and Bowen (1948) the total marginal social benefit of extra units can be found, therefore, by vertically adding the demand curves.[6] This is shown by the curve Dt. Let the service be provided under constant cost conditions, with each extra unit costing OC. Whatever quantity of the service which the residents decide to collectively provide the cost per unit (OC) must be shared between the residents.

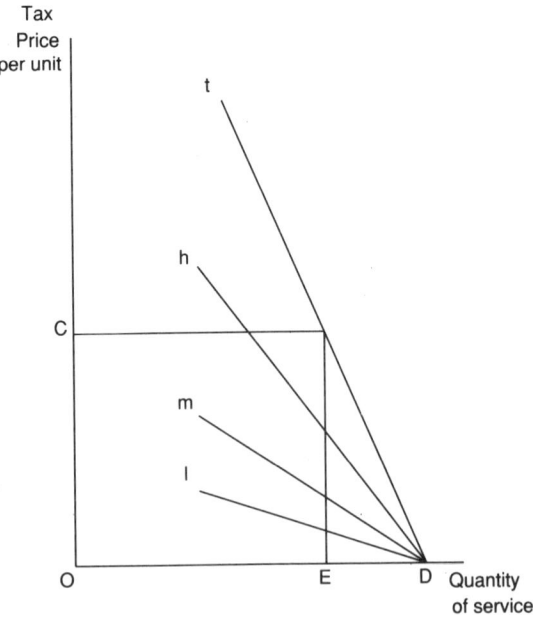

Figure 8.2: **Efficient output under collective provision**

It can be readily seen that the economically efficient output is at OE, where the total marginal benefit (that is the sum of the marginal benefits of the three residents) is equal to the marginal cost. This is the economically efficient output. The question which arises is how best to achieve it where residents must face a given structure of tax prices?[7]

The benefit principle and economic efficiency

A political decision rule for the approval of collective decisions is, of course, needed before decisions can be implemented. The Swedish economists, Wicksell (1896) and Lindahl (1919) developed a solution to the problem where unanimity was required. Although majority rule voting is a much more common requirement for collective decisions and we will use this later it is worthwhile to explore the solution to the unanimity problem. The set of tax prices which will make every resident agree that OE is their preferred output are shown in Figure 8.3 by Th, Tm, and Tl. These are the tax prices at which each resident's individual marginal benefit is equal to their marginal tax cost.

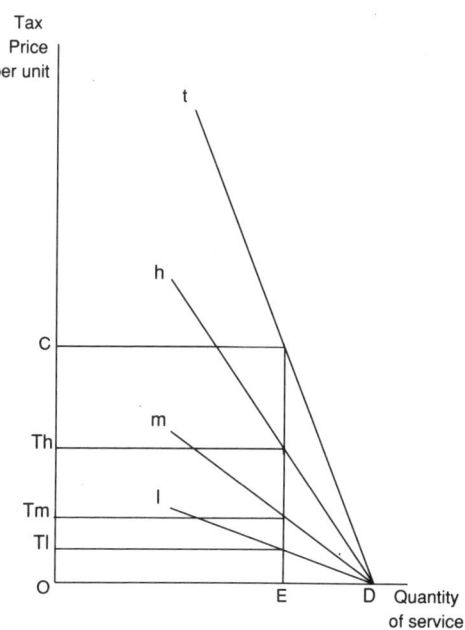

Figure 8.3: Benefit taxation

This solution was produced here, as it were, "out-of-the-hat" - visual inspection of the demand curves, which we assumed were known (but in the real world are only in the minds of the residents), provided the relevant set of benefit taxes. Discussion of how the tax prices are, or can be arrived at has much exercised economists[8], but the information requirements and the flexible institutional arrangements for introducing such benefit taxes cannot begin to be met in the real world. The realism of the model is not the main issue here, however. Rather it is that it provides an ideal, or standard, against which to measure the efficiency properties of alternative tax structures.

There is another important point to emphasise about the "benefit principle", bearing in mind that the Government has been so keen to invoke the principle as a justification for the replacement of domestic rates by poll tax on the grounds that *use* of services was better related to household size than value of property occupied. The point is that the benefit principle suggests that economic efficiency will be served if tax prices are related to the *value to the user* of services consumed - this can be very different to the cost of services and we will discuss this point further below. A further point is that benefit taxes will increase with income level if the demand for a public service increases with income. There is no necessary conflict between the benefit principle and the ability to pay principle.

Neither poll tax or rates are even close to being a benefit tax

Given the Lindahl standard model of benefit taxes it is necessary to deal with the notion that any local tax alternative matches a benefit tax. In general it is unimaginable that any real world tax structure will provide even a close fit to the Wicksell-Lindahl set of benefit taxes with respect to individual taxpayers. In particular half of British local authorities' expenditure is on education so there will be a strong tendency towards the major current benefits being received according to the number of children each household has of school age. The poll tax is a tax upon adults, not upon the number of children at school - it is therefore bound to be a very poor benefit tax.[9] However, this is not to prejudge matters because for the same reason domestic rates are clearly also not a close fit to a benefit tax.

In the real world tax bases and structures are "chosen" and imposed - on British local authorities this choice will be made "from above" and the imposed tax base and structure will provide the set of tax prices, subject to grants received, for each resident in each local authority. They cannot be individual benefit taxes. However, the benefit standard is still relevant. Alternative tax structures can be assessed on the basis of which provides a better benefit tax with respect to broad groupings - the absence of a close fit to group benefits may lead to exploitation of one group by another and economically inefficient decisions. This is especially so in the pervasive majority rule voting requirement, for approval of proposed collective action, of British central and local government.

Let us assume for the moment that there is direct democracy - rather than the actual representative democracy of British central and local government - and majority rule voting. We also assume that the franchise is restricted to adults. In this situation the median voter rule commands much support as a description of how collective decisions are arrived at.

The median voter model

Again all the essential complexity of the problem can be conveyed by a 3-person model. In Figure 8.4 (p.126) let us again have three demand curves for individuals L,M, and H, of Dl, Dm and Dh respectively, but with a set of tax prices, Tl, Tm, and Th, which leaves each individual preferring different quantities of collective provision - L wants A, M wants B, and H wants F. The median voter theorem is that if a number of voters with different views on an issue choose by majority rule voting, the outcome will be the optimum for the median voter (Tullock, 1976) - in this case M, who desires the middle quantity, B. In this situation the model is self-evidently more reasonable than alternative predictions such as A or F - B is the quantity which can most easily gain the support of two of the three voters.

Of major immediate interest is the question of whether with a poll tax the median voter rule results in efficient output decisions or under- or over-provision of collectively provided services. The answer depends (Bergstrom, 1973) on the relative tax and benefit shares of the median voter. Figure 8.5 (p.127) shows the demand curve of the median voter Dm and again let OE be the efficient output derived from consideration of the total marginal cost, OC, and total marginal benefit curve, Dt. The tax price for the median voter where the tax share is equal to the benefit share is Tb and results in efficient provision OE. With a poll tax, P, the expectation here is that the median voter's tax share is above benefit share and results in underprovision at B.[10] The reasons for this are now discussed.

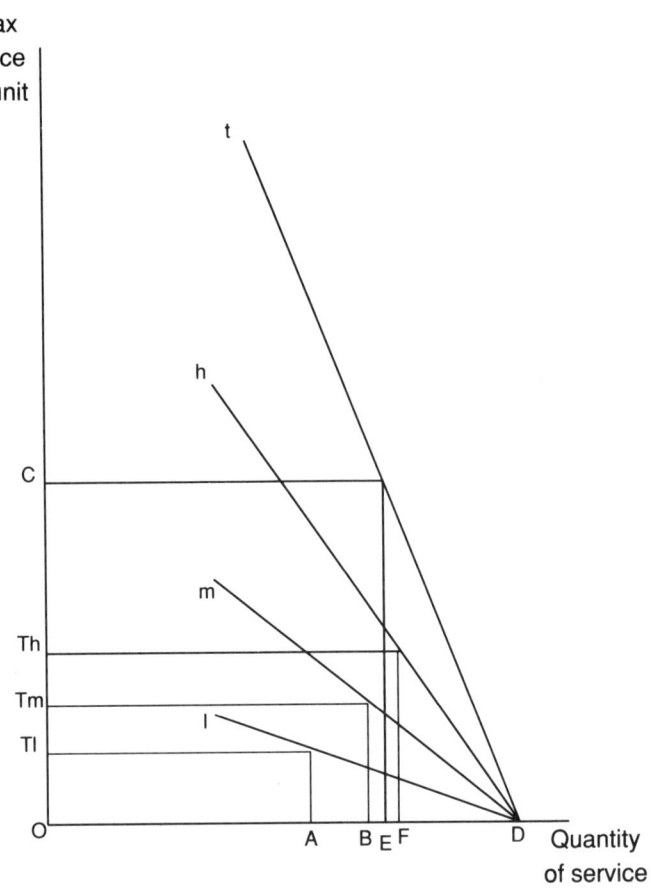

Figure 8.4: The median voter rule

Assessing alternative local tax structures

Let us now assess some alternative tax structures, staying within the framework of the median voter model. The two most important variables to concentrate on are income and household structure. The former is long established as a key influence with respect to the demand for services, and is therefore relevant to the relation of tax structure to benefits and also obviously so with respect to ability to pay. The latter is also relevant because of the fact that poll tax is particularly geared to heavier taxation of households with large numbers of adults.

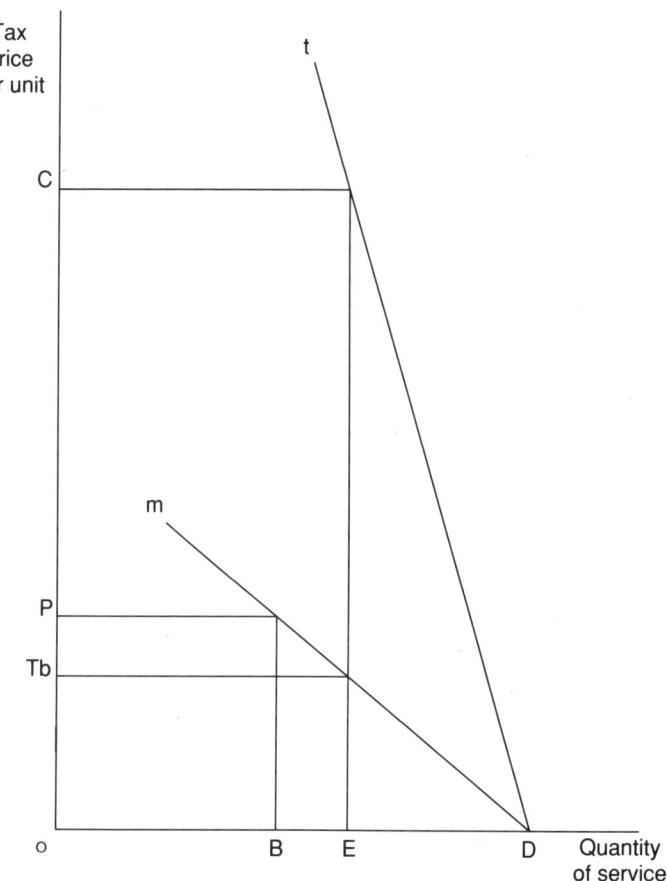

Figure 8.5: Poll tax and level of service provision

Considering the range of local government services it would commonly be expected that there are large differences between the extent to which use and benefits vary with income. For example, public housing (no longer financed by local taxation) would be expected to be more "pro-poor" and recreation and post-16 education more "pro-rich". Jackman's own verdict (Jackman, 1988) was that, overall, benefits had a positive relationship to income but increased at a less than proportionate rate. This would suggest that a moderately regressive tax such as domestic rates would be closer to a benefit tax than a flat rate tax such as poll tax.

128 The Politics and Economics of the Poll Tax

Particularly relevant here are the results given by Bramley, Le Grand and Low, 1989, of a recent survey of usage of local government services in Cheshire county which compares the use of services by five income quintiles with the tax of the quintiles under poll tax and the traditional domestic rates (ie based on the imputed rents rateable values) - both measured before rebates. Both the use and the tax side were standardised for household structure so their results are also relevant to deal with the structure question. Their results are for total household income and equivalent income and these are reproduced in Figures 8.6 and 8.7. On a use basis their results show that the less regressive domestic

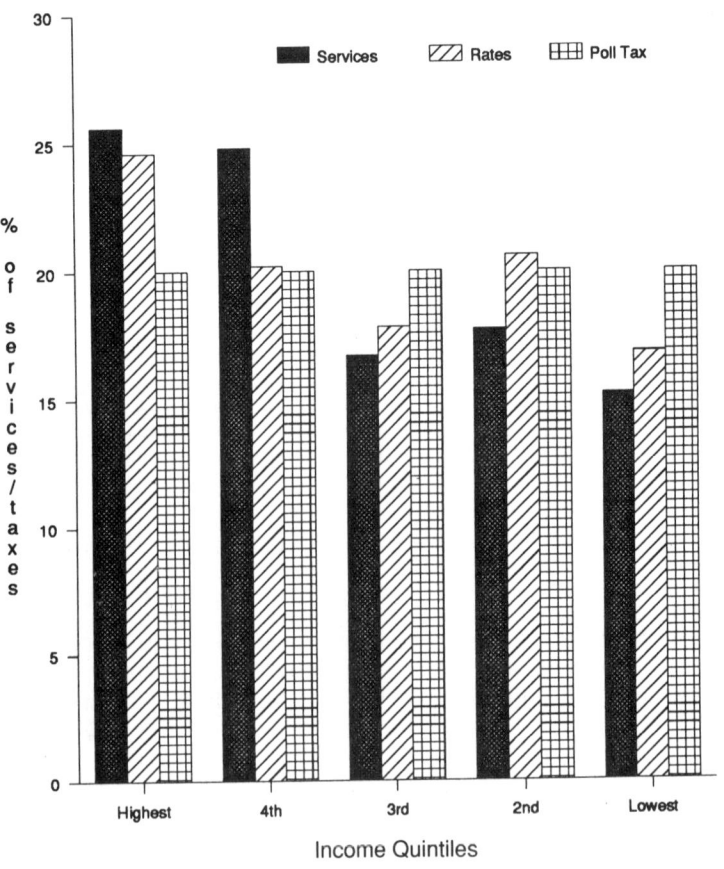

Figure 8.6: Distribution by total household income

rates provide a better fit to usage than poll tax. Rates are particularly closer to use for the top income quintile, with the largest discrepancy between tax share and use share for poll tax for the upper income quintile.

However, here it is particularly important to remember that the value placed on each unit of use - that is the benefits - varies positively with income (see also Aaron and MacGuire, 1970). This means that poll tax is even more awry as a benefit tax than appears from Figures 8.6 or 8.7 because the relative benefits shares will be higher for the

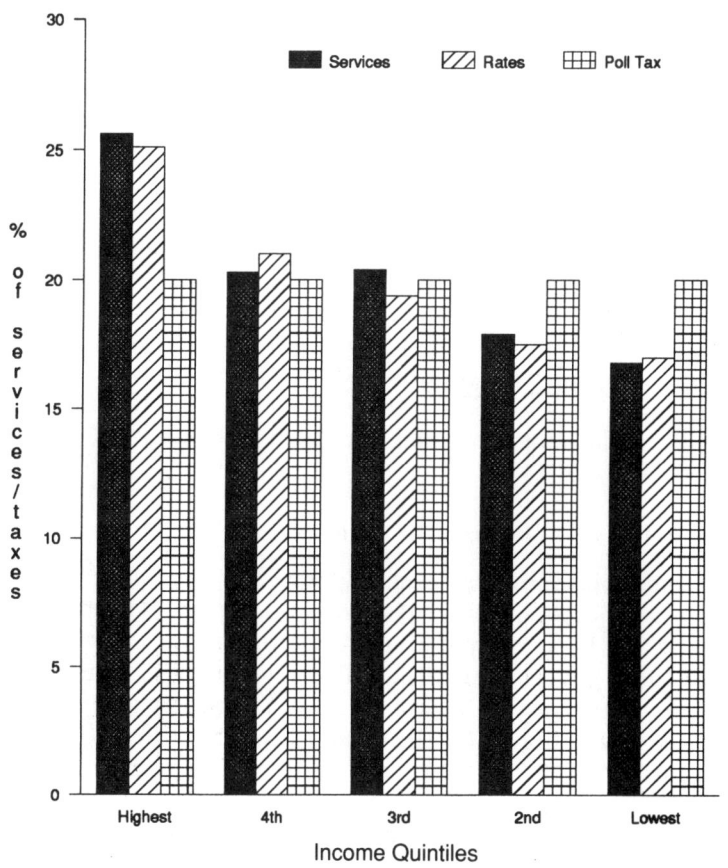

Figure 8.7: Distribution by Equivalent household income

upper income quintiles and lower for the lower income quintiles than is shown. The median voter analysis implies that the poll tax will lead to inefficient underprovision of local government services. This points strongly towards a more progressive tax than the domestic rates based on imputed rents as best meeting the benefit principle. There are two candidates - domestic rates based on capital values, which is more progressive than imputed rents, and a relatively unprogressive form of local income tax. The poll tax has no genuine claim to be a benefit tax.[11]

Rebates

Two additional topics relating to the benefit principle also merit discussion. The first is rebates. The analysis above would support the view that efficient government action is more likely when no beneficiaries are facing zero tax prices for the collective provision of services. Thus it is helpful if those on income support are put in a position where their incomes are augmented and then pay local tax according to the expenditure policies of the relevant local authorities. Representation without taxation has its dangers, especially if is widespread, and before the introduction of the minimum 20% payment in 1988 there were some local authorities in which over 50% of households received full rebates. However, one problem of the change has been that no separate item of compensation was introduced into the income support scales and given the unusual and potentially regressive nature of this change it would be a worthwhile innovation to introduce such an item in order that its annual uprating can be clearly followed and debated.

The benefits of non-domestic ratepayers

The second point is that business and non-domestic rates receive some benefits from local government services. Jackman (1986) was prepared to accept a CIPFA estimate that the non-domestic sector consumed 30% of local government expenditure - although if one treats the domestic sector as the beneficiaries of education expenditure this figure seems too high. Nevertheless it is probably true that business is responsible for 10-20% of consumer use of local government services. Given this, the fact that the marginal local contribution of the non-domestic rates is zero is a quite significant violation of the benefit principle. One line of justification is that there is no voting or representation for the business sector and therefore a local contribution

Accountability and Efficiency

is not justified. On balance I think that the present situation of getting "something-for-nothing" should be subject to some change, with the non-domestic ratepaying sector making a small contribution - pro-rata to its relative size - to marginal expenditure in their area.[12]

Lump-sum grants and efficiency

Before moving on it remains to consider whether the conclusions are affected by the existence of lump-sum grants and revenues. In the new system the level of lump sum revenues is extremely high, being nearly 75% of expenditure in 1987/88. In the block grant system there was also a substantial implicit lump-sum element. The result in both systems is that the percentage change in local tax rates is higher than the percentage change in expenditure – the so-called "gearing" effect – but it will be much more severe in the new system.

According to the basic theory, lump-sum grants should not induce inefficient output expansion, [because they do not alter marginal tax prices]. They are regarded as simply returning to local authorities an equivalent amount of revenue to that levied on residents through central taxes, to finance equalisation and other objectives achieved through such lump-sum grants. There will be some redistribution from richer and low needs areas to poorer and high needs areas. This might lead to some increase in spending but apart from this there should be no greater local government spending than if there were no central grants and the equivalent central tax reductions leaving local authorities to finance all their own spending. However, the empirical data (Gramlich, 1977) suggest that lump-sum grants do have net stimulative effects. This is of some importance because it implies that lump-sum revenues induce greater local government spending than would occur if residents compared directly the marginal benefits to the tax costs of local government spending. There has been much debate (Oates, 1979; Courant, Gramlich, and Rubinfeld, 1979; King, 1984) over the source of the bias, with a majority favouring the view that lump-sum revenues induce a fiscal illusion:- they lead the electorate to underestimate the unit costs of local government services. Thus they lead to local electors making choices as if there were a marginal subsidy on the provision of local services. This debate is not yet finally resolved, but noting that lump-sum revenues probably do induce some excess outputs (although less than direct marginal subsidies)[13] in an efficiency sense, this provides an additional consideration in assessing alterative local tax structures, which is taken up in Chapter 9.

Concluding comments

The median voter analysis and the empirical evidence considered in this chapter has markedly damaged the poll tax's claim to be most in accord with the benefit principle and serving the cause of increasing economic efficiency in the provision of local government services. However, the analysis is not complete. For various reasons the median voter analysis is unsatisfactory as a complete model of actual behaviour. In Chapter 9 we will extend the discussion by introducing some additional factors and develop a fuller public choice analysis before drawing together the conclusions of the overall analysis.

Notes

1. The approach here is different to that of Midwinter and Mair (1986), who completely reject all aspects of the Government's analysis partly on the grounds that (1) its empirical assertions are incorrect or unsupported by the evidence (a point with which there is, here, substantial agreement), but mostly on the grounds that (2) its public choice/voter rationality base is totally invalid. Rationality is dismissed by them largely on the grounds that the voter hasn't got all the information required to make the necessary calculations and there are irrational elements in voting which economics cannot explain, and therefore, because economics cannot explain everything it can explain nothing. The existence of irrational elements in voting does not mean, however, that voters will not respond to changes in incentives. The analysis by Tullock (1972) on the relationship between, and the real differences in approach between, economics and the other social science disciplines is most helpful on this point but, unfortunately, seems to be little known to British scholars. In any case Midwinter and Mair supply their own useful analysis of the workings of local government and argue effectively against those who deny responsiveness in local politics and local variations in voting. Their view that there has been increased responsiveness by local electorates to rates increases in the 1980s implies that they do, in fact, have some belief in some elements of the rational public choice model.

2. The decision to tax cap a number of local authorities in 1990/91 seems difficult to reconcile with the Government actually believing its own model of the workings of responsive local democracy.

3. British local authorities supply collectively many services which do not have the technical characteristics of "public goods", such as national defence or television, where there is non-rival consumption (i.e. additional persons can consume without adding to costs) and excluding non-payers from receiving benefits is impossible or extremely expensive (King, 1984; Brown and Jackson, 1982). However, Buchanan, 1970, and Spann, 1974, have shown that the analysis is little changed by the phenomenon of collectively provided non-public goods as long as we assume that there is a given consumption sharing rule. The simplest version of this is where, like Buchanan and Spann, it is assumed that the aggregate quantity provided by the local authority is allocated equally between households i.e all will consume the same quantity.

4. The previously cited analyses by Buchanan and Spann shows why there are inevitably efficiency costs in the collective provision of non-public goods, and the analysis shows that the most efficient solution is to employ cost based user charges in the allocation of goods and services. However, this is a book about poll tax in contemporary Britain, rather than a duplication of numerous treatises on the efficiency gains to be made from charging (Bird,1976; Maynard and King, 1972; Bailey, 1986). Adding to the latter would be a foolish allocation of this author's efforts because the Government itself rejected (without explicitly giving its reasons!) this alternative in the section of the Green Paper devoted to charging, (Department of the Environment, 1986a, para. 3.36)

> ... although there is scope for extending user charging, most local authority spending will inevitably not be financed by such charges.

5. There is a requirement that they have a unique preferred quantity, but it is most unlikely that this is not the case (see Black, 1948).

6. Vertical summation is correct because of the non-rival consumption of each unit of public good. Therefore the benefit derived each unit is the sum of each consumer's valuation of that unit. With collectively provided non-public goods where consumption is rival vertical summation is also legitimate because each unit is defined to be a bundle of units of the non-public good sufficient to allocate the collectively decided consumption share to each resident (see Buchanan, 1970; Spann, 1974).

7. I am assuming an absence of perfectly informed benevolent despots who simply impose the efficient solution on the community!

8. See Lindahl (1919), Samuelson (1954), and Bowen (1948).

9. Jackman (1988) also makes this point.

10. There will be a limit to the economic inefficiency generated here because the further this individual's demand diverges from OE then the less likely he/she is to remain the median voter - that is the more likely it is that some other voter prefers a more middling quantity and becomes the median voter. This last sentence suggests though a powerful message one can derive from the median voter model - this is that *there is real danger of large inefficiency if a majority of voters bear tax shares very different to their benefit shares. However, the danger is both ways - it may lead to inefficient underprovision or inefficient overprovision.* Thus in the 3-person model if two voters bear very little tax and have average benefit shares then they will support overprovision financed largely by the third voter. Conversely if two voters bear nearly all the tax and have average benefit shares then they will by majority support underprovision. The message is that ultimately we must, if we are concerned with the efficiency of collective government provision, beware of situations where the tax shares of groups comprising a majority of the electorate are markedly below, or above, their benefit shares.

11. Jackman (1988) knew it and most creditably pointed it out.

12. An additional consideration for some is the complete absence of fiscal incentives to local authorities regarding the attraction of business (Heald, 1978; Bennett, 1988; Foster, 1986).

13. Empirical studies have supported the theoretical prediction (Wilde, 1968) that the expenditure stimulation effects of positive matching grants are larger than from equivalent amount lump-sum grants.

9.
THE POLL TAX: FURTHER ACCOUNTABILITY CONSIDERATIONS

Introduction

The analysis in the previous chapter based on the median voter model is incomplete and unsatisfactory as an evaluation of the effects of the reforms to local government finance in a number of respects. First, representative democracy is much "lumpier" and less finely tuned than is implied by the median voter rule. In the British local government context, political parties compete for power on manifestos covering the entire range of services and a small shift in votes, if it changes the party in power, can result in much larger changes in policies and expenditure than would be implied the median voter rule with a small change in preferences.[1] The importance of this is that where there is a weak or distorted relationship between votes and seats in local elections, as was common in England in the 1980s, then the outcome from representative government will often be some distance away from the median voter's position. In areas where the Conservatives achieve excess representation output decisions will tend to be low compared to median voter preference and vice-versa in areas where Labour achieves excess representation.

Second, local electors are citizens who can also choose to take part in political activities - voting, writing letters to MPs or national newspapers, marching etc. - which bring pressure upon, and perhaps induce change, from the centre (Breton, 1974). The implicit political model in the reform of local government finance is one of automaton like behaviour by all the major participants - a tax base is decided (by central government) and local electors react to the resulting tax structure to achieve the predicted results of the median voter model.

The implicit model in the economic analysis was either (1) that there would be no other political reaction or (2) that central politicians would not respond or be diverted from their initial chosen tax and grant position for local government.

The political activity of local electors does, of course, have an important role in the Government's model of the strengthening of local accountability. Under the new system most electors will now find it costs much more in local tax bills to support high spending local authorities, and the Government's model has either (1) councillors responding to this by reducing spending or (2) being voted out of office in favour of councillors favouring lower levels of spending. This can be translated in the British context to replacing Labour councillors by Conservative councillors. Before elaborating further we can usefully consider the way some of these matters were analysed in the debate in 1986 after the publication of the Green Paper mainly between Foster, Jackman, and what I will call the "post-Layfield school" of Jones, Stewart, and Travers (the first two had been members of the Layfield committee).

Post Green Paper Evaluation - A Conflict of Views

Foster (1986) in his article was, not unnaturally as a major adviser, supportive of the reforms and emphasised the link between economic efficiency, the level of spending, and the changes in incentives at the margin (Foster, 1986, p.18):

> ... from an efficiency point of view it is not the average, but the marginal cost falling on the local population which matters. By fixing grant in advance, the Green Paper proposals oblige authorities to cover the total cost of extra spending from local sources. That is likely to be a much more effective disincentive to spend than reductions in the average proportion of spending met by grant ...

Foster's reservations about the poll tax, evident in previous writings, were absent in the 1986 article. Foster and Jackman (1982) had argued for either (a) retention of domestic rates, but with "a more equitable system of resident equalisation based on average households income rather than rateable values", or (b) the substitution of a local income tax for rates which "would improve the equivalence between those who receive benefits and those who pay for them". Now, according to Foster, expressing a commonly held view, "what matters rationally is the progressiveness of the whole tax system which taxpayers experience" (Foster, 1986).

Jackman (1986) had greater reservations about the reforms. Like Foster he noted the contrast between the emphasis in the reforms on

The Poll Tax: Further Accountability Considerations 137

increasing the domestic tax cost at the margin and the Layfield emphasis on strengthening local accountability by increasing the average proportion of local tax. According to the Layfield criteria he noted that the Green Paper did not involve any move in the direction of local accountability because it reduced the proportion of the total cost of local government services borne locally. He also noted the argument of Ward and Williams (1986) that the Layfield view had been undermined by the fact that, despite the grant proportion having fallen from 65.5% in 1975/76 to a planned level of 47% for 1986/87, there had been markedly increasing pressures for central control during this period. Jackman further stated that because the locally borne cost of local expenditure had been smaller than the nationally borne cost, central government had perceived a greater burden of local authority expenditure than had the local authorities themselves, and:

> On this interpretation, it is the absence of the full cost principle applied to marginal expenditure that is the root cause of the long-running battle between central government and local authorities over the aggregate level of local government expenditure.

These contributions evoked a critical rejoinder from Jones, Stewart, and Travers (JST), 1986. JST initially disputed what they perceived to be the Jackman view that "councillors think in marginal terms alone: economic analysis is assumed to determine political behaviour". However, they then implied some belief in such economic determinism when stating "councillors will know they have the dice loaded against them when considering whether to raise service standards". Their main attack was on the misleading signals which would be given to electors in the new system. This would be caused by the heavy gearing effect when 80% of spending was financed from grant and the national business rate. In such a situation a 1% rise in expenditure would lead on the average to a 5% rise in local tax level. The discrepancy in tax levels between local authorities would be much larger than the difference in spending - a local authority spending 10% above GRE would on average have to charge three times that of one spending 10% below. JST stated:

> Councillors and electors judge tax changes by the relative change as much as by the absolute change ... It is hard to understand what kind of local accountability flows from such a system, and whether accurate signals are being sent out to local voters about the spending decisions of their local authorities.[2]

Pressing forward the attack they stated that the marginal cost based view implied that one could have local accountability with a 99% grant, provide local authorities paid the full cost of marginal expenditure.

They predicted that with such high grant the centre would be more active in checking the expenditure decisions of local authorities: "... to make sure it was being spent wisely and not wasted. Ministers, MPs and national auditors would not let local authorities spend it as they wanted. Central control would increase".

Jackman (1986) replied to this rejoinder. He conceded that they had "serious and entirely reasonable doubts about the relevance and appropriateness of the economic analysis underlying the Green Paper". However, he disputed their claim that he had assumed that if the marginal principle were introduced, political differences would not matter because everyone would come to the same decision:

> My position is quite the opposite. I believe the introduction of the marginal principle could allow the maximum of diversity, because decisions on local expenditure need then be constrained only by what people are prepared to pay for locally, and not by interference from the centre. Jones and his co-authors appear to confuse equality of incentives with equality of outcomes.[3]

The position taken here is that there are merits in both approaches to seeking economic efficiency and strengthening local accountability. It is unfortunate that neither side saw any merit in the component stressed by the other party. In the previous chapter the view that achieving a uniformly higher domestic marginal tax cost is important was supported; but there are also desirable features in reducing the proportion of grant and other external finance, such as the national non-domestic rate, in order to avoid excessive gearing effects. The most obvious reason is that, given that empirical evidence lends support to the existence of fiscal illusion caused by lump-sum grants, there is every likelihood that in any system with a large proportion of external finance local electors will find it difficult to assess the efficiency of their own authority through the common device of comparisons with neighbouring local authorities. In such a system there is far more likelihood that there will be a weak relationship taking a class of local authorities between changes in expenditure and changes in local tax rates with a greater occurrence of perverse relationships.The reason is that when external finance is large, there will be much greater variation in fiscal pressure caused by changes in grant arising from changes in the shares of needs assessments.[4] It also gives rise to a weakness in the criterion of local accountability. Advocates of the full marginal cost principle claim that it ensures that local spending and tax decisions are taken by local electors (or, rather, their local representatives) on consideration of the marginal local benefits and the full marginal real resource costs of providing those services. However, one important point is often overlooked – that output decisions are not determined in such a model simply by a trade-off between local marginal benefits and local marginal costs. The reason is, as numerous output studies have confirmed (Ashford, Berne, and Schramm, 1976; Bennett, 1982; Foster, Jackman, and Perlman, 1980), that the level of spending chosen by local authorities is influenced quite substantially by the amount of lump sum grant received from central government. Thus the formally efficient local spending decision can never be fully local – it is bound to be a decision in which the centre exerts an influence, and the greater the proportion of external finance in the system the greater the relative influence of the centre in levels of, and changes in, local authorities' expenditure. From this perspective the conversion of non-domestic rates into an assigned revenue in effect increases the share of grant from 50 to 75% and the influence of the centre. The increase leads to changes in local tax levels being much more sensitive both to local expenditure changes and grant changes. There is an inconsistency in the position of those emphasising the importance of marginal cost to be borne by the domestic sector within the same year, but not being much concerned with the proportion of additional expenditure between different years which is financed by the domestic sector.

We will now develop a positive public choice analysis of the interacting political and economic effects predicted to follow the introduction of the proposed reforms. This will also throw light on some major problems which can be predicted because the reforms have been pivoted around a poll tax rather than an alternative, more progressive, tax. [The next section is taken from an article published in *Policy and Politics* in 1987 (Gibson, 1987c), and the tenses have been left unchanged.]

Analysis

Let us distinguish two initial impacts. First, there will be the impact upon the budgetary decisions - spending and levels of community charge - of local authorities. Second, there will be the simultaneous impact of any adverse political reaction upon central government. Let us deal with the latter first.

The best precedent here would seem to be the reaction of the Government to the outcry provoked by the revaluation in Scotland. In this case the RSG Order for Scotland was changed, at a very late stage, in March 1985 - an "unprecedented step" according to Scott, 1985 - in order to give special relief to domestic ratepayers. Domestic rate relief was increased from 5p to 8p - an extra payment of £38.5 million which reduced average rate increases from 21% to 14%. However, it has been shown elsewhere (Gibson, 1987a) that the disruption to household finances which will follow the introduction of the poll tax will be much larger than that associated with the Scottish revaluation. Our prediction is that the same central politicians will react in the same way - there will be an immediate increase in grant to local government when the new system is introduced.

In order to assess the initial impact upon budgetary decisions of local authorities we need to examine the change in average and marginal tax rates. The initial changes in the average local tax bill will be small in most local authorities, because of the operation of safety-nets to control changes in each local authority income from grant and non-domestic rates (Department of the Environment, 1986a. ch. 5). However, within this stable average, the tax share of the median income group of households will increase. This is because the poll tax is less progressive above the very lowest income group than domestic rates (see AMA; 1986, Smith and Squire, 1986) and the median income is less than the average in local income distributions (Bergstrom, 1973). The tax shares of those households at present receiving full rebates will also increase due to the introduction of the minimum 20% payment. If one adds to this the fact that, under poll tax, the average number of adults in "losing" households is greater than in "gaining" households, then the net result will undoubtedly be that the tax shares of a majority of the electorate will increase. Thus, income effects alone will be negative and cause some reduction in the demand for local government spending.[5] More straightforward, and more powerful, will be the substitution effects caused by the increase in marginal tax shares of the vast majority of households caused by the ending of marginal financing from non-domestic rates. Local politicians can be expected to immediately reflect the demands of local residents for lower levels of spending and taxation. The prediction is, therefore, that there will be an initial retreat from reliance on local taxation.

If local politicians do not quickly reduce local spending and tax levels then we may see the political effects underlying the local accountability model brought into play, namely the effect on local elections. The prediction is that with more electors paying local taxes and with the tax increase on marginal spending, there will be an increase in voting levels and a smaller proportion of electors being inclined to vote for politicians favouring high spending policies.

However, it is here that a permanent barrier to the success of any purely financial reform designed to increase local democratic accountability emerges. Bogdanor (1986) demonstrates that there is a serious mismatch between votes and council representation in many local authorities. He gives numerous examples from recent local election results ranging from clean sweeps achieved on the basis of barely 50% of votes cast to the fact that in 10 of the 36 metropolitan districts in 1978 the party winning the most votes had less votes than its nearest competitor. These distortions he argues will be far more serious and persistent than any mismatch at national level under first past the post or block vote systems because of the relatively greater social homogeneity at local authority level. The emergence of significant third party voting has only exacerbated the tendency towards mismatch. Such distortions are unlikely to be alleviated by increased voter turnout.

The second major drawback to the local accountability case is associated with the second political effect: pressure on the central government. We have already discussed the reaction to the initial disruption caused by the switch in local domestic taxation, but here we want to discuss a source of pressure which will continue after the initial disruption effects. [We assume for the sake of argument that the poll tax will survive the short term outcry]. The source of the political pressure again stems from the reliance upon such a regressive local tax. The feature to note here though is not just that poll tax is more regressive than domestic rates but also that it is markedly more regressive than grants financed from central governments ability to pay taxes. In his own evaluation of the system Foster is relying on a crucial implicit assumption that the balance between regressive and progressive tax sources will be fixed, or at least variable only to the extent that the central government's wishes to vary grant support in order to influence aggregate local government expenditure for purposes of macroeconomic management. In contrast we predict that the balance between local taxation and central government grants will be extremely variable in the early years of the new system and, as in the case of the Scottish revaluation, it will have nothing to do with macroeconomic management. Instead, it will be in response to pressure from two sources - local taxpayers and local authority employees. Let us analyse the taxpayers first.

Greene (1971) has explained the pressure caused by a system where local taxation is more regressive than central taxation. First, he introduces the fact that observed patterns of income distribution mean that a majority of the population (households or taxpayers) pay lower taxes under progressive taxes than under regressive taxes. This is because, as we noted above the majority of incomes are below the average/ mean income and progressive taxes are drawn more heavily from the minority with above average incomes. Greene concludes that the financial incentives will lead to pressures from coalitions representing the majority population, with below average incomes, to fund local spending from central progressive tax sources rather than local regressive tax sources. It was just such pressure placed upon the centre in the 1960s to fund increased local spending by grant and restrict reliance upon the unpopular regressive domestic rates which was described by the Layfield Committee. We expect that the result of introduction the poll tax will be much greater pressure upon the centre and central politicians from the electorate either to provide more grant, or take direct controls over local authorities' tax and spending decisions. We predict that the result will be an increase in grant and this will intensify two additional, but related, sources of pressure.

Local authority employees would also react to expenditure cuts in general, as well as the tendency under poll tax for large differences in service standards between areas to emerge. This is because, in the absence of matching grants, areas with higher incomes will purchase larger quantities of local government services when they are available at the same "price" in all areas (Feldstein, 1975). Argument based on the undesirability of falling and variable standards in public services will be used by local government employees, and similar arguments have exerted powerful leverage effects on the Conservative Government with respect to health and education since 1983. In addition to this pressure, there are groups representing consumers of local government services who, in the face of any decline, will ask for additional grant funding to local government both in general and to achieve minimum standards in poorer areas. If this pressure is sufficiently differentiated between services there is some likelihood that any additional grant will be tied to specific service spending. As well as this, the importance of the needs assessment (GRE) made for each local authority as a determinant of the amount of grant and level of service will be much increased. This will intensify the political conflict over the method of needs assessment, and presumably we will see a greater effort both by individual local authorities and their associations to develop arguments to change (or resist potential changes in) the indicators and the weights given to them in the needs assessment formula.

Two main strands emerge from the sequential analysis. The first is independent of the particular financial reform and is the weakness in the relationship between votes cast and seats in local elections. The second hinges not on the efficiency effects of the poll tax - but on the link between its regressiveness and the relative attractiveness of central and local funding. The problem is that the formal efficiency properties of the poll tax/full marginal cost model embody not only an explicit economic model but also an implicit political model, and the political model is faulty. The implicit political model is that politicians will supply the necessary firm and resolute behaviour to ensure that the new system will operate without major change. It is our prediction that initial local tax and spending reductions will lower the role of the poll tax to significantly below its starting point of 20% of local government spending. Following from this we expect extra grant to be forthcoming from the central government further lowering the role of poll tax. Decisions upon local spending and tax levels will be taken not only on the basis of comparisons of marginal benefits with the full resource costs per person, but will also depend upon the grant received by an local authority. Grant can be increased to local authorities in general through the standard per adult grant, or for a particular authority by an increase in its needs assessment causing an increase in needs grant. Given the emasculated role of local taxation these grant changes will become the dominant determinant of changes in local authorities' spending and tax levels. This should clearly not be described as increased local accountability. If the system were based on a local tax based on the ability to pay principle, such as local income tax, the loss of the non-domestic tax base would be much less important, because the weight supported by such a tax could be much greater. The analysis here suggests that it really does matter that the local tax is regressive.

Overall conclusions

The analysis of these two chapters on accountability suggests that some aspects of the Government's reforms can be supported, namely those which result in an increase in the domestic sector marginal tax conttribution - the nationalisation of the business rate and the conversion of grants into lump-sum form[6] – especially in areas where the previous marginal contribution was very low. However, the reliance on poll tax will, in itself, lead to inefficient underprovision because the tax share to the median voter will be above the benefit share and higher income residents will suffer a large gap between the standard of local government they would be willing to pay for and the collectively decided level of provision. This will to some extent be offset by increases in central grants, but these will alter the geographical pattern of services, in accordance with centrally assessed formulae. Given Wilson's (1988) reminder that the ability of the centre to estimate the relative spending needs of different areas is much overestimated, it is fair to conclude that this grant induced pattern will be less efficient than a pattern based more firmly on local preferences. The analysis suggests that these deficiencies would be much reduced if the new structure were combined with a more progressive, but not too progressive, local tax.

Notes

1. I do not wish to be delayed by arguing fully that politics matters so much in the British context, but one hardly needed to be more than a casual observer of British local government in the 1980s to notice a number of examples of large changes in expenditure resulting from small shifts in votes. Two examples would be the change from Conservative to Labour control of the GLC in 1981 and the changes in both directions of political control in Birmingham in the early 1980s. These were examples of parties choosing not to centre their policies upon their most marginal supporter, but to supply policies substantially closer to the middle of their supporters preferences. McLean (1982) provides a good analysis of party activists.

2. Bramley (1987a) makes a similar point.

3. Jackman concluded "Their piece contains many similar misunderstandings. In my view it obscures rather than contributes to serious analysis of the important questions on which we differ".

4. This variation in fiscal pressure has been quite marked, even in the present system with its lower external financing proportion. Thus Gibson, 1989b, found that among shire counties there was a range of variation of over 100% in the rate increase necessary to support an expenditure increase of 60% over the period from 1980/81 to 1989/90.

5. Glen Bramley has since pointed out to me that in the long run this effect may be offset by the large reduction in the aggregate domestic

contribution in some areas. Changes in the safety nets mean that this might apply to a few areas with the largest gains in 1990/91 and in 1991/92 to more areas when gaining areas are relieved of contributions to safety nets.

6. King (1988) argues that there is an inequity resulting from the fact that a 1% increase in service standards results in higher local tax increases in high needs areas, and that this exists under the rating system but will be magnified under the poll tax system. I would not wish to argue against this point but would prefer to emphasise that this inequity cost would be worth paying in return for a simplification of the structure of grants in a system based on a moderately progressive tax. Under a poll tax, however, it is worth stressing that a larger source of inequity will probably arise from the unequal level of "uncollectable" poll tax debt in different areas.

10.
RATES AND ACCOUNTABILITY: SOME EVIDENCE FROM LOCAL ELECTIONS

I had long been dissatisfied with the conventional wisdom amongst British political scientists that rate increases did not have much effect on British local election results - a conventional wisdom which lent support to the Government's view that domestic rates provided little accountability. Thus, given the fresh availability in 1986 of exhaustive compilations of local election results by Rallings and Thrasher (1986a, 1986b), I decided to test for myself whether my preconceptions that rates and services did have an effect would be supported by the evidence. [The results of my efforts presented below were published in *Policy and Politics* in June 1988.]

Introduction

The consensus view amongst political scientists is that rate increases are only rarely an important factor in determining local election results. Indeed, Newton (1976b) described local elections as "a sort of annual General Election" with "... very little that is local about them and they tell us practically nothing about the preferences and attitudes of citizens to purely local issues and events". In his report to the Layfield Committee on the impact of rates on local elections, Newton (1976a) stated that "the evidence, though not extensive, clearly indicates that rate changes have had a negligible effect on local (election) results". However, his survey covered a period when real (and nominal) rate increases tended to be low. Thus, he also added the rider that if future rate increases were larger in the inflationary conditions of the late 1970s this might result in greater responsiveness to rate increases in future. Rate increases have, in the event, been consistently above the rate of inflation since then, especially since 1979 when the

Conservative Government has, in successive years, reduced the level of grant support and imposed special grant penalties as the key part of its strategy for reducing local government spending (Gibson and Travers, 1986). However, the recent survey of the evidence on voting behaviour undertaken by Miller (1986) as part of the research programme of the Widdicombe Inquiry into the Conduct of Local Authority Business came to the conclusion that there was insufficient weight of evidence from the small number of empirical studies undertaken since 1976 to support any view that local rates have become an important influence on local elections in the last ten years. Miller's own conclusion (Miller, 1986 p.157) was that "rate rises are only likely to be salient when they are unusually high".

However, there is one awkward paradox which remains and casts a cloud over the present consensus that rates have not had much apparent influence on local elections. The paradox is that it conflicts with the findings of previous studies on the actual views and behaviour of councillors. Previous studies show that councillors are sensitive to rate increases and believe that they have a detrimental effect on their own and their party's electoral prospects (Gregory, 1969; Rees, 1967; Hampton, 1970). A survey by Newton (1976b) in Birmingham found that councillors felt that rate rises could result in reductions in electoral support. Gregory (1969), on the basis of his study in Reading, formulated a "rule of anticipated reactions" because local councillors "overestimate their own salience in the eyes of the electorate" and "try to anticipate popular reactions". The sensitivity of councillors to rate increases can also be observed in the actual pattern of council budgets. Thus, Cowan (1978) noted that in the spring of 1978 the average rate increase in the 44 authorities with elections that year was less than one-half of that in the 252 authorities without elections. Ferry (1978) in a study of rate changes in counties and boroughs between 1950 and 1974 found that "in each election year we see a reduced rate of increase, followed in the succeeding year by a steeper one, which restores the rate call to its longer term trend". In effect the interpretation of the behaviour of councillors, implicit in the consensus view, is that they are unwarrantedly risk averse to rate increases.

The consensus view is, at present, of considerable practical as well as academic importance in Britain because it lends support to the Conservative Government's current plans to abolish domestic rates and replace them with a poll tax. This connection arises from the Government's argument relating to the fact that a large majority of electors either do not receive rate bills or have their rate bills partially or fully rebated (Bramley, 1987a; Gibson, 1987c; Department of the Environment, 1986a). The Government's assertion from this is that the majority of the electorate are therefore insensitive to rate increases and thus vote in favour of local councillors advocating high spending policies.

The objective of this paper is (1) to present arguments that the academic consensus is based on work which suffers weaknesses in both its theoretical and empirical foundations, and (2) to test whether these arguments are supported by using newly available data on vote shares for some recent local elections. The view taken here is that it is only cross-section analysis of a simultaneous set of local elections which can seriously claim to test for any relationship between rate changes and voter behaviour. However, we argue that the few cross-section studies which do exist suffer from weaknesses either from the use of changes in seats rather than swings in votes as the dependent variable, or from a failure to take into account the independent effect of changes in the levels of services.

It should be made clear that we are not contesting the view that national trends play an important role in local elections. Rather, our 'a priori' view is similar to that of Jones and Stewart (1983) that local factors, such as rate changes, have important additional effects. Indeed, Jones and Stewart pointed out a number of unexplained differences in results between neighbouring authorities in the metropolitan district elections of 1978 and 1982, and Miller (1986, p.157) concluded that "there is a lot of variation round and about the overall national trend which reflects different local influences in different localities".

The next section will give a brief survey of studies of local elections concentrating on the more recent quantitative studies. We will then present our argument for the use of swings in votes as the dependent variable. There then follows our tests of whether rate changes have had an effect in three recent sets of local elections. Then we will present our argument for the inclusion of changes in service levels and test the effects of its inclusion. Finally, we summarise our findings.

A brief survey of empirical studies

Studies of local elections can be categorised into two types. First there are those studies which examine either a single election in one authority or a series of elections in one authority over time. Such studies constitute the majority of published output which has examined the question, amongst other things, of whether rates affect local elections. We agree with Ferry (1979) that the problem with such studies is simply that they do not consider a range of data which might provide evidence that different sizes of rate changes will affect electoral outcomes. Indeed, to this we must add another major problem for such studies. This is that if our later hypothesis is correct that service changes also affect local elections, then given the likelihood that service changes and rate changes are closely related at the individual authority level then it is extremely difficult to disentangle any possible negative electoral effects of a high rate increases. This is because the higher level of service provision associated with the high rate increase will result in offsetting positive electoral effects. Second there are those studies, all undertaken in recent years, (Ferry, 1979; The Economist, 1980; and Bristow, 1982) which examine the relationship between rate increases and local election results for a simultaneous set of elections for a cross-section of authorities.

Ferry's 1979 paper concentrates on presenting the relationship between rate increases and changes in seats in the 1978 elections, and finds an overall correlation coefficient of 0.6, and 0.75 for Labour controlled councils and 0.29 for Conservative controlled councils. However, Ferry actually considered the effect of rate increases on election results in London for four separate elections - 1968, 1971, 1974, 1978. He found that the importance of rates varied from election to election. Thus although he reported that the relationship was clear, but less well marked, in the 1974 elections, he also stated that no significant relationship could be found for the 1968 and 1971 elections. Later citations of Ferry's paper have tended to mention only the positive 1978 results, whereas the weight of negative results in the Ferry studies leaves room for doubt regarding the view that rates are closely related to local elections results. However, Ferry measured rate change for the pre-election year only rather than the total rate change for the four years between elections in the London boroughs. He gave the reasons for this as electors' "so-called 'short memory'", the emphasis given to the most recent events by both the media and politicians, and the fact that over a longer period many electors move residence. However, it seems that this may have reduced the level of explanation achieved by the rates variable. Thus Camden was an obvious outlier in 1978, with the controlling Labour party losing far more seats than predicted from the previous year's rate increase and led Ferry, himself, to comment:

... the bad showing of the Labour council may reflect earlier years of high rate increase rather than the small 1978 increase.

Bristow (1982) also did some cross-section analysis. He followed up a study by *The Economist* (1980) which claimed that for a sample of 41 districts in the 1980 local elections:

> The Conservatives had undoubtedly hoped that some of this year's hefty rate increases would tell against local Labour councils. It is hard to detect much difference between results in those areas run by "high-spending" Labour councils from those in Tory ones; though there does appear to have been a lower swing in some cases of profligacy (e g Newcastle, with the highest rate poundage in the country). And just a hint of a lower swing to Labour in richer (high ratepaying) wards, while the poorer wards voted Labour for public services.

Bristow found that for *The Economist's* sample there was no significant relationship between the size of an authority's rate increase and the swing in votes (r=0.17). This was despite the fact that one authority in the sample - Liverpool - had an extremely high domestic rate poundage increase, 51%, and displayed the only positive swing to the Conservatives against the national trend. Bristow's paper mainly concentrated upon an authority outside *The Economist's* sample - Wolverhampton - where there had been an extremely large rate increase (56%) and included an interesting analysis of the effect of different ward characteristics on vote swing. His analysis showed that within Wolverhampton Labour (the ruling party) increased its support in poorer wards and lost support in more affluent wards. It is notable here that although Labour gained seats there was actually a swing in votes towards the Conservatives (Game, 1981). This provides a suitable point at which to present our argument for the use of vote share data and the results of our empirical tests using such data.

Empirical tests

Although changes in seats are of primary importance in determining the political control of local authorities after elections there may be a major problem in using them as a measure of the changes in voter preferences and behaviour. Bogdanor (1986) has pointed out that there has been distorted relationship between the number of seats and the share of the vote in local elections in a large number of authorities in recent years. He gives a number of examples where the party which has won the largest number of seats has received fewer votes than its' main competitor. This also leads one to expect distortions, or at least major non-linear or unstable effects, in the relationship between swings in the vote and changes in seats.

We are raising the possibility that rate changes are an important determinant of voter behaviour, but that this is inadequately measured by changes in seats. It is notable that in both Liverpool and Wolverhampton in 1980 there was the expected swing away from the party responsible for the high rate increases, but the movement in seats was in the opposite direction. Thus Ferry's negative results prior to 1978 may simply reflect an irregular/distorted relationship between changes in seats and changes in votes. This may be viewed as optimistic, given that the one known cross-section relationship between rate changes and vote swing - that for *The Economist's* sample of 41 towns in 1980 - exhibited a very low correlation coefficient. However,it is probable that the national trend shift between the parties was operating strongly in 1980 and therefore to test for the effect of rates we would need to examine the partial correlation coefficient rather than the simple correlation coefficient given by Bristow. Therefore we should not be too discouraged by the low correlation in *The Economist's* 1980 sample.

We can investigate using vote share data for the first time because Rallings and Thrasher, (1986a), (1986b), have assembled such data for the non-metropolitan counties' elections of 1985 and the metropolitan district elections of 1984 and 1986. In addition to this we can test, using the non-metropolitan counties, whether in authorities subject to four year election cycles, like the London boroughs studied by Ferry, the total rate change is a superior explanatory variable than simply the previous year's rate increase used by Ferry.

The dependent variable we attempt to explain is the swing in the ruling party's share of the Conservative plus Labour vote. This variable is known as the 'Butler swing' as we have measured it in the Conservative controlled authorities, and our measure is the negative of the Butler swing in the Labour controlled authorities. The two party swing was chosen because the percentage share of the vote of each party, taken in isolation, was subject to variable shifts between authorities due to the trend reduction in the share of the vote taken by Independent candidates - with the reduction being particularly large in the case of the non-metropolitan counties with the largest Independent vote in 1981. This dependent variable also appears less prone to the measurement errors, pointed out by Stewart (1987), associated with the way changes in vote shares were recorded, by Rallings and Thrasher, in the large number of seats which were contested for the first time by the Alliance in the counties in 1985. This, unfortunately seems to

Rates and Accountability: Some Evidence from Local Elections 153

render the data unreliable for measuring vote swings between the Alliance and either the Conservatives or Labour. Therefore, no attempt was made to run regressions using a dependent variable involving changes in Alliance share of the vote.

We have excluded the data for the 'balanced' or Liberal controlled authorities. Of the 39 counties 21 could be clearly identified as being under Conservative control and 10 clearly under Labour control prior to the 1985 elections. Of the 36 metropolitan districts, 24 were under Labour control and 8 under Conservative control before the 1984 elections, with 25 under Labour control and 6 under Conservative control before the 1986 elections.

Table 10.1 gives the data on the swings, rate changes and changes in current expenditure per head (which we will discuss later) for the included local authorities for the three sets of elections. It can be seen there was an obvious tendency for the Labour controlled local authorities to choose higher rate-expenditure policies, but with great variation within each group as shown by the size of the standard deviation and the range of rate changes and current expenditure changes.

Table 10.1: Data summary for the three sets of local election results

Authorities: classification by pre-election control	Swing			Rate Increase			Change in current expenditure		
	Mean	Standard Deviation	Range	Mean	Standard Deviation	Range	Mean	Standard Deviation	Range
Counties, 1985									
All[a]	-0.01	2.79	10.90	41.27	18.91	79.22	22.60	4.97	15.21
Conservative	1.03	2.34	8.05	30.99	4.63	15.90	20.99	3.81	12.19
Labour	-2.17	2.23	7.90	62.85	18.43	64.40	26.00	5.15	14.58
Districts, 1984									
All[a]	0.72	2.13	8.74	5.93	4.79	24.41	4.17	2.14	9.17
Conservative	-1.91	0.75	2.32	1.90	3.45	8.04	2.83	1.19	3.26
Labour	1.60	1.66	8.74	7.27	4.40	19.89	4.62	2.19	9.17
Districts, 1986									
All[a]	0.82	2.56	9.15	41.37	15.49	70.02	29.34	7.41	42.24
Conservative	-3.62	0.27	0.85	33.69	7.40	22.13	28.98	2.99	6.45
Labour	1.89	1.50	6.00	43.22	16.26	70.02	29.43	8.09	42.24

[a] Conservative plus Labour controlled authorities prior to the election

Source: Author's computations; CIPFA (annual)

The raw data for swing and rate changes is plotted in Figures 10.1 to 10.3 and appears to indicate both that there is a negative relationship and that the national trend effect was such that the political control of authorities was much more important in the 1984 and 1986 elections than in the 1985 elections. The Figures also appear to indicate that the simple relationship between swing and rate changes was positive for one group of authorities - Conservative controlled districts in 1984. However, we will assess later whether the first order relationship, taking into account changes in services, has the expected positive relationship. [Tables 10A.1 to 10A.3 in the Appendix give the zero order correlation matrices for all the variables included in the regressions which follow and will be referred to at a number of points in the rest of the paper].

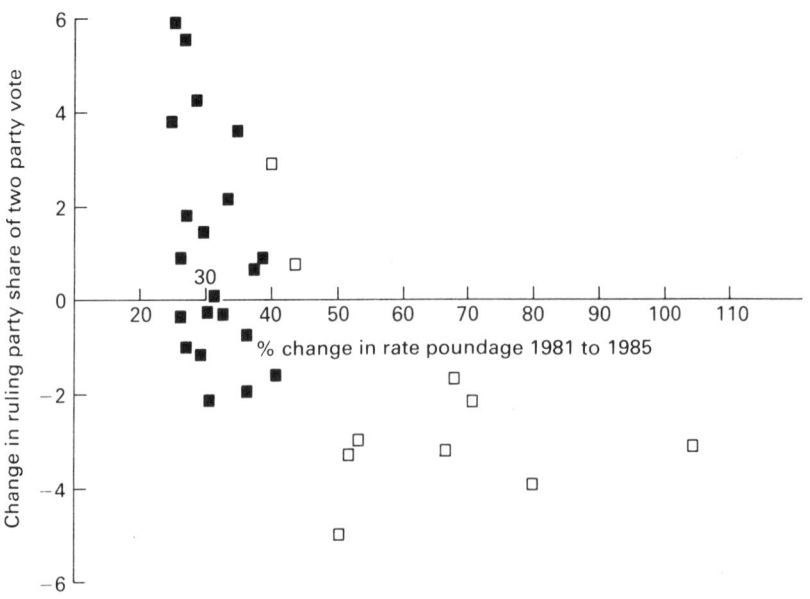

■ Conservative controlled pre-election
☐ Labour controlled pre-election

Figure 10.1: Rate changes and swing – non-metropolitan counties, 1985 elections.

Rates and Accountability: Some Evidence from Local Elections   155

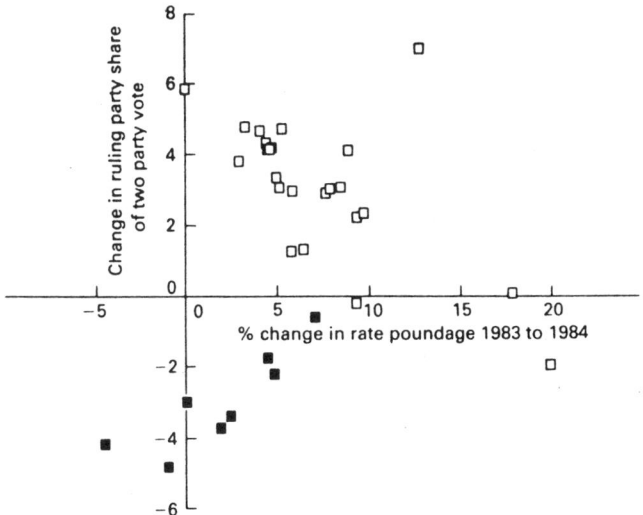

■ Conservative controlled pre-election   □ Labour controlled pre-election

Figure 10.2: Rate changes and swing – metropolitan districts, 1984 elections

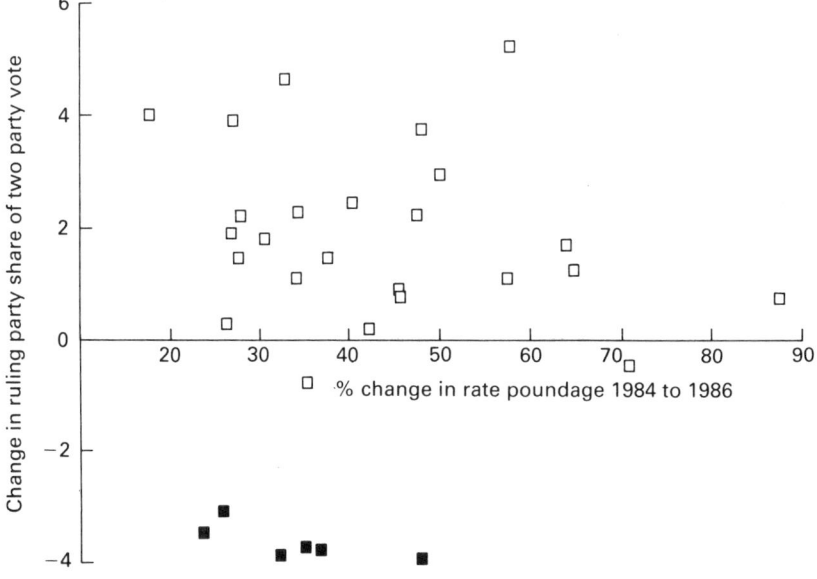

■ Conservative controlled pre-election   □ Labour controlled pre-election

Figure 10.3: Rate changes and swing – metropolitan districts, 1986 elections

The first set of regressions using the total rate change (PCHRATE) between elections are given in Table 10.2. The regressions show that rate increase is a highly statistically significant explanatory variable for all three sets of elections, although in the case of the metropolitan elections the shift variable (CON) reflecting the control of the council is the most important explanatory variable. [CON equals 1 for authorities controlled by the Conservative party prior to the elections, and equals 0 when Labour controlled]. When this is included the rate change variable is significant at the .05 level in two cases and in the .10 level in one case (using a one-tail test). The shift variable is significant at the .01 level in both sets of district elections, but appears to exert little effect in the county elections, which is as we expected after inspection of Figures 10.1 to 10.3.

Table 10.2: Swing equations

Reg. no:	Local elections	Intercept	PCHRATE	CON	R^2
1	Non-metropolitan Counties, 1985	3.739*** (3.817)	-0.091*** (-4.192)		.377
2		2.454 (1.020)	-0.074** (-2.013)	0.852 (0.586)	.385
3	Metropolitan Districts, 1984	0.809 (0.890)	0.133 (1.113)		.040
4		4.397*** (6.903)	-0.176** (-2.410)	-7.031*** (-8.716)	.735
5	Metropolitan Districts, 1986	0.256 (0.190)	0.014 (0.447)		.007
6		2.828*** (3.700)	-0.022* (-1.318)	-5.712*** (-8.835)	.738

Dependent variable = Labour/Conservative 'Butler' swing for controlling party.

t statistics within brackets

*** significant at .01 level (one-tail test)
** significant at .05 level (one-tail test)
* significant at .10 level (one-tail test)

We can now assess whether these significant results are due to the fact that we have been able to use swing data by running regressions with change in seats as the dependent variable. The variable measures the change in the percentage of Conservative plus Labour seats held in the election by the ruling party prior to the election. This variable is slightly different to that used by Ferry which simply measured the percentage change in the ruling party's seats, but gives the seats variable a better chance because it is has a closer relationship to swing. Ferry stated that in the case of the London boroughs there was a fairly close relationship between changes in seats and swing at low levels of swing but he did not give the correlation coefficient. The simple correlation coefficients for the three sets of elections are: 0.598 for the counties, 0.608 for the districts in 1984, and 0.741 for the districts in 1986. Despite these significant positive relationships it can be seen in Table 10.3 that the 'seats' results are much less supportive of the view that rates are a significant determinant of local election results. Only in the case of the counties are rate changes statistically significant; indeed, the sign on the rates variable is 'incorrect' for both sets of district elections. Given our results using swing as the dependent variable, this is surely conclusive proof that using seats as the dependent variable can give rise to underestimates of the importance of rate increases.

Table 10.3: Seats equations

Reg. no:	Local elections	Intercept	PCHRATE	CON	R^2
1	Non-metropolitan Counties, 1985	-3.279 (-0.596)	-0.120* (-1.587)	-1.886 (-0.628)	.115
2	Metropolitan Districts, 1984	4.014 (1.245)	0.036 (0.097)	-13.105*** (-3.210)	.324
3	Metropolitan Districts, 1986	3.994 (1.141)	0.003 (0.036)	-16.732*** (-5.651)	.548

Dependent variable = change in percentage of Labour plus Conservative seats held by ruling party.

*** significant at .01 level (one-tail test)
** significant at .05 level (one-tail test)
* significant at .10 level (one-tail test)

Swing data is not available for a number of London boroughs in the elections Ferry analysed, but there must be a presumption that Ferry's results were similarly affected. Overall the seats equations are much less satisfactory with dramatic falls in the amount of variable in the dependent variable explained by the regressions.

Finally, in Table 10.4 we examine the comparative explanatory power of alternative rate changes variables in elections such as the non-metropolitan counties, which like the London boroughs analysed by Ferry, are held at four year intervals. Equation 1 gives the regression from using, like Ferry, only the previous year's rate change (PCHRATE1) and equation 2 repeats our earlier result using the total rate change over the four years between the non-metropolitan counties elections. The comparative R^2 show that the total rate change has much greater explanatory power than simply relying on the previous year's rate change.

Table 10.4: Swing equations - alternative rate change variables

Reg. no:	Local elections	Intercept	PCHRATE	PCHRATE$_1$	R^2
1	Non-metropolitan Counties, 1985	3.688*** (2.689)		-0.572*** (-2.851)	.219
2		3.739*** (3.817)	-0.091*** (-4.192)		.377

*** significant at .01 level (one-tail test)
** significant at .05 level (one-tail test)
* significant at .10 level (one-tail test)

The role of services: theory and empirical tests

The results given in the previous section demonstrate that rates are a statistically significant determinant of swing in local elections. We will examine shortly the separate issue of whether the size of the rate effect is important. First, however, it is appropriate to tackle what is considered here to be an important shortcoming in the theoretical framework of research on local elections. The weakness is the omission of service levels, or changes in service levels, as an explanatory variable from election studies. It is commonly acknowledged that local authorities make simultaneous tax-expenditure decisions and that although increases in rates are unwelcome to electors, these electors place some positive value on the benefits received from increases in local government services. Thus newspapers have in recent years fairly regularly reported the results of questionnaire studies designed to elicit the preferences of the population for tax cuts versus spending on public services, and there have been a number of recent papers on this issue by social scientists (Hockley and Harbour, 1982, Game, 1984). Also, the well developed literature on expenditure models of local authorities (Foster, Jackman, and Perlman, 1980; Bennett, 1982; Barnett, 1986) is based on the fundamental idea that local politicians, aware of their electorates' preferences, use a decision process involving the "simultaneous weighing or balancing of expenditure and local tax rates" (Ashford, Berne, and Schramm, 1976, p.7). Indeed, the Government's own analysis in the 1986 Green Paper asserts that local electors vote for local politicians who advocate policies of high service provision. The only puzzle is why the effect of positive benefits from public services has uniquely been so underemphasised in studies of British local elections, when for example Bristow himself states the fiscal choice issue clearly in his paper:

... local authorities were thus faced with a clear choice. Either they could reduce their committed and/or planned expenditure on services to keep them within budgetary targets or they must set the rate at a much higher level to underwrite the maintenance of those services at planned levels.

It is, of course, the role of local politicians is to choose the rates-service combinations they wish to deliver given the preferences of the electorate and the budget constraint they face.

The nature of the preferences of the electorate presumably reflect the fact that the ratio of relative marginal benefits derived from local public services decreases relative to the foregone benefits from private consumption, as the supply of local public services is increased. The cost of acquiring these services has, however, been an increasing function of quantity supplied under the block grant system of recent years (Barnett, 1986, and Gibson, Smith, and Watt, 1987). In these years it was composed of linear branches which increased in slope (rate poundage cost) as expenditure increased. However, the description of preferences and the budget constraint is here secondary to our main focus of interest, which is the nature of voter reaction to the budgetary choices actually made. Our argument is merely that there are solid grounds for giving the level of public services an equal claim to rate levels for inclusion as a determinant of voting in local elections. In fact most studies attempt to test for a relationship between changes rather than levels - that is between changes in rates or rate poundages and changes in votes or seats.

Now we should consider what effect the exclusion of changes in services from previous studies will have had. As we stated earlier the effect in individual case studies will probably have been extremely damaging due to the close relationship between changes in rate levels and service levels for the individual authority - making it impossible to disentangle the separate offsetting effects of votes lost through rate increases and votes gained through service increases. In cross-section statistical studies, if changes in the level of public services provided does have a relationship to changes in voting behaviour, then its exclusion from models of voting is an example in regression studies of model specification error (Kmenta, 1971). This type of specification error will lead to biased estimates of the regression coefficient of the included variable (changes in rate poundage) if there is an intercorrelation with the excluded variable (changes in service level). The direction and extent of the bias depends on direction and strength of the relationship between the variables – a positive relationship leads to an underestimate of the size of the effect (positive or negative) of the included variable, and a negative relationship to an overestimate.

In a cross-section study of local authorities our 'a priori' expectation is that there will be a positive relationship between rate changes and changes in service levels. However, unlike the case of the individual authority, a study of a cross-section of authorities should give rise to sufficient independent variation between the variables to allow estimates of the independent (positive) effect of increases in services and the (negative) effect of rate increases. Thus, we would expect that the inclusion of service changes in a cross-section regression analysis would lead to an increase in the estimated sensitivity of voting to rate changes.

Service levels have been measured in terms of current expenditure per head of population over the total period between elections (PCHSERV). This is a better measure of services delivered to the population than total expenditure per head (which is more closely linked to rate poundages) because it excludes items not directly related to services delivered such as debt charges and revenue contributions to capital spending and special funds.[The correlation matrices (Tables 10A.1 to 10A.3 pp. 164-5) show that the relationship between rate changes and service changes is positive as expected for all three sets of data, but not large enough to cause serious collinearity].

Table 10.5: Swing equations - rate changes and service changes

Reg. no:	Local elections	Intercept	PCHRATE	PCHSERV	CON	R^2
1	Non-metropolitan Counties, 1985	-1.780 (-0.676)	-0.114*** (-3.184)	0.260*** (2.805)	0.872 (0.669)	.524
2	Metropolitan Districts, 1984	5.055*** (6.276)	-0.120* (-1.427)	-0.231 (-1.308)	-7.143*** (-8.912)	.750
3	Metropolitan Districts, 1986	1.606* (1.414)	-0.026* (-1.583)	0.048* (1.433)	-5.732*** (-9.029)	.756

*** significant at .01 level (one-tail test)
** significant at .05 level (one-tail test)
* significant at .10 level (one-tail test)

The regression results arising from the inclusion of service changes are given in Table 10.5 and show that services are significant for the county elections and the district elections of 1986 but have the 'wrong' sign for the 1984 elections. This explains why the estimated sensitivity to rate changes is increased in the 1985 and 1986 elections by the inclusion of services but reduced in the case of the 1984 elections. The increase in R^2 is only substantial in the counties' elections but overall the results indicate that it is worthwhile to take into account the effect of service changes.[1]

It is obvious that national trend factors had an important influence on the district elections but we will now move on to examine an issue raised by visual examination of the data, that is whether voter reactions to rate changes and service changes was different between Conservative and Labour counties. A test for the differences between two groups can be performed by running a regression with additional variables measured by the application of zero-one dummies to the observations, to enable separate estimates to made of the effect of the explanatory variables for the two groups. We call this model a "full model" because it allows for differences in the response between the two groups, in contrast to the previous restricted or "pooled model" where after taking into account a trend variable (CON) the response was specified as identical. The null hypothesis is that there is no difference between the regression coefficients for the two groups of counties, and the alternative is that there is a substantial difference. The

162   *The Politics and Economics of the Poll Tax*

hypothesis is tested by constructing an F statistic for the comparison of the goodness of fit from each model. Basically the null hypothesis will not be rejected if the full model fails to give a sufficiently better fit given the increases in the number of explanatory variables in the full model (Chatterjee and Price, 1977).

Thus in this case differences in voter reaction to rate changes and service changes was tested by running a regression with the additional variables CON*PCHRATE and CON*PCHSERV (where CON equals unity for Conservative counties and zero for Labour counties) added to the regressions. The results are reported in Table 10.6. Here, the CON*PCHRATE and CON*PCHSERV coefficients are the estimates of the difference between the effect of rate changes and service changes in Conservative authorities and that in Labour authorities which is measured by the coefficients on PCHRATE and PCHSERV respectively. The F statistic is significant at the .01 level in the case of the district elections of 1984 (F=5.790) and this reflects the differential in response to rate changes. For the other two elections the F statistic is not significant, although the data for 1985 seems to indicate that electors in Conservative controlled authorities rewarded service increases more than in Labour controlled counties. It should be pointed out that there is severe collinearity between the CON and CON*PCHRATE, CON*PCHSERV variables in the 1985 and 1986 sets of elections which renders the estimated regression coefficients unreliable.

Table 10.6: Regression results - testing for difference in voter reactions in Conservative and Labour controlled authorities

Reg. no:	Local elections	Intercept	PCHRATE	PCHSERV	CON* PCHRATE	CON* PCHSERV	CON	R^2
1	Non-metropolitan Counties, 1985	0.257 (0.078)	-0.069* (-1.427)	0.073 (0.425)	-0.103 (-0.952)	0.241 (1.151)	-0.491 (-0.092)	0.558
2	Metropolitan Districts, 1984	5.374*** (7.528)	-0.248*** (-2.864)	-0.098 (-0.562)	0.590*** (3.342)	0.380 (0.794)	-9.793*** (-6.075)	0.827
3	Metropolitan Districts, 1986	1.579* (1.324)	-0.027* (-1.503)	0.050* (1.395)	0.001 (0.012)	-0.040 (-0.206)	-4.619 (-0.665)	0.757

*** significant at .01 level (one-tail test)
**   significant at .05 level (one-tail test)
*   significant at .10 level (one-tail test)

Size and importance of the rates effect

We have shown that rate changes are a statistically significant determinant of local election results. This does not, however, guarantee the quantitative importance of any relationship. The size of the regression coefficients cannot be readily compared because they apply to different periods. However, using the results for the counties from Table 10.5 we can see in the case of the counties that each one per cent rate increase is estimated to lead to a swing against the ruling party of 0.11%. Given an average rate change of just over 40%, a relatively small deviation from the average performance could result in substantial electoral damage. It may appear from Table 10.5 that the size of the swing effect per one per cent rate increase is relatively small in the metropolitan elections compared to the national shift effect - .026 compared to 5.73 in the 1986 elections. This is true, but the range on rate changes was over 70% in these elections (from a low of 17.5% up to 70.6%) and this is sufficient in its own right to cause substantial variation in the swing between authorities.

Summary and conclusions

This paper was written with a strong underlying view that rate increases do have an effect on local election results, and that previous studies had probably underestimated this effect due to a number of weaknesses in their empirical tests and theoretical framework. Apart from the problem that the consensus view was based on case studies of individual authorities with their inherent inability to discover general relationships it was suggested that there were weaknesses in the few cross-section studies on the subject. The weaknesses suggested were the use of seat changes as the dependent variable and the exclusion of consideration of changes in service levels from cross section studies. We have found that rate changes have an important role in local elections when their effect on swing in votes is estimated. Changes in service levels were also significant in two of the three sets of elections studied. The effect of rate changes appeared to be large enough to explain why local councillors anticipate detrimental electoral effects from rate increases. A major by-product of the argument presented is to show that the present Government's interpretation of the driving force behind the voting process is biassed and incorrect. Although our results show that voters do, as the Government has asserted, respond positively to increases in services provided by local authorities, they do not support the Government's other assertion in the 1986 Green Paper that voters do not penalise local politicians for rate increases.

164 The Politics and Economics of the Poll Tax

APPENDIX 10A:

Table 10A.1: Zero order correlation matrix - non-metropolitan counties elections 1985

	SWING	SEATS	PCHRATE	PCHSERV	CON	CON* PCHRATE	CON* PCHSERV	PCHRATE
SWING	\							
SEATS	.598	\						
PCHRATE	-.614	-.322	\					
PCHSERV	-.066	.153	.595	\				
CON	.544	.191	-.801	-.480	\			
CON* PCHRATE	-.663	.128	-.722	-.490	.967	\		
CON* PCHSERV	-.035	.342	-.773	-.261	.952	.908	\	
PCHRATE	-.468	-.104	.340	-.116	-.491	-.428	-.558	\

Table 10A.2: Zero order correlation matrix - metropolitan districts elections 1984

	SWING	SEATS	PCHRATE	PCHSERV	CON	CON* PCHRATE	CON* PCHSERV
SWING	\						
SEATS	.608	\					
PCHRATE	.199	.289	\				
PCHSERV	.091	.129	.593	\			
CON	-.826	-.569	-.485	-.363	\		
CON* PCHRATE	-.199	-.046	.115	-.204	.432	\	
CON* PCHSERV	-.735	-.427	-.466	-.205	.900	.314	\

Table 10A.3: Zero order correlation matrix - metropolitan district elections 1986

	SWING	SEATS	PCHRATE	PCHSERV	CON	CON* PCHRATE	CON* PCHSERV
SWING	\						
SEATS	.741	\					
PCHRATE	.083	.184	\				
PCHSERV	.130	-.191	.184	\			
CON	-.849	-.741	-.243	-.024	\		
CON* PCHRATE	-.831	-.667	-.177	-.040	.967	\	
CON* PCHSERV	-.841	-.747	-.251	-.000	.992	.949	\

Notes

1. Unreported regressions using a lagged version of changes in service levels were run but did not improve the reported results.

11.
POLL TAX VERSUS PRIVATISATION: COMPARING TWO THATCHER "FLAGSHIPS"

[This paper, published in *Government and Policy* in August 1989, was originally conceived in late 1986, but in a very different form. The original theme was that no Government attempting to secure electoral popularity would introduce a poll tax, because it had major deficiencies which the new rent seeking approach to analysing public policies could highlight. In contrast, using this approach, the large scale privatisations were a very effective policy. This would explain with hindsight why the poll tax proposals had been withdrawn. By late 1987, it became obvious that the thrust of the paper needed to be changed. It was necessary to take on board the idea that Governments sometimes make big mistakes - and use the theory to examine the reasons why introducing poll tax would be a big mistake.]

Introduction

This paper uses a public choice framework to compare the relative electoral popularity of two important policy innovations of the Thatcher governments: privatisation and poll tax. These two policies are of major importance to the Government, and are symbolic of the substantial shift from the approach of previous British governments expressed by the term "Thatcher Revolution".

The importance of the poll tax (to be introduced in Scotland in 1989 and in England and Wales in 1990) and the associated reform of local government finance is evident from Mrs Thatcher's declaration, shortly after winning a third consecutive general election in June 1987, that poll tax was to be the flagship policy of her third term of office.

The importance of privatisation is well expressed in the following quotation (Davis, 1986):

> The success of the mass-marketed share sales such as Telecom and Gas has been the catalyst which has thrust privatisation from its former role as a minor adjunct of economic policy to its present position as, arguably, the single most potent political innovation of Mrs Thatcher's Government.

Privatisation and poll tax can therefore be seen as the flagship policies of the second and third Thatcher terms respectively.

Both policies involve widespread redistributions of wealth between gainers and losers. We use a public choice approach to examine the implications for electoral popularity of these redistributions.

A zero-sum redistribution, where total gains equal total losses does not generally have a zero effect on electoral popularity, but depends upon the characteristics of gainers and losers. An examination of the characteristics of the gainers and losers under poll tax and privatisation leads to the prediction that poll tax is likely to be a far less popular policy than privatisation.

This prediction, in itself, may not seem to be startling, as most British political commentators have already suggested that the poll tax will be unpopular and impose political costs upon the Conservative party, and indeed this unpopularity is already being registered by opinion polls. As yet no analysis of why there is a differential net political reaction from the gainers and losers from poll tax compared to the gainers and losers from privatisation has been presented by commentators. An alternative view predicts that any political unpopularity arising from the poll tax will be a "nine day wonder". Again, the minority who hold this view, tend to maintain it only on the rather unsatisfactory grounds that previous predictions of electoral costs from other controversial changes introduced by the Thatcher governments have never materialised.

The purpose of this paper is to show why, using a public choice analysis, these two policies, both involving large scale redistributions, will differ greatly in their popularity with the electorate.

The popularity of its policies with the electorate is naturally of great interest to the government, although members of governments and governing parties may have other objectives than simply being re-elected such as personal pecuniary gains, personal power, image in history, lofty personal ideals etc. (Breton, 1974; Mclean, 1982). Despite the interest of politicians in electoral popularity, the large academic literatures already generated by both privatisation (Heald 1984; Kay and Thompson, 1986; Brittan, 1983, 1984; Veljanovski, 1987) and poll tax (Foster, 1986; Jackman, 1986; Jones, Stewart, and Travers, 1986; Bramley, 1987a; Gibson, 1987c) has paid only scant attention to the voter-calculus aspects of these policy innovations.

One reason for this is that the policies of privatisation and poll tax might be expected to have major efficiency implications, and exploration of this theme has preoccupied policy-analysts. Although some papers have placed emphasis on the important redistributive effects of poll tax (Bramley, 1987a; Barrow, 1986) they have not gone on to make explicit predictions of the associated electoral effects. Brittan, 1986, expressed dissatisfaction about the incompleteness of analyses which exclude electoral considerations when he commented on the exclusive focus on efficiency aspects of privatisation by Kay and Thompson (1986), arguing that the authors:

... have given the Government a low grade, but in an examination which the Government is not actually taking.

Some perceptive observations on the question of electoral popularity of privatisation have been made by Vickers and Yarrow (1988). However, direct explicit discussion of the topic was limited to two pages in a text of over four-hundred pages. In addition, some interest in the electoral popularity of poll tax did occur early in the policy cycle with an analysis published shortly before the general election in the local government press (Gibson, 1987b), stimulating some interest in the national press and parliament (House of Commons, 1987a).

The next section of the paper suggests that the importance of redistributive implications of privatisation and poll tax is high in comparison to their likely efficiency effects. This is then followed by a brief survey of previous contributions on the electoral effects of redistributions. A general theory of the popularity of redistributive changes is then outlined using a rent-seeking approach, and this is followed by an application of this approach to the poll tax and privatisation flagships. Finally, some implications for future developments in the two policies are given.

Redistributional and efficiency aspects of the flagships

Public policies often involve large redistributions of income or welfare between different groups. Such groups can be categorised in a variety of ways, whether as producers versus consumers, or by different income levels, or as different groups of taxpayers. The redistributive effects of public policies are of vital importance to their success or failure in the political market-place. Gains in efficiency are seldom straightforward Pareto-improvements where some groups gain while there are no losers.

Recognition that nearly all public policies or projects created both gainers and losers and that the strict Pareto criterion was, in such cases, unable to approve any change from the status quo stimulated a development of the "new welfare economics". This was an attempt to devise cost-benefit criteria, based on whether hypothetical compensation of losers by gainers would generate positive potential Pareto- improvements (Hicks, 1939; Kaldor, 1939; Scitovsky, 1941). However, as Baumol (1967) pointed out, policies could not be known to result in Pareto improvements even when approved under such compensation criteria unless compensation was actually paid.

Such direct compensation payments between gainers and losers are rare in the real world. In addition, the scale of both benefits and costs may, of course, be difficult or impossible to measure with any precision.

Nevertheless, to return to our main theme regarding the relative sizes of efficiency and redistributional changes, we can in principle measure the difference between benefits and costs and the size of this net difference compared to the gross sum of gains (to gainers) and losses (to losers). This provides a measure of the relative importance of redistributional and efficiency changes. A common baseline for policies is "zero-sum" where net efficiency changes are zero.

We argue here that the redistributional aspects of both flagships appear to be large compared to their likely efficiency benefits. The largest privatisations, British Gas and British Telecom, have brought little movement towards increased competition (Kay and Thompson, 1986) and on this basis have failed to generate the efficiency gains postulated for these industries under competition (Beesley and Littlechild, 1983). There is also a significant offset to any efficiency gains from privatisation owing to the resources used in marketing the privatisation issues (Vickers and Yarrow, 1988).

The introduction of poll tax will secure efficiency gains if it brings the tax prices facing households closer into line with benefits received and also may reduce X-inefficiency if it increases the fiscal pressure bearing on local authorities (Foster, Jackman, and Perlman, 1980; Foster, 1986). However, recent empirical studies of present consumption patterns for local government services seem to indicate that the poll tax will bring no significant movement towards benefit taxation (Bramley, Le Grand, and Low, 1989). Furthermore, two costs offset any potential efficiency gains from the introduction of poll tax. First, is the extra collection and administration costs when compared to domestic rates. Even according to the Government's own estimates, administration and collection costs will be double those for the abolished domestic rates. Second, there are the resources used in any migration (King, 1984) induced by the new tax.

The above reasoning suggests that efficiency gains from privatisation and poll tax may be low. We now turn to the distributional effects.

Redistribution and privatisation

Mayer and Meadowcroft (1985) have provided a clear method for approaching the question of the amount of redistribution involved in privatisations. They regard the assets sold as part of the public sector balance sheet, the value of which is given or revealed by the value placed on the equity in the stock market. Given the offer price and the money received by the public sector from the sale after subtracting the issuing costs, the change in the net worth of the public sector can be calculated. In the case of British Telecom 3.012 billion shares were valued at 93p on the first day of trading and had been offered at 50p. Issuing costs were £263 million. Thus using Mayer and Meadowcroft's approach, the value of the assets sold was £2.80 billion, but the public sector only received £1.24 billion and the net worth of the public sector was therefore reduced by £1.56 billion.

Who owns the public sector? Mayer and Meadowcroft assume implicitly that ownership is divided equally between all British citizens. Although this may be an oversimplification, it allows a clear view of how the net loss is borne, which is therefore, as pointed out by Mayer and Meadowcroft, largely a redistribution between citizens. (They abstract from the complication that 13.7% of British Telecom shares were issued to overseas customers.) Who gains and who loses in such a redistribution depends upon the pattern of purchasing. Supposing, for example, that all the shares had been sold to one individual, this person would gain £1.56 billion, and the rest of the population might be considered to share this loss, amounting to approximately £30 per British citizen.

However, an individual could re-coup this loss by purchasing 30/0.43 = 70 shares. Anyone purchasing more than 70 shares would become a gainer. Clearly therefore, there is a large possible variation

172   The Politics and Economics of the Poll Tax

in the actual redistribution depending upon the proportion of British households that participated in the purchase the equity. As Mayer and Meadowcroft show, there were only 2.3 million shareholders in British Telecom immediately following privatisation, including institutions and overseas investors. Mayer and Meadowcroft write:

> At most then approximately 4% of the population directly shared in the windfall gain of the under-pricing, though many more clearly indirectly benefited through their investments in financial institutions. Furthermore, within the 4% there were variations in shareholdings thereby creating inequalities within this group as well as between those who did and did not participate. One would be hard pushed therefore to defend the assertion that the redistribution associated with the BT issue was comparatively insignificant.

In addition, it seems reasonable to surmise that the redistribution has been regressive.

Redistribution and poll tax

Turning to the introduction of the poll tax, it is clear that this policy will be highly redistributive, involving a large scale change in the local

Table 11.1. Households gaining and losing with full replacement of domestic rates by poll tax (Great Britain, thousand households)

	Pounds per week	Thousand households
Losers		
	10 +	50
	5 - 10	500
	2 - 5	2,525
	1 - 2	2,175
	0 - 1	4,725
	Total Losers	10,000
Gainers		
	0 - 1	5,475
	1 - 2	1,975
	2 - 5	2,450
	5 - 10	575
	10 +	100
	Total Gainers	10,575

(Numbers may not add owing to rounding)

Source: Department of the Environment, 1986a, Figure J7

tax bills of households. This contrasts with the debatable level of efficiency gains associated with its introduction. We can assess the amount of redistribution between households by comparing the weekly tax bill per household under the rates system with the tax bill per household under poll tax. The Green Paper "Paying for Local Government" (Department of the Environment, 1986a,) gives the average net local domestic rate bill (i.e. after receipt of rebate) per household in 1984/85 as £4.81 per week, and estimates the hypothetical changes in local tax if the poll tax had fully replaced domestic rates in that year. These changes are reproduced in Table 11.1 and show that nearly 10.4 million households will experience a change in local tax of over £1 per week - which amounts to over 20% of the average local tax bill.

Further data has been provided in a Parliamentary written answer (House of Commons, 1987b) which estimates the sum of the absolute amount of losses of losing households and the amount of gains of gaining households, were the poll tax to have been introduced in England in 1986/87. This aggregate change in household net local tax bills was £1,040 million, and can be compared with an aggregate net local tax bill for English households in the region of £5,000 million in that year, showing that the disturbance to bills caused by the introduction of the poll tax is very large.

Examination of the data in Table 11.2 and Table 11.3 (p.174) shows the poll tax to have regressive effects.

Table 11.2 Relationship of rates and poll tax to net household income (England 1986/87 prices)

Ranges of equivalent net household income (£ per week)

	Under 50	50-75	75-100	100-150	150-200	200-250	250-300	300-350	350-400	400-500	500+	All
Gross:												
Rates	6.07	6.17	6.72	7.32	7.95	8.31	8.72	9.27	9.95	10.54	13.64	7.40
Poll tax	6.00	6.36	7.27	8.03	8.12	8.01	7.59	7.36	7.09	7.42	7.00	7.41
Tax Ch*	-0.07	0.19	0.55	0.71	0.17	-0.30	-1.13	-1.91	-2.86	-3.12	-6.64	0.01
Net:												
Rates	1.64	3.04	5.94	7.18	7.90	8.29	8.71	9.27	9.95	10.50	13.62	6.37
Poll tax	1.63	3.13	6.31	7.64	7.91	7.89	7.52	7.31	7.03	7.34	6.89	6.25
Tax Ch*	-0.01	0.09	0.37	0.46	0.01	-0.40	-1.19	-1.96	-2.92	-3.16	-6.73	-0.12

* Tax Ch. shows change in local tax on moving from rates to poll tax.

Source: Parliamentary Written Answer, 25 January 1988

Thus in Table 11.2 the change to poll tax is seen to cause a decrease in net household income in the range £50-£200 per week, and an increase in household income in the range above £200 per week, as shown by row three in the lower half of Table 11.2.

We conclude from this discussion that the two flagship policies involve large-scale redistributions but that the patterns of redistributive effects differ. Let us now consider previous writing on the popularity of such redistributive changes, which, given the importance of the issue to governments, has been scarce from either political scientists or economists until the recent upsurge in the analysis of "rent seeking".

Table 11.3: Two adult households gaining and losing with full replacement of domestic rates by the poll tax (England 1984/85 £ per week)

	All Incomes	Incomes below £200 per week	Incomes £200 and over per week
Losers			
10+	2	1	1
5-10	86	52	34
2-5	1215	853	320
1-2	1341	1006	335
0-1	3104	2625	479
Total losers	5745	4577	1169
Gainers			
0-1	2440	1857	583
1-2	1111	649	462
2-5	1216	491	725
5-10	310	55	255
10+	52	3	49
Total gainers	5130	3054	2086

Source: unpublished 1986 Grants Working Group paper

Previous contributions on the electoral effects of redistributions

Buchanan (1967) addresses the issue of the substitution of a new tax for an old tax and the change in fiscal burdens which result and considers the adage "an old tax is a good tax" to be a good rule-of-thumb. He states that "the old tax generates less reaction than the new tax" and that higher levels of expenditure can be supported, ceteris paribus, with a continuation of existing tax structures. However, Buchanan was interested in the effects on an incumbent government rather than any resulting electoral effects.

Very similar reasoning to Buchanan's was applied by Mitchell and Mitchell (1969) to arrive at their assessment that democratic governments, when faced with the problem of securing an increase in tax revenue, would prefer to increase the rates of established taxes rather than introduce new taxes, because the latter involves larger political costs:

> [Governments] learn that active citizens prefer known to unknown costs and that, in general, change is regarded with hesitancy. Politicians, given their dependence on voters, may be inclined to overestimate resistance, if anything, so that they will be more cautious about imposing new burdens, particularly if they are major ones.

Prest (1982b), in the context of the issue of local authorities' limited reliance on user charges, also raises the phenomenon of "gainers and losers". He states that local politicians are averse to increasing charges because of the:

> electoral consequences for themselves in terms of the familiar pattern of the squawks of the losers from the new charging arrangements drowning the purrs of the gainers.

However the most fruitful source from which to develop a general theory of gainers and losers arises from the recent work by public choice theorists on rent seeking (Buchanan, Tollison, and Tullock, 1980).

The rent seeking approach

Rent seeking is the widely observed phenomenon of interest groups attempting to secure transfers or other privileges from governments. Given that such transfers do not increase the productive capacity of the economy we are at best analysing zero-sum situations. However, when account is taken of the resources devoted to lobbying and the fact that some privileges secured may reduce choice and free competition, the net result of rent seeking activities is negative sum.

A particularly useful approach is provided by Tollison (1982). He considers the question of which type of transfers and redistributions are most likely to be adopted by vote-seeking politicians and supplies an answer in terms of information cost. Tollison considers the importance of two types of information costs. First, there are the costs to individuals of finding out on how a policy will affect them. Second, there are the costs of identifying other individuals similarly affected and the costs and benefits of the formation of interest groups. Tollison's analysis concluded that policies are more likely to be adopted where gainers are more easily identified than losers. Such policies are more likely to have well organised pressure groups formed to advocate them and:

> politicians will have incentives to search for issues on which such groups gain transfers at the expense of the diffuse general polity.

Whilst based on the same methodology, the objective of our analysis is different from Tollison's. The concern is not to predict which policies will be taken up by pressure groups and which will be successful in being adopted by politicians. Instead we are analysing policies that have actually been adopted by the Thatcher governments. Also we are not directly concerned with the reactions of pressure groups but rather the effect on individual electors' voting behaviour. We are therefore only concerned with the activities of pressure groups in so far as their activities influence voters.

Thus to address our concern we must examine the characteristics that could be expected to affect the electoral popularity of public policies. We suggest the following characteristics are important: concentration; size; visibility; envy and morality; and voluntarism. We will now briefly describe what we mean by these terms and how the nature and pattern of gains and losses from a redistribution can effect voters. Then in the next section we will apply the implications to the two flagships.

The extent of concentration of gains and diffusion of losses in a redistribution can clearly vary widely. Tollison predicted that policies are more likely to be adopted where the gains are concentrated and the losses are diffuse. In this analysis we suggest, similarly, that concentrated gains and diffuse losses generate electoral popularity. A corollary of concentration of gains and diffusion of losses is that, in a zero-sum redistribution, the size of gains will be large relative to the size of losses. The smaller number of gainers are more likely to notice their relatively large gains, than the losers are to notice their relatively small losses.

Electoral popularity stems from a combination of a small number of noticed gains and a larger number of unnoticed losses. Beyond a certain point, however, size of gains may become a disadvantage as they become apparent not only to the gainers, but also to the losers.

A second relevant factor is the extent to which gains and losses are visible and perceived by individuals. There can be large differences between perceived losses and true losses. The reason for the discrepancy is that some gains and losses are complex to measure. Gains and losses may often only be measurable through the erection of a sophisticated economic theory and the use of advanced statistical tools. Examples of this sort abound in tax incidence literature, where the presence of tax shifting and capitalization leads to complexity often sufficient to lead to disputes between economists and unsettled questions. Shifting and capitalization cause particularly acute problems in the case of local taxes such as the property tax (rates) (Mieskowski, 1972; Bennett, 1986). Certainly there will often be large differences between those who are physically paying tax bills and the actual burden of the tax, and this applies strongly to both poll tax and privatisation. Somewhat in the spirit of Stigler's (1966, p.104) remark that "Historical costs have powerful sway over untutored minds" we suggest that the visible changes will tend to dominate most households' calculations of their gains and losses.

Tollison emphasises questions of identification in his discussion of pressure groups. Transfer-seekers need to have identified themselves as potential gainers under the policy their pressure group is promoting, and also need to have identified other potential gainers in order to team up with them. Identification is related to, but distinct from, the visibility characteristic because it refers to the ease with which outsiders can identify the groups or individuals which have experienced gains and losses. Identification is clearly relevant, as Tollison showed, to the formation of pressure groups. However, identification of gainers can reduce a governments popularity if the easy identification of gainers, and losers, leads to unpopularity for reasons of morality and envy.

Gains for certain groups are more likely to lead to positive voter reaction if they are felt to be deserved in some way, either as a reward for some work, or bearing of risk or to correct a previous injustice or unfairness, but they are likely to lead to a negative reaction if none of these factors are present. Whether or not gains are in some sense truly deserved is less important than whether some, at least superficially, convincing justification can be advanced for them. Tullock labels such a justification a cover story (Tullock, 1983, p. 11). A good cover story can considerably enhance the electoral popularity of a large redistribution. Tullock (1984, p. 238) asks:

> Why do pressure groups not simply aim at a low tax on the entire population that is used to pay a direct sum of money to them? ... I think the only available explanation for this is that they know that a certain amount of confusion and misdirection is necessary. ... A direct cash transfer ... would never go through because it is to blatant and obvious. It is necessary that these things be covered by some kind of deception.

Large concentrated gains that lack a good cover story and are felt to be wholly undeserved are more likely to lead to envy effects, especially where the factors of work-effort and risk bearing are absent. Identification, and visibility and simplicity are also important because they enable hostile politicians and the media to exploit morality and envy feelings amongst losers and any gainers with an uneasy conscience.

Finally, redistributions are expected to be more popular if there is an element of voluntarism in a policy. In such cases there is an opportunity for losers to escape from losses if they become aware of them. Thus losses can be concentrated on those that are unaware or at least not upset by them.

Evaluation of the two flagships

We suggest that privatisation has a number of advantages over poll tax in terms of popularity with the electorate when seen in the context of the above discussion.

Firstly, gains under privatisation are more concentrated than under poll tax. However, the losses under poll tax are more concentrated than the losses under privatisation. A large number of losers under privatisation are unlikely to be aware of their loss. They may have reacted with some unease to remarks heard about selling off the family silver, but unless they have read Mayer and Meadowcroft (1985) and understood their public sector balance sheet methodology, their perception of loss is likely to be extremely limited.

Secondly, although it is true that both policies redistribute wealth to the more well-to-do, privatisation has the important advantage of voluntarism in that the gains and losses are less predetermined than under poll tax. Thus whereas gainers under poll tax are largely determined by household size and the pre-existing rateable value of property occupied, the option of joining the gainers under privatisation involves simple voluntary action. Thus those who become aware of their potential losses under a forthcoming privatisation have the option of joining the gainers by buying shares. No such simple mechanism for avoiding losses exists for losers under poll tax. The determinate nature of poll tax gains and losses also extends throughout the range of incomes with the largest average gains accruing to those with the largest average incomes.

Thirdly, cover stories to justify the gains from privatisation are fairly easily constructed. Gainers under privatisation are seen to have undertaken the effort involved in submitting application forms on time, accompanied by payment and to have borne a risk loss on the equities purchased. The cover story combines with a grain of truth in the risk-bearing argument. Poll tax gainers, on the other hand, are not required to take any greater risk or make any additional effort compared to losers. It is at least a possible line of argument that the size of the gains from privatisation sales varies positively with effort and risk. In contrast there can be no such argument about poll tax gains and losses - most citizens will experience gains and losses which they will interpret as largely pre-determined.

A further rationalisation of privatisation that may have elements of a cover story is the benefit of widening share ownership. The rationalisation for poll tax is to spread the cost of local services more fully amongst those entitled to vote in local elections and receiving benefits from services (the latter is a cover story if the real reason for introducing poll tax is the political problem arising from the Scottish rating revaluation of 1985). Both rationalisations are fairly adequate but the privatisation rationalisation is politically superior because it concentrates public attention on gainers, whereas every time the "disciplinary" properties of the poll tax are expounded by Ministers they concentrate attention on losers.

Fourthly, although it is true that the largest gains from poll tax accrue to those with the largest incomes, in the later mass-marketed privatisations the rationing of the under-priced equity was geared in favour of smaller subscribers. No such modification of the poll tax to reduce the large gains of the wealthiest is possible without completely destroying the flat-rate principle of the poll tax.

Fifthly, a point specifically related to the electoral calculus is that the poll tax tends to impose losses on those households with more electors. Thus whereas the 1986 Green Paper showed that 82.9% of single adult households are expected to have local tax reductions under poll tax, 84.7% of households with three or more adults are expected to have tax increases. (Although these increases are borne by more adults). An estimate has been made (Gibson, 1987b) that nearly 58% of adults live in households which will lose from the poll tax, and the visibility of the tax change will enable losers to see clearly that they have lost. There is no obvious similar structural factor present with privatisation - indeed households with larger numbers have had more chances of large gains in the rationing systems used on the heavily over-subscribed pre-crash privatisation issues.

This leads to the final, and perhaps the important, difference between the policies which is the visibility and simplicity of gains and losses. Those who lose from poll tax are sent an annual bill to remind them that they are losers, those who lose from privatisation are not sent a bill which outlines or explains their losses. Vickers and Yarrow (1988) point out that J. K. Galbraith had a phrase which neatly summarises the redistribution under privatisation "few things enhance the overall feeling of wealth better than undiscovered theft".

A number of these differences between the flagships have already become evident. There have been a much larger number of newspaper stories about individuals' large gains from the poll tax compared to individuals' gains from privatisation, with the most notable stories covering members of the Cabinet, especially Mrs Thatcher, and most recently the gains of some hereditary peers who made a most unusual effort to attend the House of Lords and vote in support of the poll tax legislation. One Conservative MP (House of Commons, 1987c) has stated that he has received "hundreds of letters" from constituents who are large potential gainers from poll tax many of which object strongly to the policy as unfair.

Implications

We believe we have explained why the redistributions arising from privatisations are likely to have more positive electoral effects than the redistribution from the introduction of poll tax. Two implications of the analysis follow.

A number of analysts of privatisation (Vickers and Yarrow, 1988; Mayer and Meadowcroft, 1985) have criticised the system of asset sales, particularly the under-pricing of equities and their sale in all or one packages at a common price and have suggested partial sales by tender to maximise sales proceeds. Sales by tender, if successful would eliminate most of the redistribution by greatly reducing the possibility of receiving windfall gains from the equity. However, our analysis suggests that creating gainers is an instrument in generating electoral popularity and sales by tender would not therefore appeal to politicians interested in reaping political benefits from under-priced sales.

However, if it is true that governments use policies to generate popularity and try to avoid policies that risk imposing electoral damage then we may ask, given our analysis, why is the poll tax being introduced? It is possible to argue that a large proportion of the gainers from poll tax are likely to be Conservative voters, and that these gainers are in socio-economic groups with above average voting propensities. Given the large Conservative majority the poll tax could be seen as a device to solidify the Conservative vote in Conservative held seats at the cost of reducing the chances of gaining any further marginal seats.

However, according to the median voter theorem, it is more important to pursue the floating voter than to solidify existing support. Could the government, in this case, have simply made a mistake? If so, the analysis in this paper suggests that it can reduce the unpopularity of poll tax by increasing central grants and reducing the average level of poll tax. This will reduce the size of visible losses at the expense of less visible foregone reductions in central taxation or alterations in the size of the public sector borrowing requirement or public sector surplus.

12.
THE PRESENTATION OF THE POLL TAX

[This article was written in the autumn and early winter of 1988 and published in *Political Quarterly* in July 1989. I felt that there had been some serious shortcomings in the Government's presentation of the poll tax both to Parliament and the country, and that it would be worthwhile to try and gather them together in one article. The article turned out to be longer than I had originally expected. It could have been much longer, and if rewritten today there would be a number of substantial additions, including the Prime Minister's recent statement that domestic rate increases this year (1990/91) would have been 35% if they had been retained. (This latter statement has, in fact, been effectively criticised by Hale, 1990.)]

Introduction

In June 1987, shortly after winning her third general election, Mrs Thatcher declared that the forthcoming introduction of a poll tax, to replace domestic rates, would be the "Flagship" policy of her third term of government. The elevation of the poll tax and the associated reform of the rest of the system of local finance probably reflected both the importance of the policy to the Prime Minister and the need to rally backbench Conservative MPs, a large number of whom had doubts about the wisdom of introducing the poll tax, behind the policy. The legislation for the reform of local finance (The Local Government Finance Act) has now been passed and its flagship status provides one reason why it is worthwhile to examine the presentation of the policy by the government now, rather than leave the task entirely to historians. The second reason is that the presentation of the poll tax has much to reveal about the situation of contemporary politics in Britain, with the Government remaining unscathed and unembarrassed from a presentation bristling with shortcomings.

These shortcomings can be classified under five heads: (1) illogical arguments, (2) misleading arguments, (3) unproven assertions presented as truths, (4) untruths, and (5) inconsistent arguments. Before proceeding further we explain the distinction which we will make between these classifications. A misleading argument is where an argument contains the truth, and nothing but the truth, but omits the whole truth, and through this omission leaves a misleading impression. An untruth we interpret as containing facts which can readily be proved to be incorrect. Category (3), unproven assertion is closely related but different to category (4), untruths, by the absence of proof that the assertion is untrue. Finally we define an inconsistent argument - category (5) - as an argument in favour or against some feature which is inconsistent with the actual choices made by the Government. We will give examples of each of these in turn. Before doing this however we will discuss two preliminary points. First, the inconsistency involved in the declaration of the poll tax as the flagship policy. Second, we will analyse two alternative interpretations of the reasons for the reform of local government finance.

The Post Election Flagship

There is massive inconsistency between the post election declaration that poll tax was to be the third term flagship and the fact that it had barely been mentioned by any member of the Conservative cabinet during the election campaign. Hugo Young, the Guardian's political correspondent, certainly had this impression and had it confirmed when his request to Conservative Central Office for Ministerial speeches on poll tax during the election campaign revealed that only one speech on the subject was made by the Conservative Secretary of State for the Environment and this was merely to a constituency gathering in Streatham.[1] Given the acknowledged skill which the Conservative government has exercised in dictating the agenda of political debate in recent years there seems to have been a remarkable failure to give prominence to the potential flagship!.

This point has not just been made in a national newspaper unsympathetic to the Conservative Government. Robin Squire, a Conservative MP opposed to the introduction of poll tax, made the point in the House of Commons during the second reading debate on the Local Government Finance Bill:

> ... (in) the last election..the issue was hardly raised on the doorstep. That was my experience and that of a number of my colleagues. The matter only became

a flagship about seven or 14 days after the election - the first recorded instance of a flagship being commissioned after the surrender of the enemy.[2]

Far from being embarrassed or disconcerted by these facts Ministers, especially the Secretary of State for the Environment, Nicholas Ridley, have continued to use manifesto arguments to resist attempts to persuade the Government to compromise on the flat-rate principle of the new tax.

Reasons for reform: two interpretations

A good source for the Government's own stated reasons for the reform in terms of its political importance is the statement produced by the Secretary of State for the Environment in the House of Commons at second reading of the Local Government Finance Bill:

> The objectives of the Bill are first, to abolish the inequities of the present domestic rating system; secondly, to make local councils more responsive and accountable to their electors; and thirdly, to provide badly needed protection for business ratepayers. It will achieve those objectives first by replacing domestic rates with a fairer community charge: secondly by establishing a uniform business rate and thirdly by introducing a simpler and more stable grant system. Together, these proposals will provide the essential linkage between those who use, pay and vote for local services.[3]

After this concise introduction he proceeded to go into more detail:

> ... We have a system in which control of local government's £45 billion gross annual spending is vested in 35 million electors. Yet only 18 million are liable to pay rates and more than 3 million of those receive a full rebate. The fact is that 20 million of the local electorate make no direct contribution to the cost of local services. Under the present system half of local revenue is raised from businesses which are defenceless against exploitation by authorities, particularly those controlled by the Labour party... The domestic rating system is also unfair. Many who benefit from local services pay nothing towards them. Payments based on rental values bear little relationship to ability to pay and even less to their use of local services.[4]

The subject of avoiding the disruption of a revaluation must have a place in any discussion of the scrapping of domestic rates and the introduction of poll tax. Indeed, although the Green Paper based the case for its major reform of local government finance on the weaknesses in local accountability inherent in the present system, the main force behind the change was the Scottish rating revaluation of 1985. This might appear to be an unwarranted assertion given that the Government has a positive argument for poll tax based on the weaknesses in local accountability in the present system, but an examination of the recent historical record supports this interpretation.

First, the rating system had very recently been subject to a major review by the Conservative Government based on consideration of responses to its Green Paper 'Alternatives to Domestic Rates' published in December 1981. This also stimulated an enquiry into local government finance by the Environment Committee of the House of Commons.[5] The review led only to a White Paper in August 1983 which rejected all alternatives to domestic rates. Indeed the verdict on poll tax in that White Paper could hardly have been more negative:

> ... the tax would be hard to enforce ... A new register would ... be needed. But this would make the tax expensive to run and complicated, particularly if it incorporated a rebate scheme. Without a rebate scheme a poll tax would bear harshly on people with low incomes. The government agree with the Environment Committee that this option should be rejected.[6]

In fact, the only result of the review was the introduction of rate capping for selected local authorities rather than the replacement of domestic rates.

Second, it is clear that there were no plans after this White Paper to renew the search for alternatives within that Parliament. Thus the Secretary of State made a speech to the Conservative Central Council in March 1984 which stated that the Government had abandoned the search for an alternative to the rating system "in the course of the present Parliament".[7]

The first minor disturbance to this settled position was the publication in August 1984 of an extremely critical report by the Audit Commission on the block grant distribution system.[8] The Audit Commission was itself the recent creation of the Conservative Government and thus criticism from this source carried some weight - although the criticism was confined to the operation of the grant system and did not indicate any need to replace domestic rates. Nevertheless, the report encouraged renewed pressure from critics of the system of local finance both outside and, more significantly, inside the Conservative party. In response to this the then Secretary of State for the Environment, Patrick Jenkin, announced the setting up of an intra-departmental inquiry or set of studies into local government finance at the Conservative Party conference of October 1984. Even at this stage there was no expectation that this inquiry within Whitehall would lead to any significant change.[9] Indeed the inquiry was extremely "low-profile" throughout the autumn and early winter with Ministerial responses to inquiries from the local authority associations, as to whether they should submit any evidence, indicating very limited objectives for the internal inquiry.

However in late February and March 1985 Scottish householders began to receive rate bills based on a new set of valuations.[10] The revaluation had increased the domestic sector's share of local taxation, especially in the more affluent areas and led to much protest against rate increases. The response of Ministers was a rapid search for a solution and much more pressure being put on the inquiry. In an atmosphere of some crisis there was a much publicised weekend meeting at Chequers in March 1985 where the Prime Minister discussed the problem with the Secretary of State for the Environment and the Scottish Secretary, George Younger. The general message which emerged from this weekend was that "something was going to be done this time".[11] There quickly followed a series of public speeches by Ministers putting emphasis on the need for thorough reform on this occasion.[12] In the summer of 1985 there followed a series of Government leaks to the press suggesting that poll tax was now seriously under consideration as a replacement for domestic rates.

Thus there are two rival interpretations of the reasons for introducing the reforms. The first is that it was a rational and politically courageous decision to introduce a tax which, although bound to be unpopular with many citizens, was needed on perceived weaknesses in the present arrangements. Perhaps conscious of possible scepticism about the Government's sudden conversion to reform the Green Paper claimed that the weaknesses in local accountability, were always inherent but were only revealed now because the Government had, for the first time since the war, been seeking to exercise significant restraint over local authority spending. The alternative interpretation rather than stressing political courage stresses instead the fear of political consequences by a Government pushed into an awkward corner. Douglas Mason of the Adam Smith Institute, who as author of a monograph advocating poll tax in 1985[13] might have been tempted to claim credit for persuading the Government to introduce the reform, holds with the interpretation we have given: "It was only the outcry following rating revaluation in Scotland that eventually persuaded the government into producing an alternative to domestic rates".[14] Hugo Young also supplied a good summary of the poll tax: "its main merit is that it supplants rates which were causing the governing party ever greater political embarrassment".[15]

We can now commence our evaluation of the Government's presentation of the poll tax. The description above explains why a major feature of the Government's presentation has been a concentration not on the advantages of poll tax but on the disadvantages of the rating system.

Avoiding the disruption of revaluation

The reaction to revaluation in Scotland emphasized the potential political costs of the status quo - retention of the rating system. These costs were the unpopularity for the governing party arising from the redistribution in local tax burdens. A revaluation was more urgently overdue in England and Wales in 1985 than it had been in Scotland, because the last had occurred in 1973 whereas the previous Scottish revaluation had been in 1980. The fact that the disruption of revaluation still loomed large in Government thinking when the 'Paying for Local Government' Green Paper was published in January 1986 can be shown by two examples. First, the Secretary of State for the Environment, Kenneth Baker, stated when introducing Green Paper to the House of Commons in January 1986:

> If rates are to be kept, there will have a major revaluation and that will create a turbulence in family incomes much greater than what I am proposing to the House.[16]

Second, in discussing Scotland's rating revaluation, the Green Paper stated that based on this experience: "... an unacceptable price has to be paid in the disruption faced by ratepayers following any revaluation"[17] and later on the same page made it clear that the "unacceptable price" occurred because: "... over 100,000 householders in Scotland have faced increase of more than one third in their rate bills between 1984/85 and 1985/86".[18]

We can make a distinction between these two examples. The statement by the Secretary of State in the House of Commons is an untruth, whereas the extract from the Green Paper is misleading. Let us demonstrate this dealing with the Green Paper extract first.

The Green Paper is misleading in two ways. First, in the presentation of the statistics for Scotland, and second, and more importantly in failing to provide comparative disruption statistics for poll tax. We accept the description of the facts given in the Green Paper, but the presentation is designed to make the disruption caused by the revaluation appear very large. The 100,000 households which experienced increases in rate bills of more than 30% looks a good deal less dramatic when stated as 5.26% of the 1,900,000 households in Scotland. It also fails to point out that the trend year-on-year increase in rate bills caused by inflation and grant loss was close to 10%.

In fact there was an average increase in domestic rates in Scotland in 1985 (1985/86) compared to 1984 (1984/85) of 14%. Thus a more balanced presentation would have stated that just over 5% of Scottish households experienced increases in rate bills 20% greater than the average increase in Scotland in that year. Now let us deal with the more important point - the omission of comparative disruption figures for poll tax. Such comparative figures were provided by a study which estimated household poll tax bills and present rate bills for 160,000 households in County Durham.[19] This provided an estimate that at a national level poll tax would increase the local tax bills of over 15% of households by more than 20%. In other words the poll tax was over six times as disruptive as a rating revaluation. If the disruption of the rating revaluation was an unacceptable price then it seems an amazing oversight that the Government did not itself check the comparative disruptive properties of poll tax. The accuracy of estimates from this study have, as we shall see below, since been confirmed in Parliamentary written answer.

Also Mr Baker's statement to the House claiming that a rating revaluation would cause more turbulence to family incomes than a poll tax has been shown by the above discussion to be an untruth.

This was not the end of Mr Baker's mispresentation of the facts. A second blatant example was given by him in a major speech in May 1986 to an Association of Metropolitan Authorities' one-day conference on the Green Paper. The full text of this speech was made a Department of the Environment news release under the title 'Local Income Tax - recipe for conflict says Kenneth Baker'. In this speech Mr Baker discussed in the context of the option of retaining domestic rates the fact that it would urgently require a revaluation and that a revaluation based on capital values, favoured by many, would mean that: "Over a million households in England would see increases of 80% or more in their rate bills" and further asserted that: "Half of these would be owners of modest terrace houses - many of them first-time buyers".[20]

Mr Baker's speech uses the same technique as that in the Green Paper to make the effects of a rating revaluation appear extremely undesirable - that is giving the absolute numbers of households (1,000,000) who would suffer large bill increases rather than the proportion of households. In fact there are approximately 17,650,000 households in England, and therefore 1,000,000 households facing bill increases of 80% or more, under domestic rates with a revaluation based on capital values, represents only 5.66% of English households. Again the Durham study estimated that the introduction of the poll tax would be much more disruptive than a rating revaluation. It estimated that the poll tax would result in slightly over 15% of households (ie 3,000,000 households) facing bill increases of more than 80%.[21] In fact a later Parliamentary written answer itself confirmed that poll tax would be more disruptive than a rating revaluation. It estimated that based on 1987/88 local authorities' expenditure: "... 3 million households might face an increase of over 50% in their local tax bills: and that 1.8 million might face an increase of 80% or more".[22] In addition to this Mr Baker's remarks imply that a rating revaluation particularly discriminates against those living in poorer houses. However, the Durham study estimated that the poll tax favoured those living in the highest rateable value houses and here also a Parliamentary written answer showed that a rating revaluation increased the tax bills most of those living in detached houses.[23] Now it is conceivable that both of the misleading presentations and the untruth in this section may have, at the time they were made, simply have been oversights. However, it is difficult to see why Ministers, when they themselves finally produced figures showing the far greater disruption which would be caused by poll tax, did not apply their previous criteria and withdraw the legislation.

Voting, Electors, and Accountability

A key element in the Government's case for reforming the system of local finance has been what Ministers have described as the large gap between those who pay local tax bills and those who vote in local elections. The arithmetic was given above in Mr Ridley's second reading speech. There can be no dispute with that arithmetic, but there can with the further argument, often made by the Government, that voting in local elections is dominated by those not directly paying local tax bills and, therefore, favouring candidates and parties advocating increases in services, expenditure, and local taxes.

The further argument is an assertion because there is no objective evidence on which individuals and groups actually vote in local elections. The best evidence would be provided by a study of marked electoral registers which record such voting. However, only one study has been made using marked electoral registers and that was for voting in a national election.[24] This found a surprising lack of variation in Aberdeen between the proportion of different socio-economic groups who vote. Other survey evidence relating to local elections has also found no large variation between the voting propensities of different groups.[25]

In the Green Paper the section on this matter has the title "Those who vote and those who pay" but in the text more carefully notes that the arithmetic relates to those who are entitled to vote rather than to those who actually vote.

However Ministers have been much less scrupulous in making the direct assertion about voting. Thus Kenneth Baker when introducing the Green Paper to the House:

> In many authorities well over 50% of the voters pay no local rates and therefore have little interest in restraining spending by the local authority; indeed, they have a clear interest that it should spend more.[26]

The direct assertion that it is those who don't directly pay rate bills, rather than those who do, who vote in local elections has since been made on a number of occasions. Thus Michael Howard, in a speech to a Association of District Councils conference attracting over 300 local councillors from throughout England and Wales stated: "In Liverpool only one voter in four pays rates directly and in full. In Manchester the proportion may be slightly higher".[27]

However, this assertion is inconsistent with Michael Howard's answer to a Parliamentary question. Barney Hayhoe had asked in the House whether the minister would publish any statistical or survey evidence available to him on any correlation between the incidence of paying local taxes and voting at local elections in the United Kingdom or in any other country. The Minister's curt reply in a written answer on 24 July 1987: "I am not aware of any research into this topic".[28]

Gainers and Losers

One point on which the Government was aware that there would be great concern amongst Conservative MPs was the potential loss of votes arising from increased local tax bills. Thus Kenneth Baker's speech introducing the Green Paper to the House offered some reassurance: "Slightly more households gain than lose".[29] He was referring here to the data in Figure J7 in the Green Paper which is reproduced in Table 12.1 (p.192).

However in June 1987 it was pointed out, in a short article[30] in the local government press that because poll tax tended to raise household tax bills in households with large numbers of adults, and lower them in smaller households the number of voters in losing households exceeded the number of voters in gaining households in the ratio 56:44. In addition it was estimated that for households with net changes in bills more than £2 per week the ration of losing voters to gainers was

192 The Politics and Economics of the Poll Tax

62:38. These figures were taken up by a number of Conservative MPs in the debate on the Queen's speech in late June 1987. The bluntest expression of dissatisfaction came from Anthony Beaumont-Dark Conservative MP for Birmingham Selly Oak on BBC2's *Newsnight* programme when on the issue of gainers and losers from poll tax he stated that "Ministers should stop pretending that this is a children's tea party at which everybody leaves with a prize".[31]

The Government produced fresh evidence on "gainers and losers" in a Parliamentary written answer to a question from Labour front bench environment spokesman Jeff Rooker. Mr Rooker asked the Secretary of State for the Environment "to construct a table in the same form as figure J7... of 'Paying for Local Government'" this time showing the number of adults gaining and losing with full replacement of domestic rates by community charge" using the latest available data.

Table 12.1: Households (thousands) gaining and losing with full replacement of domestic rates by the poll tax (Great Britain based on 1984/85 data (£ per week))

	Single Pensioner	Other single adult	Two adults	Three adults	All households
Losers					
10 +	-	-	0	50	50
5 -10	-	-	75	425	500
2 - 5	0	75	1325	1125	2525
1 - 2	25	100	1625	425	2175
0 - 1	375	275	3750	325	4725
Total losers	400	475	6800	2350	10000
Gainers					
0 - 1	1700	775	2800	200	5475
1 - 2	250	350	1275	100	1975
2 - 5	350	600	1400	100	2450
5 -10	75	100	350	25	575
10 +	25	25	50	0	100
Total gainers	2400	1850	5875	425	10575

0 = less than 12500
Numbers may not add due to rounding

Source: 'Department of the Environment, 1986a,' Figure J7

A question was also asked that data was produced for households on a regional, local authority, and parliamentary constituency basis. Data was produced only by economic region and household type basis. Table 12.2 shows the data produced, based on 1985/86, given by Michael Howard in the written answer[32] and the proportion of gaining households was much higher than the comparable Table in the Green Paper. The discrepancy between figure J7 in the Green Paper and this table had no obvious explanation and none was offered in the written answer. Instead the Department of the Environment made the written answer a press release under the heading 'Many Households to Benefit under Community Charge'. This release made the most of the favourable figures. It quoted Michael Howard as stating: "Overall we expect that there will be nearly 10 million households paying less in community charge bills than they pay now in rates, whilst some 7.7 million will

Table 12.2: Households (thousands) gaining and losing with full replacement of domestic rates by the poll tax (England based on 1985/86 data (£ per week))

	Single Pensioner	Other single adult	Two adults	Three adults	All households
Losers					
10 +	-	-	98	123	222
5 -10	2	25	254	387	669
2 - 5	20	91	1291	704	2108
1 - 2	45	115	1056	292	1509
0 - 1	404	283	2217	284	3187
Total losers	471	515	4916	1791	7695
Gainers					
0 - 1	1233	634	1994	257	4122
1 - 2	185	295	1248	128	1856
2 - 5	365	514	1823	146	2849
5 -10	125	150	597	56	928
10 +	12	16	114	17	160
Total gainers	1920	1609	5776	605	9915

0=less than 12500
Numbers may not add due to rounding

Source: House of Commons, Parliamentary Debates, Written Answers 26 October 1987 cols. 39-40.

pay more ... ". The written answer also stated for this Table the number of gaining adults - 17.1 million - now exceeded the number of losing adults - 16.7 million.

The discrepancy led to a further Parliamentary question asking why the results were now so different from those in the Green Paper. To this a written answer replied that: "The figures are on different bases".[33] Briefly the new figures were for a system operating without safety net/transitional grant provisions whereas the Green Paper data included such safety nets. The removal of safety nets, which will actually take five years when the new system is introduced, has the effect of concentrating large losses in a few local areas offset by smaller average gains in the majority of areas, with of course more households and adults. Further Parliamentary questions finally ensured the supply of a comparable table to that in the Green Paper and showed again the rough equality between the numbers of gaining and losing households. This latter table did not, however, receive a Department of the Environment press release. The evidence of this episode seems to be that there was a clear intention to give a misleading impression on the number of gaining adults and households.

Regressivity

The regressivity of a poll tax has long been seen as a reason why it cannot be a major local tax source either in Great Britain or abroad - certainly not a substitute for such a substantial tax as domestic rates which amount to over 3.5% of personal disposable incomes. The reason for this has been its perceived regressivity. As we saw above the 1983 Rates White Paper had mentioned the regressivity drawback, which had also been stressed in the 1981 Green Paper and the 1982 report of the House of Commons Environment Committee. Certainly in all these recent documents poll tax was seen as a substantially more regressive tax than domestic rates. The most detailed study was included in the 1981 Green Paper and the following extract summarises the relative regressivity of poll tax and domestic rates:

> For any given household type ... lower income households would pay a higher proportion of their income in (poll) tax than ... higher income households. Moreover, since domestic rate payments tend to increase with income - though less than proportionately - replacing rates by a poll tax will mean that higher income households will gain more or lose less (in pounds per week) than the lower income households of the same type.[34]

Although the results in the 1981 Green Paper were of an unrebated poll tax, the fundamental regressivity within household type remains in a rebated system for all those income groups above rebate levels. It is useful to have established this fundamental regressivity characteristic of the poll tax before considering the Government's presentation on this issue. The reason for this is that from the outset the Government have not acknowledged that poll tax is even slightly, let alone substantially, more regressive than domestic rates.

If regressivity was a point on which the poll tax was susceptible to attack, the strategy increasingly taken by the Government since 1986 is one of attack being the best form of defence. Thus Ministers concentrated on the unfairnesses and anomalies of domestic rates. Michael Howard's speech to the Association of District Councils' conference includes a typical statement:

> 40% of homes with above average rateable values are occupied by those with below average incomes. It is unfair that a single person can pay the same as four wage earners in the house next door. It is unfair that, because rateable values are taken as a measure of ability to pay, those in high rateable value areas pay more for the same services than those in low rateable value areas.[35]

This statement is misleading in a number of ways. First, it fails to point out that incomes are positively related to household size and numbers of adults so that many households with below average incomes and living in above average rateable value houses may be better off than those with larger incomes but more dependents. It also fails to mention that the discrepancy caused by large regional variations in rateable values could be offset by using equalising grants in the present system to equalise according to average income levels in different areas rather than to average rateable values per head. Rateable values could then be used solely to determine household tax shares within authorities on a less regressive basis than poll tax - but this option has, of course, never been mentioned by Ministers.

The official presentation has absolutely avoided giving figures on the relationship between tax and income levels for a given household type. It is these figures which would have shown the substantially greater regressivity of poll tax. The nearest approach is the fifth table provided in Appendix F of the Green Paper which shows the relationship between tax bills and "equivalent" net household income - that is household income adjusted for differences in household composition. This table showed that for all income groups above £200 a week average local tax bills fell - with the largest gains of nearly £6 per week for the very highest income group (over £500 per week). However, the text of the Green paper emphasised instead the fact that the lowest income group would experience average gains of 10p a week!

Even this rather slanted treatment was much less misleading than the ruse attempted in January 1988. A Parliamentary Question from a Conservative backbencher resulted in a Department of the Environment Press Release on the same day under the title *Households to gain from the community charge*. This release was on the subject of the relationship between local taxes and income and the distributional impact of the community charge. It claimed to "update the principal tables (on this subject) in Annex F of the Green Paper..". Most important was the statement that: "community charges on the average will be less than domestic rates at all income levels up to £150 per week". Again this is a completely misleading picture due to the fact that no correction is made for household structure. As well as this there was no updated set of figures on an equivalent net income basis despite the claims in the press release that it contained updated versions of all the principal tables. Again a further Parliamentary question was necessary to obtain this information. Table 12.3 shows the data obtained from the answer to this question which indicates the greater regressivity of the poll tax.

In addition to this, it is possible from some unpublished Grants Working Group papers to derive data on the gains and losses - that is changes in tax bills - by given type of household for two broad income groups. These groups are those with net incomes under £200 per week and those with incomes £200 per week and over. Table 12.4 gives the data for two adult households and shows emphatically the greater regressivity of poll tax. The ratio of gainers to losers from poll tax is 40:60 for the below £200 a week group but 64:36 for the high income group.

Table 12.3: Relationship of rates and poll tax to net household income (England 1986/87 prices)

	Ranges of equivalent net household income (£ per week)										
	Under 50	50-75	75-100	100-150	150-200	200-250	250-300	300-350	350-400	400-500	500+	All
Gross:												
Rates	6.07	6.17	6.72	7.32	7.95	8.31	8.72	9.27	9.95	10.54	13.64	7.40
Poll tax	6.00	6.36	7.27	8.03	8.12	8.01	7.59	7.36	7.09	7.42	7.00	7.41
Net:												
Rates	1.64	3.04	5.94	7.18	7.90	8.29	8.71	9.27	9.95	10.50	13.62	6.37
Poll tax	1.63	3.13	6.31	7.64	7.91	7.89	7.52	7.31	7.03	7.34	6.89	6.25

Source: Parliamentary Written Answer, 25 January 1988

The Presentation of the Poll Tax

Table 12.4: Two adult households gaining and losing with full replacement of domestic rates by the poll tax (England 1984/85 (£ per week))

	All Incomes	Incomes below £200 per week	Incomes £200 and over per week
Losers			
10 +	2	1	1
5 -10	86	52	34
2 - 5	1215	853	320
1 - 2	1341	1006	335
0 - 1	3104	2625	479
Total losers	5745	4577	1169
Gainers			
0 - 1	2440	1857	583
1 - 2	1111	649	462
2 - 5	1216	491	725
5 -10	310	55	255
10 +	52	3	49
Total gainers	5130	3054	2086

Source: unpublished Grants Working Group papers

Finally we must consider another argument used by Ministers. This argument is the one presented by the Secretary of State at the Conservative Party Conference in October 1987 when he said of the forthcoming system:

> It is fair. The better off will pay much more for local services but everyone will pay something. The community charge will cover only a quarter of local authority spending. Three quarters will come from the central taxpayer and the business rate. Everyone in a local authority's area will pay the same community charge but the highest paid 10% of households will pay nearly 16 times as much towards the cost of local services as the lowest paid 10%.

This line of argument comes into our category (1) - illogical. It is illogical to use the progressivity of central taxation as an aid to ameliorate the regressivity of the poll tax (which in any case is not directly conceded in the statement) and not also to include this as a factor to alleviate the alleged unfairness of domestic rates.

The "Equal Bills" Principle

Under the present rating system households living in similar houses but in areas with widely differing levels of house prices and therefore rateable values pay different rate bills for the same standard of local government services. This is because the objective of the present system is to make rate poundages equal in all areas for a given standard of service.[36] This difference in local tax bills has been criticised as unfair both in the Green Paper and in a number of Ministerial speeches. Thus in the Secretary of State's speech to the Conservative Party Conference in October 1987 emphasising the drawbacks of the rating system he stated:

> In Torbay a family living in a three bedroom semi would pay £435 some 20% more than an identical family in Torridge on the opposite coast of Devon even though the level of services provided in each area was the same. A family with a three bedroom terraced house in Carlisle would pay £225 a year for the same level of service as a family with the same house in Luton - but the family in Luton would pay £435.

and in the second reading debate he emphasised that:

> ... the new system will sweep away the unfair system ... whereby those who live in high rateable value areas subsidise those who live in low rateable value areas. Instead of people paying widely different amounts for the same local services, everyone will pay the same.[37]

This is an important example of an inconsistent argument. The reason for this is that the Government is not choosing to apply equal bills in all areas. Thus local tax bills will be £178 per adult for spending at GRE (the assessed cost of providing a standard level of service in each area) in England but only £122 in Wales. The difference in tax bills has never been clearly stated by Ministers and is evident only by comparing (unadjacent) parliamentary written answers. If the Secretary of State was so concerned about a 20% difference in bills within Devon there seems to be no good reason why bills should differ by over 45% across the England-Wales border. If it is fair to remove a subsidy from residents of Luton to residents of Carlisle it seems strange to simultaneously introduce a subsidy from residents of Carlisle to residents of Cardiff.

International Experience: The Japanese Poll Tax

The final example of misleading presentation comes from the section in the Green Paper on 'Local Government Finance: International Comparisons' where the text states that:

Japan ... has an inhabitants tax - accounting for 48% of local tax income - comprising a flat rate charge and an income related element.

The reader is invited to believe that a poll tax is an important part of 48% of local tax income in what is commonly perceived as a very successful economy. Presumably the authors of the Green Paper did not expect many readers to check the facts in the annual publication of the Tax Bureau of the Japanese Ministry of Finance. The facts are that the Japanese poll tax (flat rate element) accounts for only one per cent of the local inhabitants tax and, therefore, less than one-half of one per cent of Japanese local tax income.[38] This is a final example of a misleading argument. However, it does show that there have been some bounds to Minister's presentations because it has not been repeated since the Green Paper.

Conclusions

The above deficiencies in the Government's presentation of the poll tax and the relative merits or demerits of the present and new systems sit unhappily with what Michael Howard said at the ADC conference in September 1987: "... much remains to be done to increase the understanding of our proposals and the reasons for them ... that is why Christopher Chope and I are going round the country to explain why the time is ripe for reform ...". It helps to explain, however, why the Secretary of State worried as late as the summer of 1988 that he would receive more trouble from Conservative backbenchers as they increased their understanding of the Government's proposals.

Notes

1. Hugo Young, "The furtive decision to go from bad to worse", *The Guardian*, 23 July 1987.

2. House of Commons, *Parliamentary Debates (Hansard)*, 17 December 1987 column 1311.

3. House of Commons, *Parliamentary Debates (Hansard)*, 16 December 1987, column 1115.

4. House of Commons, *Parliamentary Debates (Hansard)*, 16 December 1987, column 1115.

5. Environment Committee, (1982), *Enquiry into methods of financing local government in the context of the Government's Green Paper* (Cmnd. 8449), House of Commons, Paper 217, 1981-82.

6. Secretary of State for the Environment, *Rates*, Cmnd. 9008 (HMSO, London: 1983) para. 2.9 p.12.

7. Julia Langdon, "Tories abandon search for alternatives to rates", *The Guardian*, 24 March 1984.

8. Audit Commission, *The Impact on Local Authorities' Economy, Efficiency and Effectiveness of the Block Grant Distribution System*, (HMSO, London: 1984).

9. Tony Travers, "Finance Review deja vu", *Local Government Chronicle*, 18 October 1984.

10. Rating revaluations have been much more regular and frequent in Scotland than in England.

11. James Naughtie, "Ministers accept need for early rate reform", *The Guardian*, 28 March 1985; John Carvel, "Mrs Thatcher's ever-increasing rate of knots", *The Guardian*, 1 April 1985.

12. Department of the Environment, "Patrick Jenkin examines the way forward on local government finance reform", Press Notice 173, 12 April 1985; Waldegrave W, "Finding the best financial regime for a healthy local democracy", *Municipal Journal*, 28 June 1985.

13. Douglas Mason, *Revising the Rating System*, (Adam Smith Institute, April 1985).

14. Douglas C. Mason 'Slimming for Survival' paper presented at Institute of Economic Affairs, May 1988.

15. Hugo Young, "No green light for a juggernaut mandate", *The Guardian*, 23 June 1987.

16. House of Commons, *Parliamentary Debates (Hansard)*, 28 January 1986 col 800.

17. Secretary of State for the Environment, *Paying for Local Government*, Cmnd. 9741 (HMSO, London: 1986) para. 8.17, p.61.

18. Secretary of State for the Environment, *Paying for Local Government*, Cmnd. 9741 (HMSO, London: 1986) para. 8.20, p.61.

19. J.G.Gibson, *The Poll Tax: Its Impact on the Residents of County Durham* (Durham County Council, 1987).

20. "Local Income Tax - recipe for conflict says Kenneth Baker", Department of the Environment news release.

21. J.G.Gibson, *The Poll Tax: Its Impact on the Residents of County Durham* (Durham County Council, 1987).

22. House of Commons, *Parliamentary Debates (Hansard)*, Written Answers, 25 November 1987.

23. (As above) except for date 15 February 1988

24. M.C.Dyer and A.G.Jordan, *Who Votes in Aberdeen? Marked Electoral Registers as a Data Source,* Strathclyde Papers in Government No 42, (Department of Government, University of Strathclyde, Glasgow: 1985.

25. W.L.Miller, "Local Electoral Behaviour", in Research Volume 3 of Report of the Committee of Inquiry into *The Conduct of Local Authority Business*, Cmnd 9800, (HMSO, London: 1986).

26. House of Commons, *Parliamentary Debates (Hansard)*, 28 January 1986 col 798.

27. From 'Mr Howard's speech to the ADC', Association of District Councils, County Branch Consultative Meeting, 17 September 1987, p.4.

28. House of Commons, *Parliamentary Debates (Hansard)*, Written Answers 24 July 1987

29. House of Commons, *Parliamentary Debates (Hansard)*, 28 January 1986 col 811.

30. John Gibson, "How the poll tax will punish electors", *Public Services and Local Government*, June 1987.

31. BBC Television, Newsnight, 7 July 1987.

32. House of Commons, *Parliamentary Debates (Hansard)*, Written Answers 26 October 1987 cols 37-40.

33. House of Commons, *Parliamentary Debates (Hansard)*, Written Answers 2 November 1987 col 590.

34. Secretary of State for the Environment, (1981), *Alternatives to domestic rates*, Cmnd 8449 (HMSO, London: 1981) p.74.

35. From 'Mr Howard's speech to the ADC', Association of District Councils, County Branch Consultative Meeting, 17 September 1987, p.3.

36. There is a discount from the national poundage applying to different parts of London to compensate for higher rateable values.

37. House of Commons, *Parliamentary Debates (Hansard)*, 16 December 1987 column 1119.

38. Japanese Ministry of Finance's publication *Annual Abstract of Statistics of Local Government Finance, 1986*.

13.
POLL TAX IN OTHER COUNTRIES: THE JAPANESE POLL TAX

There is relatively little that can be written about contemporary poll taxes in other countries. However, it might surprise many readers that in the nineteenth and twentieth centuries poll taxes have been of some importance both in Africa and the southern states of the USA. In the USA poll taxes started to be introduced in many southern states in the late nineteenth century, as a device for disenfranchising blacks, rather than for the purpose of raising revenues. By 1908 payment of poll tax was a prerequisite to voting in all 11 states of the old Confederacy (Ogden, 1958). They were accompanied by other devices as prerequisites for voting qualification, such as tests of literacy and understanding of the constitution (Billington, 1975). Ezell, 1975, p.407 provides a good summary:

> ... the South deliberately set out to eliminate the Negro as a voter by the use of such techniques as the poll tax, residence requirements and the literacy test. The poll tax ... in general proved a boomerang. The small sum, from one to two dollars a year, although cumulative in some states, was not in itself sufficient to discourage anyone seriously desiring to vote. The nuisance value of having to go down to the courthouse six or more months before an election to pay probably disenfranchised more, white and black, than did the cost. ... Literacy tests proved more efficient as a means of eliminating the Negro voter, but they too had a discouraging effect upon white participation, despite the many loopholes provided to prevent such exclusion.

The civil rights movement secured some reduction in these restrictions, especially from the 1940s onwards. However, as late as 1966 payment of a poll tax was still in use by four states – Alabama, Mississippi, Texas and Virginia. February 1966 marked the end of a number of legal struggles over the tax when the US Supreme Court upheld rulings of lower federal courts that the use of poll taxes as a prerequisite to voting contravened the 15th Amendment to the US Constitution.

In contrast, a major motive in the British introduction of poll taxes in a number of African colonies was to encourage the supply of labour in agriculture for the growth of cash crops (Hailey, 1957; Hogendorn, 1975). Davey (1983) in his book on international practices in financing decentralised governments states that only a few developing countries still had flat rate personal taxes to which all adult males were subject. He cites the rural community tax in Pakistan, the communal taxes in the northern states of Nigeria (recently abolished), and the head tax in Papua New Guinea (also, I believe, recently abolished). Davey summarises (p. 69):

> Flat rate taxes are inevitably set at the capacity of the poor taxpayers and are low in incidence and yield. They are invariably of declining importance as economic differentiation grows ... and public expenditures expand. Most African poll taxes have been abolished.

Thus it was surprising to read in the Green Paper that there was a significant poll tax in Japan. The following short article was written in early 1988 for the weekly magazine, *Local Government Chronicle*, to reach a local government readership, and appeared under the title 'Japan's poll tax misleads the UK' (Gibson, 1988a).

The plan to replace domestic rates by a poll tax is the largest one step fiscal change to be imposed on the UK in the post war period. Scrapping such a significant tax, at present giving a yield of well over 3 per cent of personal incomes, and replacing it by the poll tax will cause a large scale disruption to household finances. Any government contemplating such a sizeable redistribution of the tax burden would be wise to ensure that:

(1) The change is based on a thorough analysis of the policy alternatives, including the "status quo" alternative of retaining domestic rates, and

(2) Its presentation of the advantages and disadvantages of the alternatives could not be accused of being misleading.

This does not seem to have happened. The government have consistently mislead the country on the relative disruption caused by a rating revaluation and the introduction of the poll tax.

The Japanese poll tax in the Green Paper

The poll tax was a major cause of the Peasants' Revolt in 14th century England. Although it had been introduced into a number of British colonies in the 19th century it had survived only in Nigeria and Papua and New Guinea. Thus I was somewhat surprised to read in the section in the Green Paper on 'Local Government Finance: International Comparisons' that:

> Japan ... has an inhabitants tax - accounting for 48% of local tax income - comprising a flat rate charge and an income related element.

A poll tax was thus presented as an important part of 48% of local tax income in the world's most successful economy. This seemed to be weighty evidence that a poll tax could have an important role in local finance in a modern economy.

The Japanese poll tax: the truth

However, it is a wise precaution to check the evidence. This has been supplied by Professor Akira Kobayashi of Kanazawa University in Japan - a Japanese specialist in local public finance. The data can be split into two sections.

(a) The Japanese poll tax - how many yen? (£1 = 232 yen, 25 March 1988)

The facts are derived from the annual publication of the Tax Bureau of the Japanese Ministry of Finance. Japan has two tiers of local government, prefectures and municipalities. For both levels the inhabitants tax has the two components - per capita (poll tax) and income related. Leaving aside the details of the income related component the poll tax component is:

Prefectures: 700 yen per person per annum

Municipalities:

Cities with population of 500,000 or more: 2500 yen to 3200 yen per person per annum

Cities with population of 50 to 500,000: 2000 yen to 2600 yen per person per annum

Other cities towns and villages: 1500 yen to 2000 yen per person per annum

Thus adding together the taxes payable to prefectures and municipalities the maximum possible poll tax payable by any Japanese is 3900 yen - less than £20 a year!

(b) The overall Japanese figures

Professor Kobayashi has also compiled facts from the Japanese Ministry of Finance's publication 'Annual Abstract of Statistics of Local Government Finance, 1986'. These are given in Table 13.1. There are a lot of Japanese local taxes, so the rows which show poll tax totals are in bold.

Table 13.1: Composition of Local Tax revenue in Japan in the financial year 1984 (by Outturn)

	(Billion Yen)		%	
Prefectural Taxes				
Inhabitants Tax	2,733		28.8	
Individuals - Per capita		**19**		**0.2**
Individuals - on income		1,910		20.1
Corporations - per corporation		**43**		**0.5**
Corporations - on corporate income		761		8.0
Enterprise Tax	3,610		38.0	
Automobile Tax	1,014		10.7	
Other Taxes	2,146		22.6	
Total	9,503		100.0	
Municipal Taxes				
Inhabitants Tax	6,012		50.1	
Individuals - Per capita		**57**		**0.5**
Individuals - on income		4,047		33.8
Corporations - per corporation		**182**		**1.5**
Corporations - on corporate income		1,727		14.4
Property Tax	3,942		32.9	
Other Taxes	2,037		17.0	
Total	11,991		100.0	
Prefectures + Municipalities				
Total Taxes	21,493		100.0	
Total Per Capita Taxes	**76**		**0.4**	

Source: Japanese Ministry of Finance, (1986)

Concluding remarks

It is obvious now that the section in the Green Paper was very misleading. Recall that it read:

> Japan ... has an inhabitants tax - accounting for 48% of local tax income – comprising a flat rate charge and an income related element.

Whereas an honest statement designed not to mislead would have said:

> Japan ... has an inhabitants tax - accounting for 48% of local tax income – comprising a flat rate charge and an income related element, but the flat rate element is very low, accounting for less than one-half of 1% of local tax income.

and it might also have added that property taxes in Japan raised nearly 40% of Japanese local tax revenue and were nearly 60 times larger than the Japanese poll tax.

If we have a tradition in Britain that governments attempt to provide straight information on major policy changes, then that convention has been broken by this government. It is extremely disturbing that the Government presumably believes that it will never be called to account for applying the standards of a shady second-hand car dealer to the introduction of new policies.

14.
THE ELECTORAL PROBLEM

[It had been obvious to me in 1986 that the poll tax's tendency to hit large households would result in an unfavourable electoral calculus, and I had been surprised not to have seen it pointed out in any of the dozens of newspaper or magazine articles on poll tax. The imminent general election, therefore, finally stimulated me to write this article in May 1987 for the monthly local government magazine, *Public Service and Local Government*, where it appeared under the title 'How the Poll Tax will punish electors'.]

One of the last pieces of legislation to get through Parliament and onto the statute book before the prorogation for the general election was the Abolition of Domestic Rates Etc. (Scotland) Act. The Act will, of course, introduce the community charge as a replacement for domestic rates on 1 April 1989 as well as leading to a uniform business rate throughout Great Britain once the non-domestic revaluation is completed in England and Wales. Scrapping the domestic rates was seen by Ministers as a vital aid to alleviating the Conservatives' unpopularity in Scotland.

As we know the Conservatives are also promising to introduce similar measures for England and Wales. Indeed the uniform business rate fits in with one of the Conservatives' major electoral themes of spreading jobs and economic prosperity to those parts of the country where it has not yet reached - especially the inner cities and the north, where the uniform rate will result in a reduction in business rates.

Privately, however, a number of Conservative MPs have been concerned that the community charge/poll tax will cause bigger problems for a future Conservative government than the rates ever did. These worries have not surfaced very often, although last December Timothy Raison registered his own doubts both in Parliament and in an article in *The Guardian*.

What these Conservative MPs are really worried about is what is going to happen at that crucial time - not very far away now - when the first poll tax bills hit the mats. The previous Secretary of State for the Environment, Kenneth Baker, offered them reassurance by pointing to the Green Paper figures (see Table 14.1) which showed that a narrow majority (51%) of households would actually gain from the introduction of the poll tax - that is their local tax bills would be smaller under poll tax than under domestic rates.

Table 14.1: **Households gaining and losing with full replacement of domestic rates by the community charge - by type of household (Great Britain thousand households)**

	Single Pensioner	Other single adult	Two adults	Three adults	All households
POUNDS PER WEEK					
Losers					
10 +	-	-	0	50	50
5 -10	-	-	75	425	500
2 - 5	0	75	1325	1125	2585
1 - 2	25	100	1625	425	2175
0 - 1	375	275	3750	325	472
Total losers	400	475	6800	2350	10000
Gainers					
0 - 1	1700	775	2800	200	5475
1 - 2	250	350	1275	100	1975
2 - 5	350	600	1400	100	2450
5 -10	75	100	350	25	575
10 +	25	25	50	0	100
Total gainers	2400	1850	5875	425	10575

Note : 0 = less than 12,500 households

Source: *Department of the Environment, 1986a.*

However, so far as I am aware, no Minister or political commentator has spelt out the electoral arithmetic which is implied by the household figures in Table 14.1. It is worth exploring this issue.

The electoral arithmetic

One feature to notice in Table 14.1 is that the majority of single adult households will gain from the poll tax. Conversely, the majority of households with three or more adults will find their bills are increased. From this follows the important point that the average number of electors in households where bills will increase is larger than the average number of electors in households where bills will fall. How much does it alter the 50-50 picture which Ministers have presented? Well in Table 14.2 we have converted the household numbers into the numbers of electors who are members of gaining and losing households.

Table 14.2: Electors in households gaining and losing with full replacement of domestic rates by the community charge - by type of household (Great Britain thousand households)

	Single Pensioner	Other single adult	Two adults	Three adults	All households
POUNDS PER WEEK					
Losers					
10 +	-	-	0	175[a]	175
5 - 10	-	-	150	1488[a]	1638
2 - 5	0	75	2650	3825[b]	6550
1 - 2	25	100	3250	1445[b]	4820
0 - 1	375	275	7500	1105[b]	9255
Total losers	400	475	13600	8038[b]	22438
Gainers					
0 - 1	1700	775	5600	660[c]	8735
1 - 2	250	350	2550	330[c]	3480
2 - 5	350	600	2800	330[c]	4080
5 - 10	75	100	700	80[d]	955
10 +	25	25	100	0[d]	150
Total gainers	2400	1850	11750	1400	17400

Note: [a] average size of "three +" adult households assumed to be 3.5
 [b] average size of "three +" adult households assumed to be 3.4
 [c] average size of "three +" adult households assumed to be 3.3
 [d] average size of "three +" adult households assumed to be 3.2

Source: Author's computations

The figures show that out of every 100 electors, there are 56 who live in households which will find themselves worse off under poll tax and 44 living in households where bills fall under poll tax.

Table 14.2 also enables us to compare the numbers of electors in those households which are the largest losers and gainers - say those with a change in bills of more than £2 a week/£100 a year. Here the numbers look even worse for the popularity of the poll tax. The ratio is 62 large losers to 38 large gainers - and there are over 8.3 million electors in households with bill increases of over £100 a year. [Remember as well that all this excludes the losses that will be experienced by those at present receiving full rebates, when plans to introduce a 20% minimum payment of rates are introduced.]

These are the average figures for Great Britain. The proportions of gainers to losers will vary from area to area. Perhaps there is the feeling that this will not matter too much to Conservative MPs because (1) won't the increases in bills tend to be larger in Labour controlled authorities?, and (2) within each authority won't the poll tax tend to hit opposition voters living in the lowest rateable value properties rather than their own supporters who tend to live in the better parts of the authority?

Unfortunately for MPs seeking comfort from such reasoning only the second proposition is true. It is true that ultimately the new system will increase average bills most in local authorities where there is both high spending and low domestic rateable values. However, when the new system is introduced in England and Wales on 1 April 1990 the changes in average bills which will occur will be small, because of the "safety netting" procedure which the Government will set up to control changes in local authorities' income from grants and non-domestic rates. This means that average bills do not immediately shoot up in high spending Labour authorities and plummet in low spending Conservative authorities.[1] In fact these initial changes in average bills (and it is these initial changes which will be in place as the next election approaches) do not seem to be directed at Labour strongholds.[2]

Constituency variations

The small changes in average bills lead to what we will call "constituency variations" and these are important because quite small changes in average bills can lead to the "56 to 44" ratio of losers to gainers changing quite dramatically. Luckily the DoE have recently worked out the changes in average bills in each local tax collecting authority

Table 14.3: Poll Tax - areas where more than 65% of electors live in households with increases in local tax bills on 1 April 1990 (figures in brackets = % change in average household bill)

Local tax collecting authority	Parliamentary constituencies affected
Weymouth & Portland (25.8)	Dorset South (Con)
Leominster (25.7)	Leominster (Con)
Torridge (25.2)	Devon West and Torridge (Con)
Pendle (24.4)	Pendle (Con)
Fenland (23.7)	Cambridgeshire NE (Lib)
Forest of Dean (23.3)	Gloucestershire West (Con)
Burnley (23.3)	Burnley (Lab)
South Herefordshire (22.8)	Hereford (Con)
	Leominster (Con)
Hereford (22.7)	Hereford (Con)
Aylesbury Vale (22.6)	Aylesbury (Con)
	Buckingham (Con)
Wandsworth (22.2)	Battersea (Lab)
	Putney (Con)
	Tooting (Lab)
Milton Keynes (21.7)	Buckingham (Con)
	Milton Keynes (Con)
Hyndburn (21.0)	Hyndburn (Con)
Portsmouth (20.5)	Portsmouth South (SDP)
	Portsmouth North (Con)
Bolsover (20.3)	Bolsover (Lab)
Colchester (19.4)	Colchester North (Con)
	Colchester South and Maldon (Con)
Greenwich (18.5)	Greenwich (SDP)
Hammersmith & Fulham (18.2)	Fulham (Lab)
	Hammersmith (Lab)
Braintree (17.9)	Saffron Walden (Con)
West Dorset (17.5)	Dorset West (Con)
	Dorset South (Con)
North Dorset (17.4)	Dorset North (Con)
Runnymede (17.2)	Chertsey and Walton (Con)
	Surrey NW (Con)
North Devon (16.4)	Devon North (Con)
Hastings (15.8)	Hastings and Rye (Con)
Leicester (15.5)	Leicester East (Con)
	Leicester South (Con)
	Leicester West (Lab)
North Warwickshire (15.1)	Warwickshire North (Con)
Crawley (15.1)	Crawley (Con)

Source: Author's computations; Crewe and Fox (1984).

based on the 1986/87 spending figures for local authorities. We use these to list those local authorities where average bills change by more than 15%. Where average bills rise by more than 15% we can safely estimate that more than 65% of electors will be "losers" and where average bills fall by more than 15% we can safely estimate that more than 50% of electors will be gainers.[3] The tax collection areas where there are such changes are listed in Tables 14.3 (p.213) and 14.4 along with the Parliamentary constituencies which are affected.

Table 14.4: Poll Tax - areas where more than 50% of electors live in households with reductions in local tax bills on 1 April 1990 (figures in brackets = % change in average household bill)

Local tax collecting authority	Parliamentary constituencies affected
Kensington & Chelsea (-46.4)	Chelsea (Con)
	Kensington (Con)
Westminster (-33.7)	City of London and Westminster S (Con)
	Westminster North (Con)
West Lancashire (-22.7)	Lancashire West (Con)
	Chorley (Con)
Beverley (-22.6)	Beverley (Con)
	Boothferry(Con)
Fylde (-21.9)	Fylde (Con)
South Staffordshire (-18.9)	Staffordshire South (Con)
South Buckinghamshire (-18.8)	Beaconsfield (Con)
Rushcliffe (-17.4)	Rushcliffe (Con)
Lichfield (-17.2)	Cannock and Burntwood (Con)
	Staffordshire SE (Con)
Macclesfield (-17.1)	Macclesfield (Con)
	Tatton (Con)
South Cambridgeshire (-16.6)	Cambridgeshire SE (Con)
	Cambridgeshire SW (Con)
Castle Morpeth (-16.4)	Berwick upon Tweed (Lib)
	Hexham (Con)
	Wansbeck (Lab)
Wyre (-16.0)	Wyre (Con)
	Lancaster (Con)
Brentwood (-15.9)	Brentwood and Ongar (Con)
Chiltern (-15.4)	Chesham and Amersham (Con)

Source: Author's computations; Crewe and Fox (1984).

Notes

1. In early 1987 the Government's intentions were that in the first year average bills would be unchanged apart from the factors mentioned in note 2 below. There have been numerous changes of mind since then, and the eventual implmentation of safety nets is described in the next two chapters.

2. In fact the only changes which occur are those due to alterations in the distribution of the burdens of precepts between rating authorities (precepts will be sent on the basis of number of adults rather than on rateable value) and the replacement of the domestic rate relief grant by a straight per adult grant.

3. The estimate of the percentage of electors living in losing households is based on knowledge derived from a study in Durham (The Poll Tax: Its Impact on Residents of County Durham, available from Durham County Council) which measures the percentage change in bills for 160,000 households in County Durham using data on rateable values and the number of adults in each household.

15.
THE IMPLEMENTATION PROBLEM: DESCRIPTION

The implementation problem refers here to the wider political and economic problems associated with the introduction of the reforms, as well as to the predictable problems of administering the poll tax. From mid-1989 the poll tax grew into an increasingly serious political problem for the Government. It culminated in what appeared to be a severe political crisis by the spring of 1990, with the Prime Minister setting up a ministerial review of the operation of the poll tax shortly before the local government elections of May 1990. Unexpectedly, although the overall result was the worst the Conservatives had experienced since 1979, Government ministers derived sufficient comfort from good Conservative results in Wandsworth and Westminster - where low levels of poll tax were set by local Conservatives - to secure some respite from the immediate political crisis. This was sufficient to ensure both the survival of the poll tax and that the review was limited to tinkering at the edges and not changing the fundamental flat-rate principle of the tax.

This chapter will provide a description of the implementation problem concentrating particularly on the revenue support grant settlement of early 1990. In the next chapter there will be an analysis of the main political and economic features of the crisis. In particular the question of why the Government rather than local authorities appeared to suffer most of the blame for high poll taxes will be addressed. In the final chapter there will be a brief evaluation of the reforms.

After the passage of the Local Government Finance Bill in the summer of 1988 there followed a quiet news period with respect to poll tax. The introduction of the poll tax in Scotland in April 1989 and the problems experienced there in its early months had been very much neglected by the London based national newspapers. Public consciousness in England of the imminent arrival of the new tax was rather slow to emerge and only gathered momentum with the commencement of the registration process in the spring of 1989.

There can be little doubt that many Conservative MPs were extremely anxious about the approaching introduction of the tax. The speeches of many Conservative MPs in the important second reading of the Local Government Finance Bill in the House of Commons had been critical of the Government's plans. It was obvious to many of them that the flat rate principle of the tax would be seen by many of their constituents to be not quite as "fair" as Ministers were fond of describing it. There had been an unsuccessful attempt to introduce banding, with higher taxes for those with higher incomes, through an amendment to the bill put forward by Conservative MP, Michael Mates. Despite the misgivings, the bill received a majority of 72 at second reading, with only 17 Conservative MPs voting against the measure. Ian Aitken, the Guardian's political correspondent, was probably very accurate when he stated:

> ... the truth about poll tax is that, far from there being only 17 Conservatives opposed to the idea, it would probably be very difficult to muster 17 Tory MPs who genuinely and unequivocally support it. In the Cabinet itself, I very much doubt if Mrs Thatcher can count on the wholehearted endorsement of more than one or two colleagues besides her Secretary of State for the Environment.[1]

If there were great misgivings in the Conservative party about the poll tax, the general approach of the Government was, throughout, one of confidence and attempting to offer reassurance to any doubters. There was a long string of DOE press releases giving good news about the poll tax. Given his later prominent role in criticising the implementation, even indeed the principle,[2] of the poll tax, it is interesting to note a press release highlighting a speech by Dr Rhodes Boyson in December 1986, when he was Minister of State for Local Government, (Department of the Environment, 1986c):

> People are overwhelmingly in favour of the Government's plans to abolish domestic rates in England and Wales, Local Government Minister Dr Rhodes Boyson said today.
>
> Responses to the Government's Green Paper 'Paying for Local Government' show that those who support abolition outnumber those who don't by two to one ...
>
> "... We are confident that the community charge can be implemented smoothly and effectively and we have explained in the document published today *exactly how it will work in practice* ... we are convinced that the new system will be fairer, easier to understand and, most important of all, that it will restore local accountability and thereby enhance local democracy. This is surely a common goal around which we can all unite," he concluded. [Author's italics]

Exemplifications of levels of poll tax since 1986 had always given rise to worries among some MPs because they highlighted the potential rise in bills facing some of their constituents. The response of ministers was to emphasise that the figures could be reduced if local authorities reduced their spending. The Secretary of State for the Environment Mr Ridley claimed that this was, in fact, happening, because the impending arrival of the poll tax was forcing a new realism into the expenditure plans of some of the high spending local authorities. Thus at the Conservative Party Conference in October 1987 he stated:

> The community charge is working already. Even in the most intransigent left-wing councils we hear of cuts; even Lambeth is looking for cuts now.

The exemplifications of poll tax levels based on 1988/89 local authorities' budgets showed that the average level of poll tax in England would have risen to £246, compared to £226 in 1987/88. However, the Department of the Environment news release on the subject was titled 'Latest figures show massive reductions in the highest community charges'. There was a reduction in the illustrative poll tax level for Camden of £143, and one of £113 for Hackney, and also £100 for Lewisham. However, this was hardly a triumph for the poll tax because as the Secretary of State said in the House of Commons "this is largely the result of government action to reduce the spending of the highest spending authorities in London through rate capping".

Inflation, pay, and the rising burden of local taxation 1986 to 1990

In fact the overall picture was not reassuring. The introduction of the poll tax in Scotland in April 1989 did not appear to have provided any break in the gradual upward trend of local government expenditure. The announcement about local authority expenditure and revenue support grant in Scotland for 1989/90, made in July 1988, for the first year of poll tax had provided for an increase in the amount of Aggregate Exchequer Grant of 5.5% (this was greater than the grant increases of 4.6% in England and 5.1% in Wales). Expenditure provision was for an increase of 4.6% above Scottish authorities' adjusted budgets for 1988/89, or 6% net of specific grants. The Scottish Secretary stated that the implied average poll tax in Scotland arising from the settlement was £267. However, actual tax levels for 1989/90 emerged as just over £300, around 16% higher than Government forecasts. There was in fact only a small increase in the volume of expenditure because the official figures had failed to take into account the large use of balances in the previous year in Scotland, and also had made the patently unrealistic assumption that the level of non-payment under poll tax would be the same as it had been for rates. Moreover, the reforms had brought the removal of severe grant penalties in Scotland, often over £2 per £1 of expenditure in 1988/89, and both Midwinter (1989b) and John (1989) concluded that this had encouraged some local authorities to increase spending.

One of the problems facing local authorities from the mid-1980s onwards was the acceleration in pay increases, as public sector workers attempted to catch up with the private sector (see Table 15.1), which meant that settlements based on inflation estimates such as the GDP deflator, faced local authorities with the prospect of either making large cuts in the volume of services or increasing the level of local taxes. Nor could the responsibility be placed upon local authorities as negotiations on teachers' and police pay were in the hands of central government. The teachers' pay settlement in 1986, following extensive strike action, was a major source of the rising pressure on local authority finances.

Table 15.1: Pay and Prices

	1985/86	1986/87	1987/88	1988/89
Local authority pay and prices	5.6	6.2	7.0	7.2
GDP Deflator	5.4	3.4	5.3	7.3
Retail Price Index	5.9	3.2	4.0	6.0

Source: Department of the Environment (1989)

The spring and summer of 1988 was, in fact, the start of the period when the Government started to severely underestimate the level of inflation. At first described by the Chancellor as a "blip", the increase in the RPI had risen from under 4% in the spring of 1988 to 6.5% by the fourth quarter as compared to a forecast in the March 1988 budget of 4%. This official underestimation of the rate of inflation was an important component of Scottish local government's "overspend" of 6.5% in the first year of poll tax. This overspend was mirrored in England, where total revenue expenditure exceeded provision by 6.7% in 1989/90. This had also generated a significant increase in the level of local taxation with the implied average poll tax bill rising to £275 in 1989/90, the last year of the domestic rating system.

The March 1989 Budget again included overoptimistic estimates of inflation — that it would fall to 5.5% by the fourth quarter of 1989 and to 4.5% by the middle of 1990. The background to the negotiations over the grant and expenditure provision for English local government was one where there was primacy for the Government's wish to get on top of inflation[3] and to continue the reduction in public spending as a proportion of GDP. This was more difficult than in earlier years because the growth of GDP was slowing. In addition to local government's claims for more generous central funding there were other urgent priorities for public spending, especially transport and the National Health Service. A new framework of public expenditure planning (H.M.Treasury, 1988) also ensured that increases in central grants would directly increase the planning total of central government expenditure whilst contributing, at the same time, to a reduction in the increase of local government expenditure financed by local taxes (Hogg, 1989).

The negotiations also took place against the background of growing concern amongst Conservative MPs because the problems, anticipated by some of them years earlier, were approaching ever nearer. There were a number of separate issues of concern. First, it was anticipated that the average level of poll tax would depend upon the amount of grant Government gave to local government for 1990/91 - although as we shall discuss in the next chapter this was a more difficult issue than many appreciated. Second, there was considerable resentment from politicians, local and central, over the plans for safety nets which were usually seen as a subsidy to high spending authorities provided at the expense of low spending authorities and their residents.[4] Third, there was an increasingly keen awareness that some households would be facing very large increases in bills. This was an especially sensitive issue for Conservative MPs holding seats in the north and north-west where typically rateable values were very low.

The July announcement: aggregates and safety net decisions

Thus there were conflicting pressures in making the trade-off between the level of grant provided for 1990/91 and the ultimate level of poll tax bills. The announcement of the main grant and expenditure aggregates in England for 1990/91 was made in July 1989 and included decisions on the safety net mechanism. It showed that the decision had leaned towards little easing in the fiscal pressure on local authorities. The announcement stressed the overspending and rising expenditure of local authorities. It noted that in the current year, 1989/90, English local authorities had budgeted for current expenditure of about £30.3 billion, £1.2 billion more than the Government had provided for in the last RSG Settlement. Also local authorities had budgeted to increase spending by 9% compared with 1988/89. It stated that:

> Over the last four years local authority expenditure will have increased by 13% in real terms. This is excessive.

The amount of revenue spending which the announcement deemed appropriate for local government for 1990/91 was £32.8 billion, which was £1.2 billion (roughly 3.8%) more than local authorities had budgeted for in 1989/90. The amount of Aggregate External Finance to be made available was set at £23.1 billion, an increase of 8.5% from the equivalent amount of finance in 1989/90.

There were changes in the safety net arrangements which, compared to the previous proposals, improved the first year situation of long run gaining areas and worsened the situation of long run losing areas. Instead of complete protection for losing authorities it was now proposed that they should bear £25 per adult of their initial losses in the first year. This would enable gaining areas to receive between 40% and 50% of their gains in the first year, with a ceiling on contributions to the safety net pool of £75 per adult.

In addition the July announcement included two schemes of special protection. First, there was special protection for areas with low rateable values, which would, of course, have higher domestic sector tax contributions under the poll tax. This gave a maximum protection of £25 per adult for charging authorities where average domestic rateable value per hereditament was £130 or less and a tapering scale of support where average domestic rateable value was between £130 and £150. The total cost of this was £87 million.

Second, £100 million was to be given in transitional grant to the inner London boroughs and to the City, in order to give protection against high poll taxes resulting from "wasteful expenditure inherited from ILEA", which it was argued would take the boroughs some time to eliminate.

The Secretary of State summarised as follows:

> ... under these proposals if local authorities control their spending and improve their efficiency, the average community charge need not be higher than about £275, and could be lower. We recognise the particular problems some authorities face

The Implementation Problem: Description   223

through the change to the new system, and we are providing extra help targeted on these areas. but it will be for local authorities to set their budgets, and for community chargepayers to judge whether the amount they are asked to pay is justified.

The fact that the implied average level of charge from the figures, according to the Secretary of State, was, at £275, more or less the same level as average rate bills per adult in England in 1989/90 followed the typical pattern of Settlements throughout the 1980s. This was that there would be zero or very low average local tax increases if local authorities spent in line with the Settlement expenditure guidelines or provision (Gibson and Travers, 1986). Unfortunately, it had never worked because each year the expenditure guideline had been at or below the rate of inflation, and local authorities had exceeded this guideline by increasing spending by a larger figure. The tougher the Settlement guideline expenditure increase in relation to the rate of inflation, then the lower the notional rate increase compared to inflation, but the greater the likely overspend from local government. On this criterion this Settlement for 1990/91 looked to be particularly optimistic over the level of expenditure. The increase was only 3.8% over 1989/90 budgets at a time when inflation was over 8%, and the Treasury's forecast that inflation would fall to 4.5% by mid-1990 had lost credibility.

Many Conservative backbenchers felt that the change in safety nets had not gone far enough and the simultaneous availability of exemplifications, based on local authorities' 1989/90 budgets, led to the Secretary of State being put under much pressure from nervous backbenchers. Several now objected to the need to make safety net contributions, although throughout 1988 they had voted in favour of reforms when larger safety nets payments had been planned. Sir Rhodes Boyson, who had been a Minister advocating strongly the operational aspects of those plans in 1986 and 1987, now asked in the July debate:

Does my right hon. Friend (the Secretary of State) agree that to transfer community charge money from provident to improvident authorities under the safety net arrangements is to undermine the very basis of the community charge ...

However, there were awkward exceptions to such generalisations in the English system. Although Conservative controlled authorities tended to be contributors to safety nets, rather than receivers, and vice-versa for Labour controlled authorities, there were numerous exceptions. Thus Labour members could object, in the later January 1990 debate on revenue support grant, to the safety net contributions paid by Labour controlled authorities such as Birmingham and Knowsley.

The extent of the difficulties was also shown in a contribution by Mrs Elizabeth Peacock the Conservative MP for Batley and Spen who represented an area which received safety net payments and was also worried about the impact of the poll tax on individual households:

> ... even though we receive £89 (per adult) from it (the safety net), can he (the Secretary of State) help me explain to two pensioners in my constituency, whose current rates payable are £267, why they still have to pay £624 under the new system?

The poll tax troubles had arrived. According to *The Guardian* (Travis, 1989) backbenchers now believed the poll tax to be the single issue most damaging to their general election prospects. There was also a common belief, even at this stage, that it was most improbable that local government would make cuts in spending sufficient to give only a 3.8% increase in revenue spending. Certainly the local authority associations presented a unanimous view to the new Secretary of State in September, which was that the Government's £275 average target for poll tax was completely unrealistic.

In addition it was becoming more apparent that public opinion was moving against the poll tax. An NOP survey published in September showed growing opposition to the new tax with 63% of the electorate opposing the tax and only 27% supporting the introduction of the poll tax, compared with 54% opposing and 33% supporting when a similar poll was carried out in February 1988. The survey linked opposition to poll tax with the impact the tax would have on individuals, with 66% of C2s regarding the tax as unfair, as did 43% of those in the survey who had voted Tory in the 1987 election. The implication was drawn that many losers would be marginal voters in marginal constituencies (Travers and Moon, 1989).

Undoubtedly over the late summer and early autumn there was a build up of Conservative backbencher nervousness and pressure on the Government. In September Sir Rhodes Boyson led a deputation of backbench Conservative MPs to urge the new Secretary of State, Christopher Patten, to revise the safety nets proposals. Under such pressure, the Secretary of State now had more political backing to secure extra funding from the Treasury and the Government quickly produced two concessions and announced them at the Conservative Party Conference.

First, gaining areas were to be relieved completely of contributing to the safety nets pool after the first year of the new system. This was instead to be directly funded by the Treasury at a cost of £400 million in 1991/92 and £200 million in 1992/93.

Second, a scheme of household based relief was introduced[5] to compensate one or two adult households where the notional poll tax bills in 1990/91 was more than £156 above their rates bill for 1989/90, after taking into account any rebate entitlements. In addition relief was offered to pensioners and disabled who were not ratepayers or their partners to limit their bill to £156. This relief was estimated to cost £385 million in 1990/91 in England. The scheme was also to last for a further two years, with details to be announced later. Relief was only offered on a notional poll tax bill, which the DOE calculated each authority should charge in the forthcoming Settlement, based on a standard (to be 4.64%) increase in spending (net of specific grants), compared to 1989/90 budgets. Any excess above this figure would receive no relief.

These concessions also applied to Wales[6] and Scotland. The public expenditure costs of transitional grants is shown in Table 15.2. Compared to the planned situation in July, the Secretary of State had secured an extra £385 million for 1990/91 and an extra £650 million for 1991/92 in transitional grants for England.

Table 15.2: Transitional grants – England

	1990-91 plans	1991-92 plans	1992-93 plans
Inner London Education Grant	100	70	50
Low rateable value area grant	87	475	275
Area protection grant	0		
Transitional relief	385	235	180
Total	572	775	505

Source: *The Government's Expenditure Plans 1990-91 to 1992-93, Ch. 21, Cm 1021, January 1990*

However, as Table 15.3 (p.226) shows the public expenditure plans published in January 1990 were still maintaining that Aggregate External Finance would increase by only 5% for 1991/92 and by only 2% for 1992/93.

Table 15.3: Aggregate External Finance, England

	1989-90 estimated outturn	1990-91 plans	1991-92 plans	1992-93 plans
Revenue/Rate Support Grant	9613	9490	20550	21130
Non-domestic rates	9616	10428		
Area protection grant			480	280
Specific grants	2841	3182	3230	3340
Total	22070	23100	24260	24750

Source: The Government's Expenditure Plans 1990-91 to 1992-93, Ch. 21, Cm 1021, January 1990

Negotiations on the Standard Spending Assessments

A major determinant of grant receipts in the new system was, of course, the assessment of the level of relative spending needs of each local authority. Discussions had been underway in the Grants Working Group since early 1989 on alternative methods of assessing the costs of providing a standard level of services in each authority and area - the Standard Spending Assessments (SSAs). Options had been drawn up by the Needs Assessment Sub-Group and presented to the CCLGF in July 1989. The amount of material considered may be judged from the fact that the sub-group met 41 times and discussed 142 papers.

As explained in Chapter 4, each extra £1 per adult of assessment would produce an extra £1 per adult of needs grant for an authority. An analysis of the options put forward by the different local authority associations and the DOE (AMA, 1989) showed just how much depended upon the choices made by the Government. The range between the best and the worst combinations of assessment options amounted to over £100 per adult in 32 of the 69 tax areas in London and the metropolitan areas. In Hackney the range was nearly £399 and no inner London area had a range smaller than £139. In Knowsley the assessment range was over £217 and in Birmingham £167; only 5 areas had an assessment range narrower than £50.

The provisional Settlement and the Final Report

It was, of course, a zero sum game, in that the SSAs simply determined the distribution of a fixed available amount of Revenue Support Grant - £1 of grant gained by one area would be at the expense of £1 lost to other areas. In November the Government's consultation paper on the Revenue Support Grant for 1990/91 was announced. This largely confirmed the previous grant aggregates but included SSAs for authorities and exemplifications showing the amount of grant to each charging area and the resulting level of poll tax, if the Government's spending assumptions were followed in each area. The arithmetic had changed slightly and the Secretary of State again concentrated on the poll tax for spending at Standard Spending:

> If authorities were each to spend at the level of their SSA, the community charge in each area would be about £278 ... This figure, the community charge for Standard Spending will be the benchmark for accountability. It will appear on the bill which each chargepayer will receive and will help chargepayers to assess the policies and performance of their authorities. In this way councils will be made accountable to those who must pay for their activities.

The figure of £278 was reckoned to be overoptimistic by the chairman of each local authority association. New Labour shadow Environment Secretary, Bryan Gould, stated that the gap between unrealistic assumptions and reality could mean local authorities spending £2.5 billion more than the assumed figure. He also concentrated on the threat to services and the bind in which local authorities found themselves: "... they are faced with government sanctioned pay increases to teachers, firemen and policemen far in excess of the rate of inflation, and ... they will have no option but to cut services further".

The serious potential effect on the average level of poll tax can be seen by looking at the basic arithmetic of the settlement. Table 15.4 (p.228) shows that a 5% overspend on the Government's provision (net of specific grant) would lead to an increase in the average poll tax from £277.9 to £319.2 - an increase of nearly 15%. This was the high gearing effect caused by the large proportion of external finance at the target level of spending. In addition, local authority treasurers were likely to assume at least a 5% write off on poll tax collection, further boosting the average charge to £336.

The Revenue Support Grant Reports laid before the House in January 1990 brought some minor changes from the November consultation. There was one additional concession - local authorities were to be paid 25% of their grant in the first two months of the year, which was estimated to be worth about £180 million in increased interest receipts.

Table 15.4: Revenue support grant: the basic arithmetic

	£bn.	£ per adult
Government provision for local government spending (net of specific grants)	29.8	835.0
Less revenue support grant	9.5	265.6
Less national non-domestic rates	10.4	292.5
Equals Poll Tax for Standard Spending	9.9	277.9
Plus 5% spending above Government provision	11.4	319.2
Plus 5% allowance for collection write offs	12.0	336.0

There was a significant redistribution in the needs assessments with a marked improvement in the assessments of the inner London boroughs and the south-east counties. The change in inner London was due to a large increase in the share of education assessments going to inner London at the expense of other areas. The improvement in the relative position of south-east counties resulted mainly from the decision to extend the higher cost adjustment to areas outside London. Correspondingly the needs assessments for many northern counties and cities suffered.

The large increase in inner London needs assessments narrowed the excess of assumed spending in relation to SSA there. However, there remained large differences between the assumed spending of different local authorities in relation to their SSAs. This brought with it large differences between areas in the level of the long run poll tax - with the range varying from £573 in Haringey to £95 in the Isles of Scilly. In addition contributions to and receipts from safety nets, as well as receipts of the special grants to low rateable value areas and to inner London areas, brought large differences to the assumed or guideline poll tax for 1990/91 and the long run poll tax.

Table 15.5 shows the overall regional effects of the new system and Table 15.6 (p.231) the particular effect of the changes in needs assessments.

The rapidly escalating crisis

From November there was increased media coverage, which regularly made the reforms a leading news item and put them on the front pages of the national newspapers for the next six months. There was a severe political crisis for the Conservatives measured by the rapid movement of the opinion polls against the poll tax and the Government. The Labour party had overtaken the Conservatives in the spring of 1989 and by the autumn had extended that lead to double figures. There had been a temporary abatement before Christmas, but by February an NOP survey had put the Labour lead back up to 12% and in an ICM poll in March the Labour lead was over 20%. This latter figure was extremely significant because no government had ever fallen more than 20 points behind in the polls against the main opposition party and won outright at the next election. 51% of those in the ICM sample thought that Mrs Thatcher should step down from the leadership. The March NOP poll found that poll tax was far and away the most decisive influence on people's voting intentions.

Table 15.5: Regional effects of the new local government finance system, 1990/91 compared to 1989/90

	Change in non-domestic rate income	Change in government grants	Net change in income to local authorities (before safety nets)		Safety net contribution (+)/ receipt(-)	Net change in income to local authorities (after safety nets)
	£m	£m	£m	£ per adult	£m	£m
North	52.8	-223.4	-170.5	-74	-131.9	-38.7
Yorkshire & Humberside	94.6	-207.5	-112.9	-24	-27.0	-85.9
North West	84.3	-373.8	-289.4	-78	-269.3	-20.1
East Midlands	134.0	-175.2	-41.2	-14	-36.5	-4.7
West Midlands	145.3	21.7	167.0	43	88.8	78.2
East Anglia	90.6	-49.8	40.8	27	19.4	21.4
South East	298.4	414.1	712.5	89	333.2	389.3
South West	301.1	-284.1	17.0	5	-1.8	18.8
Inner London	-1224.5	673.3	-548.2	-321	-208.1	-340.1
Outer London	23.4	201.8	225.2	67	56.5	168.7

Source: Parliamentary written answers, 12 December 1989

There had been a large number of news items on the reforms which had shown the resentment and anger of losers from the changes and, as the theory implied, it was not offset by applause from the gainers. A prime example was the effects of the revaluation of non-domestic property announced in December 1989. This combined with the introduction of the uniform business rate implied a long-term shift in the rate burden of £1.8 billion from the North to the South. This would seem to be a desirable shift both in terms of reflecting actual relative values and in providing an extra incentive to business location in the north. However, the Government got no credit. As with area safety nets and transitional relief on the domestic side, the Government had, under pressure, introduced a 5 year phasing in of the changes with limits on the annual increase of 15% for small businesses and 20% for large and medium size businesses. Consequently, reductions to long term gainers had to be limited to cuts of 10.5% in the first year and 13% in the second. The West Midlands region was the largest absolute gainer from the revaluation and the response of the West Midlands CBI working party on rates was to claim "... justice delayed for five years is effectively justice denied".

Problems intensified most though after the release of the final grant figures in January and in the immediate reaction from individual local authority treasurers, in response to media enquiries, that they expected the poll tax in their area to be much larger than the Government's guideline. Thus very quickly after the settlement the news was dominated by stories of the high poll taxes to be expected. The Secretary of State's response was to tell the House of Commons on the 18th of January that "If some of the horrendous figures for the community charge which we hear bandied about are actually set next year, we will have absolutely no hesitation in capping the councils concerned". Much of the early attention concentrated on the unexpectedly high charges in the traditionally Conservative and low spending county areas of the south and south-east. There were objections from many local authorities that their SSAs were unjust and underestimated the cost of providing services. Attention here also centred on the south-east with Berkshire County Council taking the first steps towards a legal challenge to the Government's measure of its SSA. This reflected the confusion generated in the growing crisis - Berkshire had in fact had the highest increase in its SSA of any shire county in 1990/91! Meanwhile, the media paid no attention to the northern counties where increases in SSA had been much lower than in the south-east. It was a frenetic and distorted public debate. It was even a commonly

Table 15.6: Regional effects of the changes in needs assessments 1990/91 SSAs compared to 1989/90 GREs

	Net change in income to local authorities 1989/90	Net change in income to local authorities 1990/91	Difference
	£m	£m	£m
North	-142.6	-170.5	-28.0
Yorkshire & Humberside	-55.4	-112.9	-57.5
North West	-252.8	-289.4	-36.6
East Midlands	-8.9	-41.2	-32.2
West Midlands	169.3	167.0	-2.3
East Anglia	46.1	40.8	-5.3
South East	547.6	712.5	164.9
South West	35.3	17.0	-18.3
Greater London	-338.5	-323.1	15.4
Inner London	-568.9	-548.2	20.7
Outer London	230.5	225.2	-5.3

Source: Parliamentary written answers, 12 December 1989

held view by mid-February that "it is the spending plans of the mainly Tory-led county councils which have driven up predictions of the average poll tax from the Government's £278 to £380".[7] By then the Secretary of State had announced that the SSAs - which, for the previous three years, the Government had stated would be left unchanged for 5 years in order to give stability - would be open to change if arguments of substance could be put by local authorities or their associations. The Government was hinting that it might meet what was perceived as a need for more grant to be channelled towards the south next year (1991/92). Nothing could have been more stupid - the area had the largest long-run gains from the change in the system, and the autumn decision that the Exchequer would fund the safety net contributions from 1991/92 onwards meant that it was already "built-in" that the south would fully secure the extra grant embodied in its full gains.

Embarrassment was intensified by the resignation from the party whips by numbers of Conservative councillors both in West Oxfordshire and in Beverley. By mid-February the newspapers were carrying stories that the Environment Secretary was to launch a fundamental review.

Much attention was given to tax capping, with rumours of impending widespread capping, which many, including the local authority associations, argued against on the grounds that capping would be completely against the principles of relying on local accountability which was the fundamental idea of the reforms. Eventually 20 councils were capped on the basis of exceeding two criteria - spending at £26 per adult more than the higher of 12.5% and £75 per adult above their SSA.[8] None of the capped councils were Conservative controlled, which was not surprising, even given previous ministerial talk of shire county overspending. What was surprising though was that the settlement guideline figures for several of the authorities were at levels which later were deemed to exceed the threshold levels for tax capping. The spending reductions required amounted to £200 million, reducing the national average poll tax by less than £6.

There appeared to be three pieces of good news for the Government in March. This was that the levels of charge in the Conservative controlled London boroughs of Wandsworth and Westminster, were actually below their guideline figures, at £148 and £190, respectively. Also Conservative controlled Bradford announced the lowest poll tax amongst the metropolitan areas at £276. This was at last the sort of signal the Government had been looking for - that Conservative councils cost less.

Nevertheless, the popularity of the Government did not improve and in advance of the local government elections there was a story that there were plans to introduce major amendments to the new community charge which would require legislation in the next session of Parliament. The local government elections were regarded as likely to be a major test of the public's attitude to poll tax and the Government responsible for introducing it. It was anticipated that the results would be awful for the Conservatives.

The May 1990 local elections

The election results although very bad for the Conservatives - the swing to Labour was 11% and the Conservatives had a lower share of the vote than in any previous election since 1973 - were not as bad as anticipated. Also the most striking results were swings to the Conservatives in Wandsworth and Westminster and against Labour in some London boroughs where they had set high poll taxes.

Mrs Thatcher's swift reaction was to claim this as a vindication of the community charge:

> The results in London where people have experienced the worst excesses of Labour councils, show that the message about the community charge is getting through. People want good services, efficiently and economically delivered in local government. And where they have it - in Wandsworth - they vote to keep it. And where they don't have it - in Ealing and Hillingdon - they vote for the Tories who they know are the only people to provide it.

There was also a marked increase in turnout which appeared to be over 50% in many areas - an increase of at least 6% compared to the most recent local elections. This combined to give the general impression that the introduction of the poll tax had brought some tangible increase in the interest of local electors and, therefore, in local accountability. It will be suggested later that this is to give the poll tax credit for increasing local turnout, which is largely undeserved.

Peter Jenkins (1990) concluded in *The Independent* that this was probably sufficient to lift the aura of doom which had recently surrounded the Government, and that it ought to calm the panic on the Tory back benches and quieten speculation about Mrs Thatcher's leadership.

The expenditure outcome

An analysis by the Institute of Public Finance (Ramsdale, 1990) showed that total local authority net revenue expenditure was budgeted to rise by 11.9% in England and Wales. This was estimated to be a 3.5% real increase in spending, after allowing for inflation. However, given the rise in local authority pay and prices the increase in the volume of current expenditure was only 2% - see Table 15.7 (p. 234). Nearly all of the net volume increase stemmed from new duties imposed on local authorities by central government. It was estimated by CIPFA that implementing new duties, such as the national curriculum and local management of schools, would add 1.5% to local authority budgets. Nearly one-third of the volume increase was due to the extra resources used in local tax collection. Thus, collecting community charge and community charge rebates was budgeted to cost £588 million in England and Wales compared to £219 million for rate collection costs in 1989/90. Some further issues arising from the administration of the poll tax will be dealt with in the final chapter.

Table 15.7: Net current expenditure, 1990/91 compared to 1989/90

	Net current expenditure: 1989/90	1990/91	Year on year difference: cash	volume
	£m	£m	%	%
Inner London (exc. City)	2701.2	2602.1	-3.7	-10.8
Outer London	2917.9	3310.1	13.4	5.0
Metropolitan districts	7005.9	7560.0	7.9	-0.1
Metropolitan joint authorities	2780.5	3145.8	-13.1	5.0
Non-metropolitan counties	n.a	n.a	n.a	n.a.
Non-metropolitan districts	2560.2	2963.4	15.7	7.1
England	33249.7	36614.9	10.1	1.9

Source: Ramsdale (1990)

Notes

1. It also led Aitken to reflect:

    So what are we to make of a constitutional system which can throw up a political party which just six months after a near-landslide victory, is prepared to march en masse into the division lobby in support of a proposal which most of them regard as questionable, many of them regard as grossly unjust, and virtually all of them regard as a catastrophic vote-loser? Certainly it makes it difficult to retain the comfortable view that a system founded on the supposed supremacy of Parliament provides any effective protection against intellectual corruption

2. By April 1990 Dr Boyson was regretting on *Newsnight* the support he had previously given to changing from domestic rates.

3. Young (1989) writing in July 1989 judged that the Government's problems in order of importance were inflation, poll tax, the NHS, the environment, and water privatisation.

The Implementation Problem: Description 235

4. As the analysis in Chapter 4 demonstrated, this was a great oversimplification; in many cases it was a payment from gaining high rateable value areas to losing lower spending low rateable value areas.

5. The 1986 Green Paper had contained proposals that the poll tax should replace domestic rates gradually during a transition period, lasting up to 10 years where rates were highest. However, this had been abandoned for England, following a similar decision for Scotland because local government had objected to the increased complexity, bureaucracy, and expense of running two systems in parallel. This had been rather predictable from the start and it was little surprise when the proposal was abandoned during the introduction of the legislation for Scotland. Thus all the earlier work discussed in this book was written on the basis of no household level transitional relief.

6. In Wales transitional relief was a grant similar to the low rateable value areas grant in England.

7. This was reported by Travis (1990) but was the responsibility of Environment ministers themselves.

8. A useful guide to this and other features of the implementation of the reforms is provided in LGIU, 1990.

16.
THE IMPLEMENTATION PROBLEM: ANALYSIS

Given the Government's underlying objectives in introducing the poll tax and the associated reforms in local government finance, it presumably hoped that the poll tax would lead to a general reduction in local government expenditure, and induce pay restraint and efficiency savings in local government. This would keep the average level of poll tax down, whilst not having a severe effect on the provision of the main services. Nevertheless, it might not be too harmful if there were some high poll taxes as long as they could be seen to be the result of profligacy by Labour controlled councils. A few high poll taxes in Labour authorities would, according to the underlying rationale behind the reforms, encourage the final element of the Government's theory of local accountability to come into play - local electors turning out in greater numbers and switching their vote to the Conservatives in local elections.[1] What the Government surely didn't want was what actually happened - generally high levels of poll tax with them, rather than local councils, getting most of the blame. Given the Government's explicit, and implicit, objectives this chapter will assess how consistent and competent it has been in its implementation of the introduction of the poll tax.

The political crisis

There are two theoretically separate questions in relation to the political crisis:

(1) why was the political crisis caused by poll tax so large?

(2) why did the Government, rather than local authorities, get most of the blame?

The most common answer given to the first question has been that the crisis occurred because the average level of the charge was too high. Whereas, the average domestic rate bill was £275 per adult in 1989/90 the increase to over £360 in 1990/91 was, using this argument, the reason that the poll tax caused so much trouble. According to this view, if only the Government had provided more central grant - sufficient to leave the average tax bill close to £275 - then there would have been little political trouble. This interpretation is largely rejected here because, as has been emphasised in this book, the extent of the redistribution is too large - losers were bound to complain and cause trouble whether the average poll tax was £378, or even £278. It is true, of course, that a reduction in the average charge would have reduced the aggregate number of visible losers and the average losses of losers, but many of those regarding £278 as the "trouble-free" goal substantially underestimated the cost of securing tax reductions. They thought that £3 billion extra grant (£84 per adult) would have been sufficient to bring the average charge down by £84 per adult. This atheoritical figure had, unfortunately, been introduced into the public debate, by a prominent local government spokeswoman.[2] It was a massive underestimate of the cost of securing reductions in poll tax levels because it completely overlooked the fact that a substantial proportion of any extra grant would either be spent or added to reserves. A recent estimate by Barnett, Levaggi, and Smith, 1990,[3] is that close to 40% of real grant increases will be spent, which suggests that, taking into account likely replenishment of reserves, poll tax bills would have been reduced by less than half the £84 per adult. The original poll tax target could only have been attained at a cost of, at least, £5 billion - equivalent to over 3p on the standard rate of income tax.[4]

The reason why the Government incurred most of the blame is first the obvious one that it was responsible for the introduction of the poll tax. However, it could have turned out that this would be dominated by anger against local authorities with high poll taxes caused by overspending. So the question we have to answer is why the vast majority of the anger was directed towards the Government. The answer is, I think, that the Government made some crucial mistakes in the implementation of the poll tax.

First, it directed public and media attention towards a poll tax figure of £278 whilst at the same time introducing a grant settlement which guaranteed that nearly all local authorities would exceed this figure and especially that many Conservative controlled areas would exceed this figure. The parsimony of the expenditure guidelines, which were based on an increase in local budgets of 4.7% net of specific grants was an important contributory factor. Even in July 1989 this was patently overoptimistic, given the fact that inflation appeared very likely to be much higher than the official forecasts, and local authorities were being given additional responsibilities. Later, in November 1989 and by January 1990, the Chancellor of the Exchequer had revised the inflation forecast upwards and the necessary cuts appeared larger. An unusual intervention by CIPFA, sending a letter to MPs - indicating that the cuts of the order of 8-10% would be necessary to meet the £278 average poll tax target - added substantial weight to making the Government appear unreasonable.

Second, the safety nets and the payment of the special grants (for low rateable value areas and the inner London education grant) significantly helped to reduce the difference in actual levels of poll tax between Conservative and Labour controlled areas. As Table 16.1 shows the underlying differential in long run average poll tax was £65.4, but the safety nets and special grants reduced this to £18.7. This very much helped to ensure that a significant number of actual poll tax levels in Labour areas would be lower than actual levels in Conservative areas.

Table 16.1: Differences between poll tax levels in Conservative and Labour controlled areas (by lower tier) – (£ per adult per year)

	Conservative	Labour	Difference
Long run poll tax	246.5	311.9	65.4
Safety Nets and special grants – net contribution (+)/receipts(-)	16.9	-29.8	-46.7
Poll tax guideline	263.4	282.1	18.7
Actual average poll tax	345.7	387.1	41.4

Source: author's calculations

An additional contributory factor was the failure to take into account the extent to which local authorities had used balances and reserves to reduce their rate call in 1989/90. This reduced recorded expenditure in 1989/90, according to the new definition and authorities were given spending guidelines for 1990/91 based on this reduced figure. This made the spending guidelines even tougher in general, as local authorities had withdrawn £600 million from balances in 1989/90, but especially hurt a number of the shire counties where substantial drawings from balances had been made in advance of the county elections of May 1989. However, there were great differences between individual authorities and this made the spending guidelines and the consequent poll tax guidelines – and also safety net contributions and receipts – subject to a large random element. It ensured that several Conservative controlled authorities were in severe trouble and that several Labour controlled authorities gained. It was a bit of a lottery and hardly a secure basis on which local electors should judge their local authorities.

Another reason why the Government got most of the blame might seem to be that so many backbench Conservative MPs were critical of the implementation of the poll tax. A distinction emerged between "Mark 1" critics - those who had warned of the dangers during the passage of the Local Government Finance Bill and in a number of cases voted against the proposals - and a larger number of "Mark 2" critics who had voted for the bill in 1988. This criticism from within the party did not help the Government, but it is worth reflecting that the Conservatives might have been worse damaged if their backbenchers had shown no response to the hostile messages they were getting from the electorate.

More important was the impression of inconsistency given by Government ministers and what appeared to be surprise at the level of poll taxes. In the initial stages of the crisis when most of the attention centred upon the southern shire counties, there were rapid changes in ministerial positions. One day it was stated that only authorities which kept their spending down could hope to receive extra grant, then the emphasis was put on the need for capping, and later that the Government would be more ready to consider extra funding for next year. However, when capping came none of the southern counties was involved.[5] Ministers also irritated large numbers of the public by insisting on using the term "fair" to describe the poll tax. Large number of losers did not regard as fair the fact that the richest adults in their area, or the adults living in the most valuable house (or castle), were now paying the same poll tax as those with the lowest incomes above the level qualifying for rebates. It was also noticeable how little weight losers gave to the argument - often put forward by Ministers on radio and TV - that the rich were paying much more for local government services when their national tax contributions were taken into account. However, the importance of presentation, relative to the real effect of the flat-rate tax must not be exaggerated. In any case there were some real issues of mistakes or lack of competence in the introduction of the reforms which must be analysed.

Incompetent and inconsistent

The most serious deficiency in the Government's handling of the reforms is that it has a built-in inconsistency. This was emphasised by the stress the Secretary of State put on the fact that the shire counties were following a traditional cycle of overspending and replenishing balances in the year after their county elections and this was a prime reason for driving up poll tax levels. The fact that there was such a cycle was acknowledged in Chapter 10 (see also Gibson, 1985). The non-metropolitan counties are responsible for over half of English local government current expenditure and it was extraordinarily incompetent, given the crucial role of local elections in the Government's theory of local accountability, for it not to have introduced annual elections for the counties. As it is, there is no chance for the electors to deliver a verdict on the shire counties until 1993. Similarly, electors now have no further chance to vote in the London boroughs or the Scottish regions until 1994.

In any case the Government has been inconsistent on this point. Tax capping has been retained on the grounds that temporary protection of local taxpayers might be necessary until local elections could be held, but in the event 18 local authorities were capped just four weeks ahead of their local elections.

A further inconsistency is the fact that transitional relief is tied to guideline poll tax levels, when in most areas electors have, because of the absence of local elections, no ability to influence actual poll tax levels by voting.

Also the basic idea of safety nets had severe deficiencies. It is clear that Ministers, and many MPs, have seen safety nets both as a necessary protection for local authorities and an important device for protecting local taxpayers from too rapid a change in their bills and high levels of poll tax. This combines a number of mistakes. First, it provides inaccurate and insufficient protection for losers. For example, in an area where the average domestic tax payment rises by £100 per annum from £300 to £400 per adult the safety net gives £75 per adult protection. However, the receiving local authorities might well spend £30-£40 of this grant, and given the data we considered in Chapters 6 and 7, many households will lose more than £150 per adult. This leaves the safety nets relatively ineffective. Furthermore, even in a losing local authority there will be many gainers and the safety net grant will benefit them equally, per adult, to losers. Safety nets are an inefficient use of funds for the protection of local taxpayers.[6]

It is the redistribution between households and individuals which is the main source of political trouble and it would have been more effective to put extra resources into transitional relief for households. This would have been a much more politically competent use of the available funds.

The initial plan in the Green Paper, devised by Kenneth Baker, to directly protect households by phasing poll tax in, and domestic rates out, over a period up to 10 years, was deficient in involving the extra administrative costs of running two local tax systems and no targeting towards losing households. The plan was opposed by many in local government because of the extra administrative burden and under pressure it was dropped for Scotland and later for England when enthusiasm for poll tax was running high in sections of the Conservative party backed by the Secretary of State, Mr Ridley and the Prime Minister.[7] It was an extraordinary error to proceed to introduce the poll tax with no plans for household level transitional relief, given the continued use of safety nets, an error relieved extremely late in the day only by the new Secretary of State, Mr Patten after pressure from Conservative backbenchers from the summer of 1989 onwards. Scotland had had to go through the introduction of poll tax without the aid of transitional relief.

Safety nets were the biggest mistake. There was no need to protect local authorities against losses of external finance - they had the power the tax - and safety nets substantially distorted the poll tax levels which were supposed to form the basis of the operation of local accountability. If an effective scheme of household relief had been in place there would have been, and would now be, less pressure for general grant increases to local government. As it is the Government is set to spend £540 million on transitional grants protecting local authorities, but only £235 million on grants protecting households in 1991/92. This is a big mistake.[8]

The local elections

There was some consensus in early analyses that there was a local poll tax effect in the local elections, although it was usually thought to be spasmodic because whilst Wandsworth and Westminster with their low poll taxes had been retained by the Conservatives, Bradford also with a low poll tax had been lost. What was overlooked was that even the low poll tax imposed tax increases on the majority of households in low rateable value Bradford.

It is too early yet for the publication of any completed analyses of the effects of the local elections, but the importance of this was stressed by Butler (1990):

> Finding out how far this week's vote was decided by the level of tax, and taking appropriate action, may yet determine the outcome of the next election.

There are, however, some interesting interim findings which point to a more pessimistic interpretation of the local elections for the Government. Game (1990) has drawn attention to some important evidence on voting intentions in local versus national elections. Throughout the 1980s, MORI asked a sample of voters one week before each set of local elections how they would vote in the impending local election and if there were an immediate general election. The responses in the 1980s revealed a *relative local electoral advantage* to Labour over the Conservatives: 10% in 1983, 8% in 1984, 10% in 1986, and 7% in 1987. In 1990 there seems to have been a big shift: Labour's local advantage had slipped to 2%, and as Table 16.2 (p.244) shows, it was now the SLD which had the big local advantage.

This shift in the relationship between local and national voting means that the Conservatives are under greater electoral threat than from previous good local results for the Labour party. This shift in the relationship could, of course, be due to the dropping by Labour of unpopular national policies, especially defence.

Some early research using ward data for Birmingham has also shown that the relative shifts in votes against the Conservatives are much higher in the wards where local tax prices have risen most under poll tax. This is the very opposite trend to that implicitly forecast in the Government's theory of accountability, and shows no increased readiness as yet by electors to use their local votes to register their local preference. In addition, the increase in turnout, in Birmingham at least, was not much greater than that experienced in local elections in the general election years - with increased media interest - of 1983 and

Table 16.2: Local versus General Election Voting Intentions

Question:	Which party are you most inclined to support ... (a) if there were a General Election tomorrow (b) in next Thursday's local elections				
	Con.	Lab.	Alliance/ Lib. Dem.	Labour lead over Con.	Labour's local electoral advantage
1986					
General Election	38	46	23	-2	+10
Local elections	33	41	22	+8	
1990 (all GB)					
General Election	30	56	5	+26	+2
Local elections	25	53	10	+28	
1990 (London only)					
General Election	38	48	6	+10	+2
Local elections	34	46	11	+12	

Source: MORI/Sunday Times opinion polls

1987. Much of the increased turnout must also be credited to by far the largest post-war annual real increase in the aggregate of domestic sector tax bills.[9]

The Review and the second settlement

Fear of electoral disaster provided the spur for announcement of the setting up of a review by Ministers of the operation of the poll tax. The fact that the headlines were taken by the electoral triumphs in Wandsworth and Westminster ensured that the flat rate principle of the poll tax was retained and the results of the ministerial review, announced simultaneously with the provisional RSG statement in July 1990, promised only minor changes. These were much less significant than the change in the RSG aggregates. Aggregate External Finance was to be increased by £2.95 billion - 12.8% - much above the rate of inflation. This was to support a level of total standard spending 7% above actual 1990/91 budgets. This was by historic standards a generous settlement. The Government had reluctantly accepted much of the 1990/91 "overspend". However, the level of poll tax in 1991/92 which would result, if the spending plans were met, would be £379. An increase of grant of nearly £3 billion, far from securing a reduction in the average poll tax, was only sufficient to keep the increase in average poll tax level down to £22 per adult.

As well as securing extra grant from the Exchequer for general support of local government the July announcement also significantly extended transitional relief by reducing the threshold loss from £3 to £2 a week. This increased the planned level of relief in 1991/92 from £260 million to £570 million.

This was a skilful settlement, limiting or reducing the political damage caused by poll tax. Unfortunately, it also presages the loss of local accountability, which the electorate was told was the rationale behind the reforms. It also ignored the problem predictably emerging - always the achilles heel of poll taxes - of administration and enforcement. It is to these topics we turn in the final chapter.

Notes

1. The reforms made it more expensive for a significant majority of the population in nearly all areas to support high spending policies and, therefore, for them, made it more expensive to vote Labour.

2. The £3 billion figure was reported in various national newspapers in early April and attributed to Rita Hale, who also repeated it on television.

3. The quite large number of local government officers I have discussed this matter with suggested a consensus that the "leakage" would be over 50%.

4. A precise estimate is not possible and, it is likely that as any change in grant gets larger, local authorities' propensity to spend reduces. In

addition any fall in poll tax levels consequent upon extra grant will lead to reductions in expenditure on community charge benefit.

5. It might be wondered why there was no such crisis to the Government arising from the introduction of the poll tax in Scotland one year earlier. I suggest two reasons, one obvious and one more technical. The first reason why this did not cause a problem was because there were relatively few Conservative voters and seats in Scotland. The second reason is that because there were many fewer actual or potential Conservatives voters, as a proportion of the electorate, they tended, far more than in England, to live in properties with relatively high rateable values for Scotland and their tax shares went down under poll tax. Paddison (1989) provides some relevant evidence on the spatial impact of the poll tax in Scotland.

6. Mr Ridley and/or his speech writers never seem to have mastered this point. Thus in his July 1989 grant announcement he linked (in para. 10) payment of safety nets to local authorities with the justification that "people should have some protection".

7. The Insight Team, 1990, provides an interesting account of the background to the dropping of the transition plan in England.

8. This mistake has been somewhat alleviated in the July 1990 announcement on the 1991/92 grant settlement.

9. See Gibson and Stewart (1991).

17.
IN CONCLUSION: ACCOUNTABILITY, EVASION, AND EQUITY

The "abandonment" of accountability

Numerous press stories throughout the early summer of 1990 had suggested that the Prime Minister strongly wished to introduce new legislation to extend the Government's formal capping powers and in her only interview during this period, with disc jockey Jimmy Young, she argued that the majority of the public, including those in areas where local elections had recently been held, would have supported greater use of capping in the spring of 1990. There could be no doubt that the Prime Minister did not subscribe the theory of local accountability delivered through the local ballot box, outlined so frequently by her Secretary of State and other ministers during the passage of the bill. We now know that the drive for fresh legislation was resisted by other ministers - on the grounds that existing powers were sufficient and there would be political costs in giving renewed prominence to the poll tax in Parliament. Nevertheless the result is still that the accountability objective has been abandoned. This is shown by the continual reiteration by ministers, throughout the late summer, of the threat to use capping powers more extensively in 1991/92. The threat featured prominently in the announcement for 1991/92:

> I expect authorities to pass on the benefit (of extra grant) to their chargepayers in their bills, rather than increase spending too much once again. ... Those local authorities which are not prepared to budget sensibly should know that *I shall be prepared to make vigorous use of my powers for charge capping next year.* (Author's italics)

The use of tax capping in 1990/91 and the apparent need by ministers to threaten its greater use in 1991/92 surely means that the poll tax has been less than marvellously successful. A leading article in *The Times* following the April 1990 announcement of capping just a few weeks before the May local elections neatly summarised the issue. Reflecting that these elections would include the "high-spending" London boroughs, the leader said:

> ... Here in operation is precisely the principle for which Conservative ministers and backbenchers voted: ... local democratic choice over spending levels. They could not have been more explicit. ... More voters would pay the tax, restoring the (presumed) lack of accountability inherent in the rates

and regretted the fact that ministers:

> do not trust the purpose-designed, larger poll tax electorates to exercise a democratic verdict on local spending. ... even to the extent of permitting a first year's trial period.

It questioned whether a British Government had ever been so lacking in the courage of its own convictions. However, what may have been lacking was not courage, but strength of conviction. The question presumes that there were ministers with strong prior commitment to the local democratic verdict under poll tax,[1] whatever the level chosen. Given the accuracy of Ian Aitken's view that, in 1987, few MPs or ministers believed in the wisdom of the poll tax, it is difficult indeed to imagine that among the small number who did, there were many who were really committed to accepting the local electorate's verdict, if it wasn't the verdict they desired. Throughout, Parliament and the British public were expected to believe in the strength of the Government's commitment to their theory of greater local accountability through the poll tax. Greater local accountability has turned out to be only a "cover-story" - a cover for the only real objective: to cut expenditure.

Administration

In any evaluation of the poll tax, the administration of the tax must be taken into account. This has only been mentioned in passing in the main body of the text, because although many analysts had predicted from the outset much greater problems than with the administration of the rating system, only by the summer of 1990 did reasonably clear data emerge.

There are several aspects of administration to consider - registration, costs, and collection shortfall or written-off debts. Although there were claims that initial registration was 98% in Scotland and 99% in England, any non-registration is a problem if only on the grounds that it is a device for evasion and will lead to inequity between residents. A study of electoral registration by Blair (1989) indicated that there had been a sudden reversal of a rising trend over the rest of the decade, with the number of registered electors falling by 0.2% in England between 1988 and 1989 and by 0.9% in Scotland. The figure for Scotland probably reflected the greater imminence of the poll tax there in 1989. There is also additional cause for concern if registration is uneven between areas. This could influence relative area SSAs, grant receipts, and tax levels (King, 1989), especially if it is a prelude to the understatement of population in the forthcoming 1991 census. Here, Muir (1989) reported that the fall in registered electors for the four largest Scottish cities - Glasgow, Edinburgh, Dundee, and Aberdeen - was over twice the national average at 2.1% with demographic changes accounting for less than a third of the fall. A survey by the newspaper *Scotland on Sunday* reported falls in registration on the poorest housing estates of up to 15%. Blair's data also indicates similar trends in English cities.

The costs and difficulties of administration appear to be even larger than initially anticipated. The figures given previously show that English local authorities have budgeted for costs to be nearly 2.7 times larger than rate collection costs. The extra costs of £369 million amounts to over £20 per household. In Scotland the difficulties of administration have been larger than initially anticipated, with an important factor being the unexpectedly large number of changes in the register. Tait (1990) reports that in Scotland there were changes to between 45-50% of the register, about two million in the first year. This supports the interpretation of Ridge and Smith (1990) that there will be only minimal reductions in administrative difficulties and costs once the system is installed in England.

The most important aspect of administration, though, is the issue of non-payment. It has taken some time for conclusive information from Scotland to emerge and data reported in July 1990, four months after the end of the first financial year of poll tax indicates that revenue not yet collected for that year stands at 18.6% (Begg, 1990) and is likely to outturn at around 10%. In Scotland poll tax is collected by the nine regional councils and levels of non-collection varied from over 20% in the more urban regions to 7.6% in rural Galloway. One major problem which makes collection difficult with reluctant payers is that it costs more in additional administration costs to collect than the extra revenue derived, especially in cases where the charge is a lower rebated sum than the full poll tax. The level of non-collection is an extremely serious problem for local government as a whole and local taxpayers, because it is uncompensated by central government and therefore necessarily either drives up the average level of poll tax or reduces expenditure upon services. Again, however, it is variations between areas which are even more serious, because this has differential effects on poll tax levels and taxpayers in different areas. The problem in England will probably be much worse than is indicated by the data from Scotland. This is because the regional data from Scotland conceals much wider variation between districts. In England there will be obviously be great differences in non-collection between large parts of the more affluent shire counties and the inner cities. This will create major inequities between local taxpayers in cities like Birmingham and shire districts such as Wokingham. In a system where the standard charge is £278 for spending at SSA, the charge has to be £327 in areas where non-collection reaches 15%, as opposed to £293 where non-collection is 5%, in order to achieve the same revenue. Non-collection renders spurious any claim that the new system gives equal charges in each area for spending at SSA. Final proof of the dangerous nature of the problem is the news from Scotland that collection rates in the first three months of the second year of poll tax are below those achieved in the first year. (Begg, 1990)

Evaluation

Thus an important drawback of the poll tax is that it introduces a substantial inequity between taxpayers in different areas arising from differential non-collection rates - differentials much bigger than those existing under a property tax. To this can be added the violation of the principle of equal treatment of equals living in different areas arising from the fact that tax rates are necessarily higher in high needs areas for equal percentage improvements in services (King, 1988). This inequity existed under domestic rates, but has been greatly intensified under the new system.

The above factors will intensify the tendency, anticipated by the analysis in Chapters 8 and 9, of the system to generate inefficiently low levels of services due to the fact that there is a more substantial mismatch between benefit and tax shares under poll tax than under domestic rates, and the majority of low and middle income electors have a tax incentive to provide services at a level below that desired by the high income minority. In the first year of operation of poll tax there has been in England a sharp brake put on the discretionary volume increases of the late 1980s.[2] However, the 1990 local election results probably indicate that electors will, if given the opportunity, punish councils with high poll tax levels thus soon enforcing the lower spending levels predicted earlier.

Under such a regressive local tax regime expenditure levels will become very grant dependent and the increase in aggregate external finance for 1991/92 exhibits the response from central politicians predicted earlier. Also predicted were increased pressures for favourable changes in aggregate and relative needs assessments (SSAs). This is precisely what has been observed during the summer of 1990. It is damaging to the objective of local accountability when levels, and changes in levels, of local tax and services depend excessively upon central decisions rather than local preferences and information.

There are some positive benefits from the reforms to offset against these costs. One positive benefit of the reforms is the substantial reduction in uncertainty facing non-domestic ratepayers. Also desirable is (1) the fact that there has been a non-domestic revaluation and that rate payments are now more closely aligned to the underlying value of assets, and (2) rate payments are not tied to the level of local expenditure and tax rates. This latter has led to a redistribution of non-domestic rates which removes a somewhat artificial incentive for new investment and jobs to be located in the south-east. Unfortunately against this benefit must be offset the undesirable rise in house prices and possible intensification of regional house price differentials (Muellbauer, 1987) caused by the replacement of domestic rates by poll tax.[3]

Another positive benefit of the reforms is that they remove the substantial differences in spending incentives between areas which existed in the previous system, caused by the large differences in the contribution of non-domestic rates. There is, of course, the offset to this gain, mentioned above, in the intensification of the greater relative cost to high needs areas of equal percentage service improvements.

Neither of the positive benefits of the reforms has been dependent upon the introduction of the poll tax. They could have been achieved using a different local tax base. The analysis here has suggested that a less regressive local tax would be more efficient. The review of the operation of the poll tax has left the regressive nature of the tax unchanged.

Finally, let us return to the "realpolitik" of the poll tax. Inevitably, by the midsummer of 1990, after the earlier massive coverage, the poll tax was receiving much less media attention. Despite this the poll tax has decisively held first place among issues of importance to voters in the

MORI/NOP opinion polls - this despite the fact "the economy" is felt by most of the major political commentators to be the issue on which the next general election will be decided. However, the electoral influence of the economy depends not so much on the absolute performance of the economy, but on the net electoral judgment on the relative competence of the parties in their management of the economy (Riddell, 1990). Here, given the difficulties of the Conservatives in securing early reductions in the rate of inflation the electorate might soon not perceive much distance between the parties. However, the Labour party has now committed itself to a speedy return to the rating system. Here, there is a marked difference between the parties. In giving poll tax its flagship status Mrs Thatcher may, however, have been correct. It might turn out to be the most important policy of her third term. In a tight electoral contest it could lead to the loss of enough marginal seats to lose the next general election. It will have justified its flagship status.

Notes

1. Career considerations must have held sway over inner belief with many ministers.

2. Hughes (1989) thought that local authorities would take advantage of the confusion caused by the change in tax base to increase their expenditure. A number of aspects of this study have been criticised in Midwinter (1989a), to which I might add that Hughes' estimates of the incidence effects of the poll tax underestimate its regressivity. This leads Hughes to understate the importance of the change in the domestic tax base.

3. Muellbauer, like Fender (1986), was primarily interested in housing and other economic issues rather than the efficiency considerations applying to local government. These were also ignored by Hughes (1988), as were extra administration and collection costs of the poll tax, in reaching the conclusion that:

> even using a social welfare function incorporating a large degree of income inequality aversion any adverse distributional effects are swamped by the welfare gains accruing to households as they adjust their housing consumption to relative price changes.

The cavalier use of social welfare functions in argument leaves many economists uneasy (Rowley, 1987), but in any case the empirical bases of this conclusion are incorrect. First, Hughes underestimates the regressivity of the poll tax and, therefore, the degree of income equality to which the social welfare function has to be averse. Second, due to the rapid house price inflation of the late 1980s, what Hughes diagnoses as undesirable relative overtaxation of housing (through domestic rates) had disappeared by 1988. Certainly the public seem to have been slow to appreciate being "swamped by welfare gains".

18.
MRS THATCHER'S DOWNFALL: THE FUTURE OF THE POLL TAX

[The dramatic events of November 1990 and the return of Michael Heseltine to the cabinet as Environment Secretary with the task of sorting out the poll tax suggested that a postscript needed to be added to the book]

On 14 November 1990, Michael Heseltine announced that he was to challenge Mrs Thatcher for the leadership of the Conservative party. As we now know, his challenge resulted in the unprecedented removal in peace time of an incumbent Conservative Prime Minister in good health - one moreover with the remarkably successful record of winning three out of three contested general elections.

Mrs Thatcher lost the leadership of the Conservative party and resigned as Prime Minister, when Michael Heseltine secured enough MPs votes - 152 compared to Mrs Thatcher's 204 - to deny her a first round victory, and had a good prospect in a second round contested with Mrs Thatcher alone of securing the necessary majority of eligible Conservative MPs votes (187 out of 372) to become leader.

The occasion for the challenge was the disunity within the Conservative party over policy towards Europe, brought to the surface by the resignation of the deputy leader Sir Geoffrey Howe, and his scathing criticism of Mrs Thatcher in his resignation speech delivered in the House of Commons on 13 November 1990. However, in the actual election contest Europe became relegated to a minor role and domestic issues, especially the poll tax, emerged as much more important.

Mrs Thatcher was vulnerable because the Conservatives were so far behind in the opinion polls at a late stage in the Parliament, and her personal unpopularity in the country was felt by many Tory MPs to be a serious block to any prospect of recovery. This feeling had been reinforced by some dreadful results in autumn Parliamentary by-elections. In Eastbourne on 18 October a seat with a majority of 16,923 in 1987 had been lost to the Liberal-Democrats on a swing of 20%. In Bradford North on 8 November the Conservatives vote had been similarly decimated when they were relegated to third place. Thus, Michael Heseltine who had for some time stated that he expected Mrs Thatcher to lead the party into a fourth general election and win it, now stood for the leadership because, as he put it:

> I am persuaded I would now have a better prospect of leading the Conservatives to a fourth electoral victory.

Few would argue with Lord Blake's post election judgement (Blake, 1990) that:

> She was ousted because she was believed to be a vote-loser, not because of arcane differences about the EC.

Also few would argue that the poll tax - she was uniquely associated with this policy, having declared it to be her flagship - was the most important component of this vote-losing quality. Far from receding as a problem over the summer and the early autumn, the continuing potency of the issue had been confirmed in the November by-election in Bradford North. In a post leadership-election analysis on BBC radio's *The World Tonight* the Chairman of the mid-Staffordshire Conservative party stated that:

> The community charge is the bugbear .. we had a by-election in March when a 14,500 majority was turned into a 9,000 Labour majority and that campaign was on the poll tax .. going round the constituency today there is still the same resentment at what people think the unfairness, and there is a lot of unfairness in it.

On the same programme Hugo Young concluded:

> It is clear that although the economy and interest rates affect most voters much more than the poll tax, the poll tax has become the great demon of modern Conservative politics ..

These verdicts were backed up by opinion poll results. In an NMR poll, appearing in *The Independent on Sunday* on the Sunday prior to the first round of the leadership election, 38 % of respondents had named poll tax as likely to be the most important issue at the next general election, with the next most important issue, inflation, trailing at 15%.

Michael Heseltine realised the potency of the poll tax issue with his fellow MPs and he promised urgent reform of it if he were made leader. He had, in fact, opposed the introduction of the poll tax in England (although he had voted in support of the Scottish legislation) and supported the Mates amendment for a banded charge in April 1988, when the Government's majority had fallen to 25. In May 1990 he had proposed in an article in *The Times* (Heseltine, 1990) that the poll tax should be banded upwards, by which he meant higher payments by top rate taxpayers, and that councils whose budgets exceeded by a given percentage the Government's calculations of the sum needed to provide a proper service, should be required to hold an election for the whole council. By November he was also suggesting, if no other reform were possible in the short term, that in order to halve the level of the poll tax he would favour the centre taking over the entire funding of school education.

Undoubtedly the fact that he was not associated with current Government policies contributed to his much higher rating in the opinion polls compared to Mrs Thatcher - the NMR poll referred to above suggested he would bring a 6% swing to the Conservatives from Labour compared to Mrs Thatcher. This, combined with the high priority he gave to reforming the poll tax, must have significantly improved his vote in the leadership contest and ensured the downfall of Mrs Thatcher. Once this was achieved, the other leadership candidates in the second round, Douglas Hurd and John Major, also indicated a readiness to examine and undertake reform of the poll tax. John Major's victory was followed by the appointment of Michael Heseltine as Secretary of State for the Environment, the post he had held between 1979 and 1983 under Mrs Thatcher's premiership.

Those Conservative MPs taking the view that the poll tax was going to lead to losses of large numbers of Conservative seats had a very strong case. The geographical redistribution of the local tax burden outlined in Chapter 4 and reinforced by the 1990/91 grant distribution with its relatively favourable SSAs for the south-east, combined with the electoral geography in an extremely disadvantageous way for the Conservatives. It is commonly acknowledged that the Labour party must capture seats in the south and London, if they are to have any chance of a majority after the next election. However, what is less commonly known is that, even without any losses in London and the south, the Conservatives could lose their overall majority on a loss of 5% of the vote to opposition parties in the rest of the country. Table 18.1 (p.258) shows that in the four English regions worst affected by the poll tax - the north, Yorkshire & Humberside, the north west, and the south west - there are 32 seats which would fall on such a swing. This far outweighs the 18 marginals in London and the south east.

When the detail of the impact of the poll tax in 1990 is examined the picture is even more ominous for the Conservatives. There are a large number of the Conservative marginals outside the south, where the impact of the poll tax in 1990 has been much higher than the average increase of one-third. Thus in Lancashire, three marginals - Hyndburn, Pendle, and Rossendale and Darwen - cover areas where average bills have risen by over 75%. Similarly in the south west there are 5 marginals - Cornwall North, Falmouth & Camborne, Devon North, Plymouth Drake, and Plymouth Sutton - where average bill increases have been above 60%. In the country's most marginal seat - York - the average bill increase was over 60%. In Nottingham, with two close Tory marginals, a similar increase applied. Of course, these figures exaggerate the impact on Conservative voters, given that within each area they will tend to live in higher rateable value houses, but nevertheless there must have been substantial impact on their marginal voters.

Table 18.1: Regional distribution of Conservative marginal seats

	Number of seats		Seats lost to second placed party 1987 on % swing of:	
	All	Conservative held	0 to 5	5.1 to 10
North	36	8	5	1
Yorkshire & Humberside	54	21	4	6
North West	73	34	13	12
East Midlands	42	31	4	10
West Midlands	58	36	8	8
East Anglia	20	19	3	5
South East	108	107	8	15
Greater London	84	58	10	12
South West	48	44	10	18
ENGLAND	523	358	65	87
SCOTLAND	72	10	6	4
WALES	38	8	3	4

Source: Author's computations; Butler and Kavanagh (1988).

In addition, there are an even larger number of seats in the areas worst affected by poll tax which would be lost on swings to the second placed party of between 5 and 10%. The problem is also made worse by the fact that nearly all the marginal seats in these areas will suffer additional poll tax increases due to the withdrawal of safety net grants in 1991 and 1992.

The future: reforming the poll tax

Upon Mr Heseltine taking up his appointment to reform the poll tax, his predecessor, Christopher Patten, warned that the task would be like "defusing a bomb". Apparently no legislation can be introduced before the autumn of 1991, so unless it had retrospective aspects there could be no effect from this source upon the level of poll tax before April 1992. There are, however, a number of possible options being discussed for reforming the poll tax or ameliorating its effects, all of which have drawbacks in that they increase central funding and/or damage the underlying accountability objective.

The first option is for the Government to take over the funding of school education. This has been examined and rejected on a number of occasions, but now has increasing support because of the recently introduced reforms in education with devolved management of budgets to schools and the opting for grant maintained status by a number of schools. This appears to have opened up the possibility of direct central funding of schools based on pupil numbers. There are, however, three drawbacks to this policy, of which only two were pointed out by cabinet ministers supporting Mrs Thatcher in the first round. The first drawback is that in order to use central funding to halve poll tax in Great Britain would cost over 5p on the standard rate of tax. The second is that the centre would be ill equipped to allocate for capital purposes between over 30,000 schools - the inefficiency of centrally planned economies would be mirrored in civil servants deciding on the relative urgency of repairing a school roof in Bury compared to a new playground for a school in Birmingham. In this situation local interests would have every incentive, with no local tax price attached, to exaggerate their needs. There might appear to be a way out through direct funding based on pupil numbers with the price per pupil including a sum to cover capital and repairs. However, schools would still require general permission to borrow for capital purposes. This leads to the final drawback of direct per pupil funding. This is that, at present, the education SSAs effectively give far greater sums per pupil to those local authorities containing pupils in socially deprived categories. This filters through to schools in an approximate way through the formula funding introduced by local authorities, and is supplemented to a highly variable degree by authorities' exceeding SSA levels of spending by different amounts. Any move to direct funding based on a standard amount per pupil would greatly worsen the position of pupils in high spending areas and raises difficult issues regarding schools' ability to exclude certain pupils.

A second option is simply to increase general grant. This is again being presented incorrectly in the media as costing £1 billion to reduce the poll tax by £28. For the reasons given on (p.238) this is likely to be a substantial underestimate. It also suffers the important defect that it provides equal assistance to gainers as well as losers. The cost of bringing poll tax levels down from next year's projected level of £400 to £300 would be at least £5 billion.

A third option is to target extra assistance in the form of increasing rebates. Exempting the 6 million adults at present paying the minimum 20% would cost about £500 million and local authority treasurers have argued that in these cases collection costs often exceed revenue collected. Increasing the generosity of rebates to reach those further up the income scale is another option. However, this policy does not target losers and adds to assessment costs.

The option which targets losers exclusively is to increase transitional relief. Here, a key issue is whether to remove the ceiling provided by poll tax figures based on the Government's notional expenditure levels. For the reasons given in Chapter 16 this would be a worthwhile improvement, within a framework where poll tax continues.

Finally, there is banding. The problem here is that banding would involve large changes in tax liability as small changes in incomes involved movement across different bands. This would have damaging disincentive effects. Also there would remain large discontent about the unfairness of a flat-rate tax within what would be large income bands. Banding would bring extra administrative costs without the benefits of a genuine income tax.

However, all of these ameliorations damage the local accountability objective, and add to the already high administration costs at the same time as reducing the revenue raised. Also the now published evidence on the 1990 local elections shows that the disappointingly small impact of the poll tax on voting - average turnout in the metropolitan districts was a still disappointing 46.3%, not so much higher than the 39% in 1988 (Rallings and Thrasher, 1990) - in a year when average domestic tax bills rose by nearly 25% shows that little would be lost by abandoning the idea that a local tax system must ensure that every adult directly receives a bill.

All this leads one back into fundamental questions about the viability of poll tax, when - as argued in Chapters 8 and 9 - it is inferior on both the benefit and the ability-to-pay principle to either a property tax or a proportional income tax, and also when it is extremely expensive to collect with even partially satisfactory success. The experience with poll tax, with its unexpectedly high average level, suggests that a less regressive tax such as a property tax based on capital values could finance a considerable proportion of local government spending. The higher the proportion, the greater the prospect of strong local accountability and efficiency pressures on local authorities. There are other possible ingredients, including structural reform, but undoubtedly the forthcoming review, under Mr Heseltine, should decide to abandon the poll tax.

BIBLIOGRAPHY

Aaron, H., and McGuire, M., (1970), Public goods and income distribution. *Econometrica.* 38: 907-920.

Aitken, Ian, (1987), A party that chose to swallow the bitter bill. *The Guardian.* 21 December.

ACC, (annual), *Rate Support Grant (England).* London: Association of County Councils.

AMA, (1986), *Paying for Local Government: a response to the Green Paper.* London: Association of Metropolitan Authorities.

AMA, (1989), *Needs Assessments.* London: Association of Metropolitan Authorities.

Ashford, D.E., Berne, R., and Schramm, R., (1976), The expenditure Financing Decision in British Local Government. *Policy and Politics.* 5: 5-24.

Audit Commission, (1984), *The Impact on Local Authorities' Economy, Efficiency and Effectiveness of the Block Grant Distribution System.* London: HMSO.

Bailey, S.J., (1986), Paying for Local Government: Charging for Services. *Public Administration.* 64: 401-419.

Barrow, M., (1986), Reforming local government finance. *Public Money* 6 (3): 14.

Barnett, J., (1982), *Inside The Treasury.* London: Andre Deutsch.

Barnett, R.R., (1986), Local authority expenditure reactions to losses in grant aid: the case of metropolitan district councils. *Government and Policy.* 4: 131-143.

Barnett, R.R., Levaggi, R., and Smith, P., (1990), Does the flypaper model stick? *Public Choice* (forthcoming).

Baumol, W.J., (1967), *Welfare Economics and The Theory of the State.* London: Bell.

Beesley, M., and Littlechild, S., (1983), Privatization: Principles, Problems and Priorities. *Lloyds Bank Review* 149: 1-20.

Begg, David, (1990), Why Pay When Others Don't? *Local Government Chronicle.* 27 July.

Bennett, R.J., (1982), *Central Grants to Local Governments.* Cambridge: Cambridge University Press.

Bennett, R.J., (1986), The impact of non-domestic rates on profitability and investment. *Fiscal Studies* 7: 34-50.

Bennett, R.J., (1988), Non-domestic rates and local taxation of business. In Bailey, S.J., and Paddison, R., (eds) *The Reform of Local Government Finance in Britain.* London: Routledge.

Bergstrom, T.C., (1973), A note on efficient taxation. *Journal of Political Economy.* 81: 187-191.

Billington, M.L., (1966), *The Political South in the Twentieth Century.* New York: Charles Scribner's Sons.

Bird, R.M., (1976), *Charging for Public Services: A New Look at an Old Idea.* Toronto: Canada Tax Foundation.

Birdseye, P., and Webb A.J., (1981), Why the rate burden on business is a cause for concern. *National Westminster Bank Review.* February, 2-15.

Birmingham City Council, (1988a), *Impact of the Community Charge on households in Birmingham.* Report of the City Treasurer to the Finance and Management Committee.

Birmingham City Council, (1988b), *Summary of studies of the impact of the poll tax on individual authorities.* Treasurer's Department.

Black, D., (1948), On the rationale of group decision making. *Journal of Political Economy.* 56: 23-34.

Blair, P., (1989), Poll tax may be responsible for shrinking electoral rolls. *Local Government Chronicle.* 23 June.

Blake, Robert, (1990), In the top half dozen of history. *The Times.* 30 November.

Bogdanor, V., (1986), *Electoral Systems in Local Government.* Inlogov: University of Birmingham.

Bowen, H.R., (1948), *Toward Social Economy*. New York: Holt, Rinehart, & Winston.

Bramley, G., (1985), Incrementalism Run Amok. *Public Administration*. 63: 100-107.

Bramley, G., (1987a), Horizontal Disparities and Equalization: A Critique of 'Paying for Local Government'. *Local Government Studies*. 13 (1): 69-89.

Bramley, G., (1987b), Paying for Local Government. In Brenton, M., and Ungerson, C., (eds) *The Year Book of Social Policy 1986-7*. Harlow: Longman.

Bramley, G., Le Grand, J.E., and Low, W., (1989), How far is the poll tax a 'community charge': the implications of service usage evidence. *Policy and Politics*. 17: 187-205.

Breton, A., (1974), *The Economic Theory of Representative Government*. Chicago: Aldine.

Bristow, S., (1982), Rates and Votes - The 1980 District Council Elections. *Policy and Politics*. 10: 163-180.

Brittan, S., (1983), *The Role and Limits of Government*. London: Temple Smith.

Brittan, S., (1984), The Politics and Economics of Privatisation. *Political Quarterly*. 55: 109-128.

Brittan, S., (1986), Privatisation: a comment on Kay and Thompson, *Economic Journal*. 96: 33-38.

Brown, C., (1984), *Black and White*. Aldershot: Gower.

Brown, C.V., and Jackson P.M., (1979), *Public Sector Economics*. London: Martin Robertson.

Brunner, K., (1978), Reflections on the Political Economy of Government: The Persistent Growth of Government. *Schweizerische Zeitschrift fur Volkswirtschaft and Statististic*. 3: 649-680.

Buchanan, J.M., (1967), *Public Finance in Democratic Process*. Chapel Hill: University of North Carolina Press.

Buchanan, J.M., (1970), Notes for an Economic Theory of Socialism. *Public Choice*. 8: 29-43.

Buchanan, J.M., Tollison, R.D., and Tullock, G., (Eds), (1980), *Towards a Theory of the Rent-Seeking Society*. College Station: Texas A & M University Press.

Butler, David, (1990), Why didn't Wandsworth go the way of Bradford? *The Times*. 5 May.

Butler, D., and Kavanagh, D., (1988), *The British General Election of 1987*. Basingstoke: Macmillan.

Carvel, John, (1985), Mrs Thatcher's ever-increasing rate of knots, *The Guardian*. 1 April.

Chatterjee, S., and Price, B., (1977), *Regression Analysis by Example*. New York: John Wiley.

CIPFA, (annual), *Finance and General Statistics*. London: Chartered Institute of Public Finance and Accountancy.

CIPFA, (1975), *Local Government Trends*. London: Chartered Institute of Public Finance and Accountancy.

CIPFA, (1987), *'Paying for Local Government': Beyond the Green Paper*. London: Chartered Institute of Public Finance and Accountancy.

CIPFA, (1988a), *Block Grant Statistics*. London: Chartered Institute of Public Finance and Accountancy.

CIPFA, (1988b), *'Paying for Local Government': Community Charge and Ringfenced" Housing Revenue Accounts*. London: Chartered Institute of Public Finance and Accountancy.

Courant, P.N., Gramlich, E.M., and Rubinfeld, D.L., (1979), The stimulative effects of intergovernmental grants or why money sticks where it hits. In Mieszkowski, P., and Oakland, W.H., (eds) *Fiscal Federalism and Grants-in-Aid*. Washington DC: Urban Instititute.

Cowan, M., (1978), The old election-year phobia - but do the rates matter?, *Municipal Journal*. 9 June.

Crawford, M., and Dawson, D., (1982), Are Rates the Right Tax for Local Government? *Lloyds Bank Review*. 145: 15-35.

Crewe, I., and Fox, A., (1984), *British Parliamentary Constituencies*. London: Faber and Faber.

Davey, K.J., (1983), *Financing Regional Development*. Chichester: Wiley.

Davis, John, (1986), Will Sid always fall for these cynical sell-offs?, *The Independent*. 25 November.

Department of Employment, (monthly), *Employment Gazette*. London: HMSO.

Department of the Environment, (1977), *Local Government Finance*. Cmnd. 6813. London: HMSO.

Department of the Environment, (1980), *Local Government Finance: The Rate Support Grant Report (England) 1981/82*. London: HMSO.

Department of the Environment, (1981), *Alternatives to domestic rates*. Cmnd. 8449. London: HMSO.

Department of the Environment, (1983), *Rates*. Cmnd. 9008. London: HMSO.

Department of the Environment, (1985), *Patrick Jenkin examines the way forward on local government finance reform*. Press Notice 173. London: Department of the Environment.

Department of the Environment, (1986a), *Paying for Local Government*. Cmnd. 9741. London: HMSO.

Department of the Environment, (1986b), *Paying for Local Government: the community charge*. London: Department of the Environment.

Department of the Environment, (1986c), *Rate Reform - Government Proposals The Way Forward Says Dr Boyson*, News Release, 15 December. London: Department of the Environment.

Department of the Environment, (1989), *Local Government Financial Statistics England No. 1*. London: HMSO.

Department of Health and Social Security, (1985), *Reform of Social Security, Volume 1*. Cmnd. 9517. London: HMSO.

Dobson, R.B., (1970), *The Peasant's Revolt of 1381*. London: Macmillan.

Dowle, M., (1987), The Year at Westminster. In McCrone, D. (ed) *The Scottish Government Yearbook*. Edinburgh: University of Edinburgh Press.

Dyer, M.C., and Jordan, A.G., (1985), *Who Votes in Aberdeen? Marked Electoral Registers as a Data Source*. Strathclyde Papers in Government No 42, Glasgow: Department of Government, University of Strathclyde, Glasgow.

Environment Committee, (1982), *Enquiry into methods of financing local government in the context of the Government's Green Paper*. Cmnd. 8449. House of Commons Paper 217, Session 1981-82. London: HMSO.

Esam, P., and Oppenheim, C., (1989), *A Charge on the Community*. London: Child Poverty Action Group and Local Government Information Unit.

Ezell, J.S., (1975), *The South Since 1865*. New York: Macmillan.

Feldstein, M., (1975), Wealth, neutrality and local choice in public education. *American Economic Review*. 65: 75-89.

Fender, J., (1986), Local taxation and housing finance: a proposal for reform. *Lloyds Bank Review*. 162: 17-36.

Ferry, J., (1978), Politics and the rates. *Centre for Environmental Studies Review*. 4: 57.

Ferry, J., (1979), Rates and Elections. *Centre for Environmental Studies Review*. 5: 7-9.

Flannery, K., (1987), *More than just a poll tax*. Manchester: Centre for Local Economic Strategies.

Foster, C.D., (1982), Alternatives to Domestic Rates - a Comment on the Government's Green Paper. In *Enquiry into methods of financing local government in the context of the Government's Green Paper*. Volume 2. Cmnd. 8449. House of Commons Paper 217, Session 1981-82. London: HMSO.

Foster, C.D., (1986), Reforming local government finance. *Public Money*. 6 (2): 17-22.

Foster, C.D., (1988), Reflections on the Green Paper. In Bennett, R.J., and Zimmermann, H., (eds) *Local Business Taxes in Britain and West Germany*. Anglo-German Foundation.

Foster, C.D., and Jackman, R.A., (1982), Accountability and Control of Local Spending, *Public Money*. 2 (2): 11-14.

Foster, C.D., Jackman, R.A., and Perlman, M., (1980), *Local Government Finance in a Unitary State*. London: George Allen and Unwin.

Fraschini, A., (1989), Local autonomy, accountability and a new local tax: the Italian debate. *Policy and Politics*. 17: 155-163.

Fry, V., and Stark, G., (1987), The take-up of supplementary benefit - the gaps in the safety net, *Fiscal Studies*. 8(4): 1-13.

Game, C., (1981), Local elections, *Local Government Studies*. 7 (2): 63- 68.

Game, C., (1984), Axeman or Taxman: Who is now the more unpopular, *Local Government Studies*. 10 (1): 6-11.

Game, C., (1990), Local Elections: The perils of prediction. *Local Government Policy Making*. 17 (2): 41-52.

Gibson, J.G., (1985), Why Block Grant Failed, in Ranson, P.S.R., Jones, G.W., and Walsh, K., (eds) *Between Centre and Locality*, London: Allen and Unwin.

Gibson, J.G., (1987a), *The Effects of the Poll Tax on Residents of County Durham*. Durham: Durham County Council.

Gibson, J.G., (1987b), How the poll tax will punish electors, *Public Service and Local Government*. June. 14-15.

Gibson, J.G., (1987c), The reform of British local government finance: the limits of local accountability, *Policy and Politics*. 15: 167- 174.

Gibson, J.G., (1988a), Japan's Poll Tax misleads the UK. *Local Government Chronicle*. 1 April.

Gibson, J.G., (1988b), Rate Increases and Local Elections: A Different Approach and a Different Conclusion, *Policy and Politics*. 16: 197- 208.

Gibson, J.G., (1989), The Presentation of the Poll Tax, *Political Quarterly*. 60: 332-348.

Gibson, J.G., (1990), Why did precepts rise so steeply. *County Councils Gazette*. October. 82: 150-151.

Gibson, J.G., Smith, P., and Watt, P.A., (1987), Measuring the fiscal pressure on English local authorities under the block grant system. *Government and Policy*. 5: 157-170.

Gibson, J.G., and Stewart, J.D., (1991), Electoral accountability and the poll tax: an analysis based on 1990 ward results. *Local Government Studies*. (forthcoming).

Gibson, J.G., and Travers, A., (1985), Block Grant: the story of a failure. *Public Money*. 5 (2): 17-22.

Gibson, J.G., and Travers, A., (1986), *Block Grant: a study in Central-Local Relations*. London: Public Finance Foundation.

Gibson, J.G., and Watt, P.A., (1989), Privatisation versus poll tax: a public choice analysis of two Thatcher flagships. *Government and Policy*. 7: 341-351.

Gramlich, E.M., (1977), Intergovernmental grants: a review of the empirical literature. In Oates, W.E., (ed) *The Political Economy of Fiscal Federalism.* Lexington: Lexington Books.

Greene, K.V., (1970), Some institutional considerations in federal-state fiscal relations. **Public Choice.** Reprinted 1972 in Buchanan, J.M., and Tollison, R.D., (eds), *Theory of Public Choice: Political Applications.* Ann Arbor: University of Michigan Press.

Gregory, R., (1969), Local elections and the rule of anticipated reactions. *Political Studies.* 17: 31-47.

Hale, R., (1990), The make believe world of what might have been. *Public Finance and Accountancy.* 2 March. 13-16.

Hailey, W.M.H., (1957), *An African Survey.* London: Oxford University Press.

Hampton, W., (1970), *Democracy and Community: A Study of Politics in Sheffield.* Oxford: Oxford University Press.

Heald, D.A., (1980), The Scottish Rate Support Grant: how different from the English and Welsh? *Public Administration.* 58: 25-46.

Heald, D.A., (1984), Privatisation: analysing its appeal and limitations. *Fiscal Studies.* 5: 36-46.

Heald, D.A., (1989), *Charging by British Government: Evidence from the Public Expenditure Survey.* Studies in Public Policy 173. Glasgow: University of Strathclyde.

Hepworth, N., (1984), *The Finance of Local Government.* London: Allen & Unwin.

Heseltine, Michael, (1990), The poll tax: let the people choose. *The Times.* 10 May.

Hicks, J.R., (1939), The Foundations of Welfare Economics. *Economic Journal.* 49: 696-708.

HM Treasury, (1988), *A New Public Expenditure Planning Total.* Cm 441. London: HMSO.

Hockley, G., and Harbour, G., (1982), People's Choice: public spending, taxation and local rates. *Public Money.* 1 (4): 11-14.

Hogendorn, J.S., (1975), Economic Initiative and African Cash Farming: Pre-Colonial Origins and early Colonial Developments. In Duignan, P., and Gann, L.H., (eds) *Colonialism in Africa 1870-1960.* Cambridge: Cambridge University Press.

Hogg, Sarah, (1989), A ripe time for fiscal choices. *The Independent.* 26 June.

House of Commons, (1987a), Debate on the Address. *House of Commons Parliamentary Debates - Session 1987-88 Official Reports (Hansard).* volume 118, columns 141 and 434 (HMSO, London).

House of Commons, (1987b), Written answers. *House of Commons Parliamentary Debates - Session 1987-88 Official Reports (Hansard).* volume 123, column 316w (HMSO, London)

House of Commons, (1987c), Local Government Finance Bill. *House of Commons Parliamentary Debates - Session 1987-88 Official Reports (Hansard).* volume 124, column 1282 (HMSO, London)

Hughes, G., (1988), Rates reform and the housing market. In Bailey, S.J., and Paddison, R., (eds) *The Reform of Local Government Finance in Britain.* London: Routledge.

Hughes, G., (1989), The switch from Domestic Rates to the Community Charge in Scotland. *Fiscal Studies.* 10 (3): 1-12.

Insight Team, (1990), The history of the poll tax. *The Sunday Times.* 1 April.

Jackman, R.A., (1982), Memorandum. In *Enquiry into methods of financing local government in the context of the Government's Green Paper.* Volume 2. Cmnd. 8449. House of Commons Paper 217, Session 1981-82. London: HMSO.

Jackman, R.A., (1986), Paying for Local Government. *Local Government Studies.* 12 (4): 51-58.

Jackman, R.A., (1988), Accountability, Redistribution and Local Government Expenditure: is Poll Tax the Answer? Paper presented at Conference on *Local Finances in the Contemporary State.* Oslo.

Japanese Ministry of Finance, (1986), *Annual Abstract of Statistics of Local Government Finance.* Tokyo.

Jenkins, Peter, (1990), Lucky escape will lift Tory aura of doom. *The Independent.* 5 May.

John, P., (1989), *Introduction of the Community Charge in Scotland.* London: Policy Studies Institute.

Jones, G.W., and Stewart, J.D., (1982), The Layfield Analysis Applied to Central-Local Relations under the Conservative Government. *Local Government Studies.* 8: 47-59.

Jones, G.W., and Stewart, J.D., (1983), *The case for local government.* London: Allen and Unwin.

Jones, G.W., Stewart, J.D., and Travers, A., (1986), A Rejoinder to Jackman. *Local Government Studies.* 12 (4): 59-62.

Kaldor, N., (1939), Welfare Propositions in Economics. *Economic Journal.* 49: 549-552.

Kay, J.A., and Thompson, D.J., (1986), Privatisation: a policy in search of a rationale. *Economic Journal.* 96: 18-32.

King, D.N., (1984), *Fiscal Tiers.* London: George Allen and Unwin.

King, D.N., (1988), The Future Role of Grants in Local Government Finance. In Bailey, S.J., and Paddison, R., (eds) *The Reform of Local Government Finance in Britain.* London: Routledge.

King, D.N., (1989), The choice of population figures in the new system of local government finance. *Local Government Studies.* 15 (2): 29-47.

Kmenta, J., (1971), *Elements of Econometrics.* London: Collier Macmillan.

Langdon, Julia, (1984), Tories abandon search for alternatives to rates. *The Guardian.* 24 March.

Layfield Committee, (1976), *Report of the Committee of Inquiry into Local Government Finance.* Chairman Frank Layfield (QC), Cmnd. 6453. London: HMSO.

Lindahl, E., (1919), Just Taxation - a Positive Solution. reprinted in Musgrave, R.A., and Peacock, A.T., (eds) (1958), *Classics in the Theory of Public Finance.* London: Macmillan.

LGIU, (1990), *Guide to the Poll Tax.* London: Local Government Information Unit.

Lynch, B., and Perlman, M., (1978), Local authorities predictions of expenditure and income. *Centre for Environmental Studies Review.* 3: 13-24.

MacGregor, S., (1988), *The Poll Tax and the Enterprise Culture.* Manchester: Centre for Local Economic Strategies.

Mason, Douglas, (1985), *Revising the Rating System.* London: Adam Smith Institute.

Mason, Douglas, (1988), *Slimming for Survival.* Paper presented at the Institute of Economic Affairs, May 1988.

Mayer, C.P., and Meadowcroft, S.A., (1985), Selling Public Assets: Techniques and Financial Implications. *Fiscal Studies.* 6 (4): 42-56.

Maynard, A.K., and King, D.N., (1972), *Rates or Prices?* Hobart Paper 54, London: Institute of Economic Affairs.

McLean, I., (1982), *Dealing in Votes.* Oxford: Martin Robertson.

Midwinter, A., (1984), *The Politics of Local Spending.* Edinburgh: Mainstream.

Midwinter, A., (1989a), Study claims poll tax is not to blame for higher bills. *Local Government Chronicle.* 2 June.

Midwinter, A., (1989b), The Politics of Local Fiscal Reform. *Public Policy and Administration.* 4 (2): 2-9.

Midwinter, A., and Mair, C., (1986), *Rates Reform.* Edinburgh: Mainstream.

Midwinter, A., Mair, C., and Ford, C., (1987), Rating Revaluation Revisited. In McCrone, D., (ed) *The Scottish Government Yearbook.* Edinburgh: University of Edinburgh Press.

Mieszkowski, P., (1972), The property tax: an excise tax or a profits tax, *Journal of Public Economics.* 1: 73-96.

Miller, W.L., (1986), Local Electoral Behaviour. In Research Volume 3 of *Report of the Committee of Inquiry into The Conduct of Local Authority Business.* Cmnd. 9800. London: HMSO.

Miller, W.L., (1988), *Irrelevant Elections.* Oxford: Clarendon Press.

Mitchell, W.C., (1988), Government as it is. Hobart Paper 109, London: Institute of Economic Affairs.

Mitchell, J.M., and Mitchell, W.C., (1969), *Political Analysis and Public Policy.* Chicago: Rand McNally & Co.

Muellbauer, J., (1987), The Community Charge, Rates and Tax Reform. *Lloyds Bank Review.* 166: 7-19.

Muir, Kate, (1989), Poll tax prompts the poor to 'disappear' from society. *The Independent.* 31 May.

James Naughtie, (1985), Ministers accept need for early rate reform. *The Guardian.* 28 March.

Newcastle upon Tyne City Council, (1988), *The distributional impact of poll tax.* Report to Policy & Resources Committee.

Newton, K., (1976a), The impact of rates on local elections. In Appendix 6 of *Local Government Finance: Report of the Committee of Inquiry*. Cmnd. 6453. London: HMSO.

Newton, K., (1976b), *Second City Politics*. Oxford: Oxford University Press.

Nugent, N., (1979), The Ratepayers. In King, R., and Nugent, N., (eds) *Respectable Rebels*. London: Hodder and Stoughton.

Oates, W.E., (1972), *Fiscal Federalism*. New York: Harcourt Brace Jovanovitch.

Oates, W.E., (1979), Lump-sum intergovernmental grants have price effects. In Mieszkowski, P., and Oakland, W.H., (eds) *Fiscal Federalism and Grants-in-Aid*. Washington DC: Urban Institute.

Ogden, F.D., (1958), *The Poll Tax in the South*. Montgomery: University of Alabama Press.

Paddison, R., (1989), Spatial Effects of the Poll Tax. *Public Policy and Administration*. 4 (2): 10-21.

Prest, A.R., (1982a), Greener Still and Greener. *Local Government Studies*. 8 (3): 61-74.

Prest, A.R., (1982b), On Charging for local government services. *Three Banks Review*. 133: 3-23.

Rallings, M., and Thrasher, C., (1986a), *The 1985 Non Metropolitan County Elections in England*, Plymouth: Plymouth Polytechnic.

Rallings, M., and Thrasher, C., (1986b), *The 1986 Metropolitan Borough Council Election Results*. Plymouth: Plymouth Polytechnic.

Rallings, M., and Thrasher, C., (1990), *Local Elections Handbook 1990*. Plymouth: Plymouth Polytechnic.

Ramsdale, P., (1990), Local authority spending 1990/91, *Public Finance and Accountancy*. 1 June.

Rees, A., (1967), West Hartlepool. In Sharpe, L.J., (ed) *Voting in Cities*. London: Macmillan.

Richards, P.G. (1988), The Recent History of Local Fiscal Reform. In Bailey, S.J., and Paddison, R., (eds) *The Reform of Local Government Finance in Britain*. London: Routledge.

Riddell, P., (1990), *The Thatcher Decade*. Oxford: Basil Blackwell.

Ridge M., and Smith S., (1990), *Local Government Finance: The 1990 Reforms*. IFS Commmentary No. 22, London, Institute for Fiscal Studies.

Rowley, C.K., (1987), The Calculus of Consent. In Rowley, C.K., (ed) *Democracy and Public Choice*. Oxford: Basil Blackwell.

Samuelson, P.A., (1954), Pure theory of public expenditure and taxation. *Review of Economics and Statistics*. 36: 387-389.

Scitovsky, T., (1941), A Note on Welfare Propositions in Economics. *Review of Economic Studies* 9: 77-88.

Scott, David, (1985), Scottish RSG to be raised, *Local Government Chronicle*. 15 March.

Scottish Secretary, (1986), *Abolition of domestic rates Etc. (Scotland) Bill*. London: HMSO.

Smith, P., (1987), Optimal local authority budgeting strategies under block grant. *Applied Economics*. 19: 891-905.

Smith, S., and Squire, D., (1986), *Who will be Paying for Local Government*. London: Institute for Fiscal Studies.

Smith, S., and Squire, D., (1987), *Local Taxes and Local Government*. London: Institute for Fiscal Studies.

SCT, (1981), *Block Grant Indicators 1981-82*. Reading: Society of County Treasurers.

Spann, R.M., (1974), Collective Consumption of Private Goods. *Public Choice*. 20: 63-81.

Stewart, J.D., (1987), Local elections. *Local Government Studies*. 13 (2): 25-30.

Stigler, G.J., (1966), *Theory of Price*. New York: Macmillan.

Tait, A., (1990), Struggling Uphill. *Local Government Chronicle*. (Supplement) 1 June.

The Economist, (1980), Swing Low. *The Economist*. 10 May.

Tollison, R., (1982), Rent Seeking: A Survey. *Kyklos*. 88: 575-601.

Travers, Tony, (1984), Finance Review deja vu. *Local Government Chronicle*. 18 October.

Travers, Tony, (1986), *The Politics of Local Government Finance*. London: Allen and Unwin.

Travers, Tony, and Moon, Nick, (1989), Battle Axe for Tax. *Local Government Chronicle.* 6 October.

Travis, Alan, (1989), Ridley fails to ease poll tax fears. *The Guardian.* 20 July.

Travis, Alan, (1990), Patten accuses shires on poll tax. *The Guardian.* 20 February.

Tullock, G., (1972), Economic Imperialism. In Buchanan, J.M., and Tollison, R.D., (eds), *Theory of Public Choice: Political Applications.* Ann Arbor: University of Michigan Press.

Tullock, G., (1976), *The Vote Motive.* Hobart Paperback 9. London: Institute of Economic Affairs.

Tullock, G., (1983), *Welfare for the Well-to-do.* Dallas: Fisher Institute.

Tullock, G., (1984), How to do well while doing good! in Colander, D.C., (ed), *Neoclassical Political Economy.* Cambridge, Mass.: Ballinger.

Veljanovski, C., (1987), *Selling the State.* London: Weidenfeld and Nicholson.

Vickers, J., and Yarrow, G., (1988), *Privatisation: An Economic Analysis.* London: MIT Press.

Waldegrave, W., (1985), Finding the best financial regime for a healthy local democracy. *Municipal Journal.* 28 June.

Ward, I., and Williams, P., (1986), The Government and Local Accountability since Layfield. *Local Government Studies.* 12 (1): 21-32.

Wicksell, K., (1896), A New Principle of Just Taxation. reprinted in Musgrave R.A., and Peacock A.T., (eds) (1958), *Classics in the Theory of Public Finance.* London: Macmillan.

Wilde, J.A., (1968), The expenditure effects of grant-in -aid programs. *National Tax Journal.* 21: 340-348.

Wilson, T., (1988), Local Freedom and Central Control - A Question of Balance. In Bailey, S.J., and Paddison, R., (eds) *The Reform of Local Government Finance in Britain.* London: Routledge.

Young, Hugo, (1987a), No green light for a juggernaut mandate. *The Guardian.* 23 June.

Young, Hugo, (1987b), The furtive decision to go from bad to worse. *The Guardian.* 23 July.

Young, Hugo, (1989) Five ways to lose and one way to win. *The Guardian.* 13 July.

Young, K., (1988), Local Government in Britain: Rationale, Structure and Finance. In Bailey, S.J., and Paddison, R., (eds) *The Reform of Local Government Finance in Britain.* London: Routledge.

AUTHOR INDEX

Aaron, H., 129
Aitken, Ian, 218, 233
Ashford, D.E., 139, 169

Bailey, S.J., 133
Barrow, M., 169
Barnett, J., 11, 12
Barnett, R.R., 159, 236
Baumol, W.J., 170
Beesley, M., 170
Begg, David, 249, 250
Bennett, R.J., 33, 39, 134, 139, 159, 177
Bergstrom, T.C., 125, 140
Berne, R., 139, 159
Billington, M.L., 203
Bird, R.M., 133
Birdseye, P., 20, 38
Black, D., 133
Blair, P., 248
Blake, R., 256
Bogdanor, V., 141, 151
Bowen, H.R., 133
Bramley, G., 13, 88, 128, 144, 149, 169, 171
Breton, A., 135, 168
Bristow, S., 150, 151, 159
Brittan, S., 169
Brown, C., 93
Brown, C.V., 133
Brunner, K., 50
Buchanan, J.M., 133, 175
Butler, D., 240, 260

Carvel, John, 200
Chatterjee, S., 162

Courant, P.N., 131
Cowan, M., 148
Crawford, M., 111
Crewe, I., 213, 214

Davey, K.J., 204
Davis, John, 168
Dawson, D., 111
Dobson, R.B., 6
Dowle, M., 6, 97
Dyer, M.C., 48, 201

Esam, P., 92
Ezell, J.S., 203

Feldstein, M., 142
Fender, J., 252
Ferry, J., 150
Ford, C., 97
Foster, C.D., 15-18, 32, 33, 49, 74, 111, 115, 134, 136, 139, 159, 169, 170
Fox, A., 213, 214
Fraschini, A., 77
Fry, V., 92

Game, C., 151, 159, 243
Gibson, J.G., 12, 19, 32, 139, 140, 144, 148-149, 159, 169, 180, 200-201, 204, 223, 229, 241, 246
Gramlich, E.M., 131
Greene, K.V., 141
Gregory, R., 148

Hale, R., 183
Hailey, W.M.H., 204
Hampton, W., 148

Harbour, G., 159
Heald, D.A., 2, 134, 169
Hepworth, N., 24
Heseltine, M., 256
Hicks, J. R., 170
Hockley, G., 159
Hogendorn, J.S., 204
Hogg, Sarah, 221
Hughes, G., 252

Insight Team, 95, 243

Jackman, R.A., 15-16, 32-33, 48, 111, 115, 127, 133-134, 136, 138-139, 144, 159, 169-170
Jackson P.M., 133
Jenkins, Peter, 232
John, P., 220
Jones, G.W., 13, 47, 137, 149, 169
Jordan, A.G., 48, 201

Kaldor, N., 170
Kavanagh, D., 258
Kay, J.A., 169-170
King, D.N., 131, 133, 145, 171, 250
Kmenta, J., 160

Langdon, Julia, 4, 200
Le Grand, J.E., 128, 171
Levaggi, R., 236
Littlechild, S., 170
Lindahl, E., 123, 133
Low, W., 128, 171
Lynch, B., 10

MacGregor, S., 97
Mair, C., 97, 132
Mason, Douglas, 187, 200
Mayer, C.P., 171, 178, 180
Maynard, A.K., 133
McGuire, M., 129
McLean, I., 144, 168
Meadowcroft, S.A., 171, 178, 180
Midwinter, A., 33, 97, 132, 220, 252
Mieszkowski, P., 177
Miller, W.L., 45, 148, 149, 201

Mitchell, J.M., 175
Mitchell, W.C., 175
Moon, Nick, 224
Muellbauer, J., 252
Muir, Kate, 249

Naughtie, James, 200
Newton, K., 147
Nugent, N., 8

Oates, W.E., 95, 131
Ogden, F.D., 203
Oppenheim, C., 92

Paddison, R., 243
Perlman, M., 10, 32-33, 111, 139, 159, 170
Prest, A.R., 77, 175
Price, B., 162

Rallings, M., 147, 152, 260
Ramsdale, P., 233-234
Rees, A., 148
Richards, P.G., 32
Riddell, P., 252
Ridge, M., 249
Rowley, C.K., 252
Rubinfeld, D.L., 131

Samuelson, P.A., 133
Schramm, R., 139, 159
Scitovsky, T., 170
Scott, David, 139
Smith, P., 32, 159, 236
Smith, S., 85, 140, 249
Spann, R.M., 133
Squire, D., 85, 140
Stark G, 92
Stewart, J.D., 13, 47, 137, 149, 152, 169, 246
Stigler, G.J., 177

Tait, A., 247
Thompson, D.J., 169-170
Thrasher, C., 147, 152, 260
Tollison, R., 175-176

Author Index

Travers, Tony, 19, 32, 137, 148, 169, 223, 224
Travis, Alan, 234-235
Tullock, G., 132, 175, 178

Veljanovski, C., 169
Vickers, J., 169-170, 180

Waldegrave, W., 24, 200
Ward, I., 137

Watt, P.A., 159
Webb A.J., 20, 38
Wicksell, K., 123
Wilde, J.A., 33, 134
Williams, P., 137
Wilson, T., 144

Yarrow, G., 169-170, 180
Young, Hugo, 184, 199-200, 234
Young, K., 47

SUBJECT INDEX

ability to pay **see** taxation
abolition (of councils) 33, 53
Abolition of Domestic Rates Etc. (Scotland) Act, 1987 209
Act 22, 118, 183, 209
Adam Smith Institute 187
Africa 203
Aggregate Exchequer Grant 12, 25-27, 219
area protection 225, 226
assessed spending need (ASN) 27, 28
Association of County Councils (ACC) 23, 26, 32
Association of District Councils (ADC) 191, 195, 199
Association of Metropolitan Authorities (AMA) 98, 99, 104, 112, 140, 189, 226
Audit Commission 23, 32, 186

Baker, Kenneth 24, 98, 99, 102, 104, 106, 107, 112, 188-191, 210, 242
balances 73, 219, 239-241
Barnett, Joel 11, 12,
Beaumont-Dark, Anthony 192
benefits from services 1, 15, 17, 35, 40, 44, 45, 48, 118-134, 136, 138, 139, 143, 159, 170, 171, 178, 185
benefit principle **see** taxation
block grant 14, 15, 17, 19, 22-25, 28-32, 41, 50, 52, 53, 59, 70, 72, 74, 75, 120, 131, 159, 186
Boyson, Rhodes 218, 223, 224
Bramley, Glen 144
Brittan, Leon, 33

business rates **see** rates
by-elections 256

capital expenditure 2, 11, 21, 25, 26, 130, 160,
capping **see** rates and poll tax
cash limits 25
Consultative Council on Local Government Finance (CCLGF) 226
central government 2, 7, 9, 10, 13-15, 20, 35, 38, 39, 95, 117, 135, 137, 139, 141, 143, 220, 221, 233, 249
charges 2, 25, 26, 133, 160, 174, 196, 219, 231, 250
charging 174, 222, 227
Chope, Christopher 199
Chartered Institute of Public Finance and Accountancy (CIPFA) 9, 19, 76, 130, 233, 239
clawback/flowback **see** grants
collection **see** poll tax
collective provision 117, 121-123, 125, 130
community charge 1, 40-42, 44, 50-52, 88, 100, 104, 139, 185, 192, 193, 196, 197, 209-211, 218, 219, 222, 223, 227, 231-233
compensation 37, 92, 130, 170
Conservative Party 2, 4, 5, 7, 8, 12-15, 18-20, 22, 24, 93, 94, 111, 136, 142, 148, 150, 152, 153, 156, 157, 161, 162, 168, 179, 180, 183-186, 191, 192, 196-199, 209, 210, 212, 217, 218, 219, 221, 223, 224, 231, 232, 238-240, 242, 244, 248

Cunningham, John 92, 112
current expenditure 11, 14, 21, 22, 25, 26, 40, 153, 160, 222, 233, 234, 241

Department of the Environment (DOE) 14, 78, 79, 97, 102, 104, 107, 109, 121, 140, 149, 172, 189, 193, 194, 196, 201
disincentive 14, 32, 136
domestic element 8, 25, 26
domestic rateable value 53
domestic rates *see* rates
domestic ratepayers *see* rates
domestic sector tax contribution 57, 75, 81-83, 85

education 13, 35, 40, 53, 124, 127, 130, 142, 225, 228, 239, 258, 259
efficiency 11, 39, 46, 49, 117, 118, 120, 121, 123, 124, 131, 132, 134, 136, 138, 143, 168-172, 222, 237
elections/electorate/electors 1, 6, 8, 10, 18, 35, 40, 45, 46, 93, 94, 118, 131, 135, 140, 142, 147-153, 156-164, 168, 177, 178, 185, 190, 191, 217, 224, 232, 233, 237, 240, 241, 243-245, 247, 248, 252
Environment Committee 4, 186, 194
equalisation 15, 17, 25-27, 29, 30, 36, 37, 41, 42, 58, 59, 70, 115, 131, 136
equity 112, 171, 172, 178, 180, 247
evasion 247, 248
expenditure, local government 1, 2, 7-15, 17-23, 25-32, 35, 36, 40-42, 44, 45, 49, 52, 53-56, 59, 70, 72, 85, 97, 113, 118-120, 124, 130, 131, 135, 137-139, 141, 142, 153, 158-160, 174, 190, 219, 220, 221-223, 225, 226, 233, 234, 237, 239-241, 248, 250, 251

fixed element 31
flagship 4-6, 167, 183, 184, 252

Galbraith, J.K. 179

general election 2, 8, 12, 20, 92, 147, 167, 169, 183, 209, 224, 243, 244, 252
Gould, Bryan 227
Grant Related Expenditure (GRE) 22, 29-32, 37, 41, 42, 44, 52-56, 58-70, 72, 75, 76, 137, 142, 198
grants 7, 9, 13, 14, 25, 26, 29, 38, 41, 42, 52, 90, 115, 124, 131, 138, 141-143, 174, 180, 195-197, 212, 219, 221, 225, 226, 228, 229, 239, 242
  clawback/flowback 36, 47
  feedback 14
  lump sum 26, 27, 30, 42, 70, 131, 139
  matching 26, 30, 44, 142
  penalties 19, 20, 22, 32, 72, 74, 148, 220
Grants Working Group 90, 174, 196, 197, 226
Green Papers:
  Local Government Finance (1977) 10, 11, 18, 111
  Alternatives to Domestic Rates (1981) 3, 20, 47, 85-87, 194
  Reform of Social Security (1985) 91
  Paying for Local Government (1986) 4, 5, 7, 35-42, 44, 45, 47, 52, 73, 74, 88-92, 95, 97-102, 104, 106, 109, 117, 121, 133, 136, 137, 159, 163, 172, 178, 185, 187-189, 191, 193-196, 198, 199, 204, 205, 207, 210, 218, 242

Hale, Rita 183
health 91, 142, 221
Heseltine, Michael 13, 255-259, 261
Hayhoe, Barney 45, 191
Home Office 97
House of Commons 1, 3, 20, 45, 98, 169, 173, 180, 184-186, 188, 193, 194, 218, 219, 231
House of Lords 180
house prices 251
housing 2, 13, 17, 25, 53, 73, 92, 93, 111, 112, 127, 249
Housing Revenue Account (HRA) 76

Subject Index

Howard, Michael, 191, 193, 195, 199
Howe, Geoffrey 255
Hurd, Douglas 257

ICM 229
incentive 41, 45, 55, 230, 250, 251
incidence 45, 101, 176, 191, 204
income tax 3, 10, 11, 18, 20, 40, 44, 104, 130, 136, 143, 189, 238
inflation 2, 8, 10-12, 19-21, 92, 99, 147, 188, 219-221, 223, 227, 233, 239, 245, 252
inner cities 4, 76, 81, 209, 250
ILEA 16, 21, 53, 71-73, 76, 222
Inner London Education Grant 225, 239
Italy 77

Japan 198, 199, 204-207
Jenkin, Patrick, 4, 22, 24, 186, 187

Kobayashi, Akira 205, 206

Labour Party 1, 7, 8, 11, 12, 14, 18, 52, 72, 92-94, 111, 135, 136, 150, 151, 152, 153, 56, 157, 161, 162, 185, 192, 204, 212, 223, 227, 229, 232, 233, 237, 239, 240, 243, 244, 252
Layfield Committee 7-10, 15, 44, 111, 136, 142, 147
Liberal Party 153, 244
local accountability 1, 5, 7, 9, 10, 15, 18, 24, 35, 37, 38, 41, 42, 44, 49, 50, 97, 117, 118, 121, 136-138, 140, 141, 143, 185, 187, 218, 232, 233, 237, 241, 242, 245, 247, 248, 251
local electorate/elections/electors 1, 6, 8, 10, 35, 40, 44-46, 55, 93, 118, 131, 135, 136, 138, 140, 142, 147-151, 158, 159, 163, 178, 185, 190, 191, 232, 233, 237, 240, 241, 243, 244, 247, 248
Local Government Finance Bill 1, 52, 184, 185, 217, 218, 240
local income tax 10, 11, 18, 20, 40, 44, 104, 130, 136, 143, 189

London 3, 9, 14, 16, 19, 25, 27, 28, 30, 31, 51-53, 55-58, 70, 71, 72-74, 76, 85, 87, 113, 114, 150, 152, 156, 158, 214, 217, 219, 222, 225, 226, 228-230, 232-234, 239, 241, 244, 248
Low rateable value area grant 225
lump sum see grants

macroeconomic policy 33, 141
Major, John 257
marginal seats/constituencies 180, 224, 252, 257, 258
marginal rate of grant 13, 30, 32, 42, 44, 47, 72
marginal tax cost 44
   domestic sector 15, 36, 53, 55, 59, 70, 118-120, 136-140, 143
   non-domestic sector 15, 36, 118, 120, 130, 140
matching see grants
median voter 117, 125, 126, 130, 132, 135, 143, 180
migration 171
MORI 243, 244, 252

national standard rateable value (NSRV) 26
national taxes 2, 241
needs assessment 142, 143, 226
Needs Assessment Sub Group 226
needs element 14, 26-28
Nigeria 4, 204
non-domestic rates see rates
NOP 224, 229, 252

opinion polls 4, 168, 224, 229, 244, 252, 256, 257

Papua New Guinea 4, 204
Parliament 3, 4, 52, 74, 169, 183, 186, 209, 232, 247, 248
Patten, Christopher 224, 225, 227, 231, 232, 241, 242, 259
pay awards 219, 220, 227

Peacock, Elizabeth 224
Peasants' Revolt 4, 204
penalties **see** grants
poll tax 3-6, 24, 32, 35, 44, 46, 50, 51, 53-56, 59-72, 74-76, 81, 83, 84-88, 90-95, 97-99, 101, 102, 104, 106, 107, 111, 114, 115, 117, 121, 124-130, 132, 135, 136, 139-143, 148, 167, 168-173, 176-180, 183-199, 203-207, 209-214, 217, 218, 219-222, 224, 225, 227-229, 231-233, 237-245, 247, 248, 249-252
   administration 111, 171, 233, 245, 248, 249
   capping 231, 232, 240, 241, 247, 248
   collection 57, 75, 171, 214, 227, 228, 233, 248-250
   registration 218, 248, 249
precept 19, 25, 78, 215
privatisation 6, 167-172, 176-179
public choice 117, 132, 139, 167, 168, 174
public expenditure 2, 11, 13, 21, 25, 221, 225

Raison, Timothy 209
rate support grant (RSG) 8, 12, 13, 24-26, 74, 226
rateable value 17, 24-34, 37, 39, 41, 48, 50-79, 83-85, 93, 98, 106, 107, 112, 113, 177, 195, 198, 212
rates
   capital valuation 111-115, 130, 189
   capping 22, 186, 219
   domestic rates 1, 3-5, 8, 18, 20, 21, 24, 35, 36, 38-42, 44, 46, 51, 52-56, 70, 73-76, 81, 83, 85-88, 90, 92, 93, 95, 97, 99, 102, 104, 106, 113, 117, 118, 120, 121, 124, 127-130, 136, 139-142, 147, 171-174, 183, 185-187, 189, 192, 193, 194-197, 204, 209-212, 218, 226, 228, 242, 250, 251
   domestic ratepayers 2, 8, 15-17, 20, 25, 36, 41, 44, 72, 119, 139

non-domestic ratepayers 17, 36, 72
non-domestic rates 35, 36, 38, 39, 41, 42, 44, 52, 55, 70, 73-76, 117, 118, 120, 130, 139, 140, 212, 226, 228, 251
rate poundage 8, 15, 17, 23, 25-31, 37, 41, 50-53, 58, 59, 70, 74, 75, 83, 93, 151, 159, 160
Rates Act 1984 22
Rates White Paper (1983) 3, 4, 20, 21
rental valuation 1, 111, 185
rate support grant (RSG) 8, 12, 13, 21, 24-26, 30, 74, 222, 226,
rebates 17, 18, 36, 39, 46, 82, 91-93, 118, 119, 128, 130, 140, 212, 233, 241
redistribution of local taxation 5, 8, 27, 46, 49, 50, 52, 53, 73-75, 81-83, 85, 90, 93, 102, 131, 168, 171, 172, 175, 176, 179, 180, 188, 204, 228, 238, 242, 251
registration **see** poll tax
relevant expenditure 2, 7, 20, 25, 26, 31
rent seeking 167, 173-175
reorganisation 8, 217
reserves 8, 238, 239
resources element 13, 14, 26-28, 30
revaluation 5, 8, 24, 46, 73, 74, 97-99, 104, 106, 107, 111, 112, 114, 117, 139-141, 178, 185, 187-190, 204, 209, 230, 251
Revenue Support Grant 217, 219, 223, 226-228, 245
Ridley, Nicholas 1, 92, 95, 112, 113, 184, 185, 190, 192, 197-199, 218, 219, 222, 223, 242
Rifkind, Malcolm 219
Rooker, Jeff 192
RPI 21, 39, 220

safety nets 52, 81-83, 85-87, 90, 91, 93, 101, 102, 194, 221, 223, 224, 228, 230, 239, 241, 242
sales tax 40
Scotland 2, 4, 5, 24, 92, 97-99, 101, 139-141, 167, 178, 185, 187-189, 209, 217, 219, 220, 225, 241, 242, 248-250

Subject Index

services, local government 1, 2, 9, 10, 13, 29, 35, 36, 38, 40-42, 44, 45, 59, 112, 117, 118, 121, 124-128, 130-132, 135, 136, 139, 142, 144, 147, 149, 151, 154, 158-161, 163, 170, 178, 185, 190, 195, 197, 198, 220, 226, 227, 231, 233, 237, 241, 250, 251
Shore, Peter 12
SLD 243
Social Services 13, 40, 95
specific grants 25, 26, 42, 97, 142, 219, 226-228, 239
spouses 40, 46
standard grant 42, 44
Standard Spending Assessment (SSA) 53, 227, 228, 231, 232, 250
supplementary benefits 95
swing 151-153, 156-158, 161, 163, 164, 232

targets 19-22, 32, 159
taxation
  ability to pay 1, 3, 10, 39-41, 88, 112, 121, 124, 126, 141, 143, 185, 195
  benefit principle 123-134
  progressivity/regressivity 81-83, 85-92, 111, 113, 127-130, 136, 139-144, 172, 173, 194-197, 251-253
  tax base 26, 28, 29, 42, 50, 52, 53, 83, 124, 135, 143, 251

tax price 118-125, 131
tax share 125, 129, 140, 143
Thatcher, Margaret 2-5, 97, 98, 112, 167, 168, 175, 179, 183, 187, 217, 218, 229, 233, 242, 247, 252
threshold 14, 29-32, 53, 119, 232, 245
Transitional arrangements 97, 108, 235
Transitional relief 225, 230, 241, 242, 245
transport 13, 14, 221
Treasury 97, 221, 223, 224

unemployment 17, 20, 74
uniform business rate 1, 185, 209, 230
United States 4

valuation 24, 111, 112
voters/voting 4, 5, 15, 17, 18, 35, 36, 38, 44, 45, 118, 123, 125, 130, 137, 140, 141, 148, 159, 160, 163, 175, 176, 180, 181, 191, 203, 212, 218, 224, 229, 241, 243, 244, 248, 251

Waldegrave, William 24
Wales 2, 4, 8, 9, 11, 25-27, 29, 167, 188, 191, 198, 209, 212, 218, 219, 225, 233
Widdicombe Committee 148

Younger, George 5, 97, 187